GROWING CHRISTIANS IN SMALL GROUPS

GROWING CHRISTIANS IN SMALL GROUPS

JOHN MALLISON

Scripture Union

London   Sydney   Cape Town

Copyright © John Mallison 1989

Jointly published by:

Scripture Union Books
ANZEA PUBLISHERS
3–5 Richmond Road
Homebush West, NSW 2140
Australia

ISBN 0 85892 407 2

Scripture Union
130 City Road
London EC1V 2NJ

ISBN 0 86201 583 9

Printed in Singapore by Singapore National Printers

DEDICATION
to
GLOSTER STUART UDY

Minister of the Christian gospel, Methodist in experience, faithful pastor, scholar, Christian educator, visionary, initiator, inspirer of young people, campaigner for justice, advocate for the needy, who has consistently encouraged me in my own ministry, particularly when I was taking some first steps in working with small groups.

Acknowledgements

A great deal of material in the small group movement is becoming common domain; ideas have originated in one place and have been varied, changed, or used as a basis in others. We are indebted to such work. A small amount of material in this book has been adapted or copied from roneoed sheets, received from a variety of sources on which there was no indication of copyright.

We are indebted, too, to a number of pioneers and leaders in the small group movement for their inspiration and encouragement and to those who have shared new insights and thinking on fellowship, prayer and Bible study with the church today. We have acknowledged all sources on which we have drawn, either in the text or in a list of references at the end of a chapter. We acknowledge in particular the work of William F Barclay, Dietrich Bonhoeffer, John L Casteel, Lyman Coleman, Gordon Cosby, Robert M Cox, Robert C Leslie, Sara Little, Thomas Merton, Keith Miller, Leslie Newbiggin, Elizabeth O'Connor, Lawrence Richards, Roslyn Rinker, Charlie Shedd, Samuel M Shoemaker, Ross Snyder, Helmut Thielicke, Walter Wink and Paul Everett. We acknowledge also the insights shared by participants in my small group training courses and workshops.

We acknowledge with thanks the Joint Board of Christian Education, Australia and New Zealand, for permission to quote from *Teaching and Christian Faith Today* by D S Hubery; the Bible Reading Fellowship, London, for permission to quote from *Introducing the Bible* by William F Barclay; Abingdon Press, Nashville, Tennessee, for permission to quote from *A Handbook for Know Your Bible Study Groups* by Charles M Laymon, © 1959; Zondervan, Grand Rapids, Michigan, for permission to quote from *A New Face for the Church* by Lawrence O Richards; Augsburg Publishing House, Minneapolis, Minnesota, for permission to quote from *Find Yourself in the Bible* by Karl A Olsson, © 1974; Collins Publishers, for permission to quote from *A Plain Man Looks at the Lord's Prayer* by William Barclay; Harper and Row, Publishers, Inc., New York, for permission to use and abridge excerpts from *With the Holy Spirit and With Fire* by Samuel M Shoemaker; to Ross Snyder for permission to use the outline of his Bible study method.

We acknowledge with thanks permission to adpat material from *Sharing Groups in the Church*, Robert Leslie (Abingdon Press, Nashville (1971)), *Conversational Prayer*, Roslyn Rinker (Zondervan), and *Three Times Three Equals Twelve*, Brian Mills (Kingsway Publications, 1986).

Front cover design by Earl Hingston of Pilgrim International.

Cartoons by Madeline Gianatti.

Diagrams by Lynelle and Matthew Mallison.

Contents

Introduction

Anyone with a basic knowledge of church history is aware of the significant role played by small groups across the centuries in the growth and renewal of the Christian church. Every time we read from the New Testament we need to remind ourselves that we are being exposed to a small group movement which multiplied at an astounding pace throughout the Roman world. For the first two hundred years of its existence, the church had no large public buildings available in which to meet. During that time small groups were not an extension of the church—they *were* the church. When Paul wrote his letter to the church in Corinth, Ephesus or Rome, he was writing to a federation of small groups meeting in scattered locations in those cities.

When the church has great institutional strength and widespread influence and acceptance in society, the emphasis on small groups tends to diminish. It is replaced by a focus of attention on activities within church buildings where the populace is expected to rally. This occurred during the Middle Ages, and continued in Europe from the Reformation until the emergence of the Pietists in Europe and John Wesley and the Methodists in England.

However, the *increasing secularisation* of Australasia, Europe and North America has led to the marginalising of the church from the mainstream of life. Only a small proportion of the population go to church on a weekly basis—in some countries less than 10 per cent—and a shrinking periphery claim any allegiance to a particular denomination or local church. The lapsed Christian of yesterday begets the nominal and notional Christian of today, who in turn begets the secularist of tomorrow.

At least that is how it appears on the surface. At a deeper level there remains a hunger for spiritual reality, which finds expression in various forms of folk religion. If the church fails to develop flexible and dynamic structures for outreach to these people—many of whom are asking religious questions but are not coming to the churches in search of answers—then other religions and ideologies which are making their presence felt 'in the market-place' will begin to claim their allegiance.

As a consequence of this social dynamic the old methods employed by the church, of advertising worship services and developing on-campus programmes and activities to which people are invited, become less and less effective. There has to be a switch from a stance of inviting to one of infiltrating. That is where the small group plays such a significant role. To be more precise, it plays two roles: one is to mature and equip the existing members in order to face the world and survive in a hostile environment, and the other is to establish small-group, commando-like task-forces to undertake the ministry of Christ in the world. It comes as no surprise to discover that the overwhelming majority of churches which are making a significant impact in communities which are culturally distanced from the church use small groups as the main structures for their strategies.

Even churches which still enjoy social acceptance and community identity, such as the Lutheran churches of Scandinavia or the Presbyterians of Scotland, are increasingly recognising the role of small groups to help their committed membership demonstrate the radical claims of the gospel of the Kingdom of God, as distinct from the predominant life-style of the culture with which they are so closely identified.

If these observations in any way approximate to the truth of the situation faced by the contemporary church then it is evident that there is a strategic challenge facing us which has to be tackled as a matter of urgency. The problem centres on the fact that many church leaders have had little or no training in the establishing, leadership, resourcing and multiplying of small groups on anything like the scale which the present opportunities demand. The majority of ordained ministers are over 50 years of age and were trained at a time when church leaders were only dimly, if at all, aware of the significance of small groups, and little or no training was provided in our theological colleges. Consequently the majority of pastors are learning as they go, and find themselves having to 'fly by the seat of their pants'. Fortunately, some ministers have done some reading in the area and may have attended courses and obtained small group learning resources. But overall it is a case of too little too late.

Quality materials are becoming available and there are growing numbers of experts in the field, but you have to know where to find them, and for them to be available at the time when they are needed.

John Mallison has come to the rescue with what I believe to be the most comprehensive and valuable manual in the field of small groups to be written to date. There is no one more qualified to write in this specialised field, and his reputation stretches far beyond Australia. He writes with a breadth of vision, because not only has he worked with small groups in the local parish setting but at training conferences as well, as in the context of city and nation-wide Billy Graham campaigns. It was in connection with the last-mentioned that I first became aware of John Mallison's extraordinary gifts. He did such a great job in setting up the 2 500 nurture groups in connection with the 1979 Sydney Crusades that I invited him to visit England in 1982 to help us develop a similar strategy for our seven Billy Graham missions in 1984 and 1985. The materials produced for those occasions are now being widely used in revised forms in other evangelistic endeavours in many countries around the world.

Growing Christians in Small Groups is a distillation of much that John Mallison had learned over the years. Here is an author with unassailable credibility, because he has done the kinds of things he is describing in many different settings. This is the most comprehensive book on the topic of which I am aware. He describes many different kinds of groups; contact, evangelism, nurture, prayer and task groups. He provides insights on how to set them up, the kind of people to select as leaders (and those to avoid!), how to resource them, ensure that they diversify and expand the church's ministry, whilst avoiding the fragmentation which can so easily result, and as an added bonus he includes a number of creative programme ideas in the Appendices. He also stresses the need for small groups to function as launching pads for mission, and not to become retreat pods from the world. While many churches have benefited from their contribution to nurture and growth, very few have realised their potential for evangelisation and service in the community.

Some books are worth the price we pay for a one time reading but, having read them once, we happily leave them to gather dust. John Mallison's book represents far greater value for money. Its contents cannot be assimilated at one sitting. It is the kind of volume that the busy minister will want to keep within reach. The contents are helpfully organised to form the basis for developing training courses for new and established small group leaders. I would like to see *Growing Christians in Small Groups* on the bookshelf of every small group leader in the English-speaking world. If its contents were widely assimilated and applied, then the church would be equipped for a renewal and evangelistic outreach to rival that of eighteenth-century Methodism.

This is not just a polite wish, it is an earnest prayer.

Eddie Gibbs
Professor of Evangelism and Church Renewal
Fuller Seminary
Pasadena, California, USA

October, 1988.

Preface

After twenty years of using small groups extensively in my parish ministry in rural, industrial, inner-city and developing suburban areas, and nearly seventeen years in full-time Christian education, I am now more committed than ever to the belief that the church will not become a true worshipping, serving community of love, unless small groups are an integral part of its ongoing life.

Where churches (in many countries) are growing in quality of Christian life and witness and in numbers, in almost every instance small groups are the heartbeat of that new life.

The small group is the most flexible and versatile structure we have within the Christian church. It can be adapted to almost any situation to meet a wide variety of needs.

It is my hope that all who read this book will catch the vision of the possibilities of small groups for bringing renewal to the Christian community and gain some understanding of how to commence and maintain these life-giving cells.

Much of the material in this book is the outcome of my own parish ministry and my leadership and membership of a variety of small groups, all refined in the workshop atmosphere of the small group leadership training courses I have conducted throughout Australia and in many other coun-tries. I am grateful to many key people in the world-wide small group movement, to the leaders and members of the small groups in my parishes and to course participants who have helped me in my thinking.

The motivation to write this book came from a great number of people who have urged me to update my previous work, which went into four reprints and three different editions, and to include my more recent insights. It therefore contains what I consider to be the best of the original Small Group Series, completely revised and updated. I have also incorporated much new material.

Although I believe this book will be helpful to educators, I have written it essentially to enable anyone to commence and maintain an effective group in most cultures.

Having conducted small group leadership training in fourteen countries around the world, I am aware that each country presents a different situation. I have consciously written this book with this fact in mind, knowing it is to be published in at least two countries, and will be widely distributed.

I am grateful to Rod Denton, a national leader in ministry with young people, who contributed the chapter on small groups in youth ministry, and to Tony Neylan, who contributed the Bible study method, Praying the Scriptures.

I have incorporated some of the work contributed to the original series by Gordon Dicker, Graeme Beattie, Ross Kingham and Athol Gill. I continue to be appreciative of their significant material.

I wish to acknowledge the help of a number of people in the preparation of this book. My secretary, Mary Butler, typed the manuscript and made helpful comments. Emlyn and Trish Williams read the manuscript and gave useful advice. My son Paul made corrections and my daughter Lynelle and son Matthew drew the diagrams.

This book has been made possible by the support of the council who oversees my present ministry and the hundreds of people who so faithfully support me, both financially and prayerfully in this work.

Without the love, patience and support of my wife June, this book would never have been possible.

We offer this book in love to all those who are dedicated to the renewal of the life and service of the Christian community.

John Mallison

October, 1988.

Chapter 1

Christian Small Groups– the Basic Building Blocks

The Gospel must be brought back to where people live, in simple forms, and in terms of small and manageable fellowships. — Stephen Neill

The small group is the basic building block of the life of the local congregation and is fundamental to the development of individual and corporate Christian lifestyle.

The small group has always been a significant force for renewal in the Christian church, but its place is being rediscovered again in our time. In the last three decades or more, what Hobart Mowrer calls 'quiet revolution' has been taking place. Around the world, one of the signs of hope in the Christian church has been the renewal being brought to individuals and Christian communities through the formation of small groups.

In the Base Ecclesial Communities in Latin America, small groups of impoverished Catholic Christians meet regularly to pray, sing, study Scripture and apply it to their

own situations. In China, house centred groups have been the key to the remarkable growth of the church despite the suppression and persecution of the church since the cultural revolution. Other areas of rapid church growth, such as South Korea and Central Africa, have hundreds of thousands in Christian cells. In Eastern Europe, networks of small groups are bringing new life and hope to the church, despite the restrictions imposed on Christian gatherings. In the United States and the United Kingdom, there has been a dramatic increase in groups studying the Bible.

In Australia, there is also significant growth in people gathering in small groups. A few churches are reporting 75% of their membership actively participating in house centred cells. In a neighbouring Catholic parish, 50 home based prayer cells meet weekly. In a Catholic rural parish, more than that number gather regularly. Relational Bible Study resources for use in small groups are in incredible demand. Large national gatherings are being held specifically to equip people to establish and more effectively lead groups.

Some of these small groups, through which God is bringing a new spiritual awakening around the world, are linked together through large national movements. Others are part of local church or parish level networks, having only loose links with other aspects of the wider movement. Many are isolated groups of people, meeting out of a deep sense of need to take seriously the Lordship of Jesus Christ.

These small fellowships of renewal are to be found in factories and offices, schools and universities, and city restaurants and suburban homes. They meet at a variety of times, some over breakfast or lunch. There are morning and afternoon groups, some later in the evening. Some meet well before dawn to avoid the distractions of the daily routine. Within the church and outside the church, men and women are exploring together the deep things of the Spirit and, in many cases, bringing a new influence to bear upon society.

The witness of ministers, leaders and participants in this new movement is most encouraging. They testify that such groups have an amazing ministry to those who take them seriously. Homes and churches are being changed, lives transformed, a new sense of unity reached and a growing commitment to a world in need.

The testimony of Scripture, the record of history and the witness of our contemporaries make it very clear that spiritual renewal does come to the church whenever a nucleus responds to Christ in depth and when they do this together in intimate fellowship. The Holy Spirit works with revolutionary power when small companies of Christians reach new levels of openness and expectation and respond to his inner promptings in obedience and faith. 'If such groups will act as a kind of spearhead of awakening, strive constantly to be humble and teachable, and let the Holy Spirit be the Strategist that forms them all into "an exceeding great army" under His leadership alone, there is literally no telling what might happen in our day.'[1]

However, small groups in the Christian church have not always had an impressive history. While many have been successful, many have failed. There is no magic in the small group itself. On occasions I meet people who respond to my vision of the potential of small groups in the Christian church with 'Oh, we tried them years ago and they didn't work'. Small groups in the church have not always fulfilled the expectations of the participants because they have either not understood, or not put into practice, certain basic principles which help to keep group life vital. Even a limited understanding of group dynamics would have helped some groups achieve their purpose. Many groups in the church have not developed into real communities of care and concern because it was not in God's timing or because they were launched with the wrong motives.

Many have looked upon small groups as another gimmick to get the church back on the rails again, to prop up ailing structures. Dietrich Bonhoeffer has described much of the conventional concept of discipleship in terms of what he calls 'cheap grace'. 'Cheap grace' in small group life is Bible study without action, prayer without creativity, fellowship without care and concern, sharing without honesty and community without accountability. 'Cheap grace' is grace without repentance, discipleship without the Cross, togetherness without a living, ever-present Christ.

Spiritual renewal requires our co-operation and participation, but it is essentially the work of God. God always makes the first move; if he chooses not to act then all our organisation is fruitless in producing vital, growing spiritual life.

When we talk about small group structures, 'small' suggests a size which permits and encourages face-to-face relationships. It is not so large that any will be cut off from deeply and personally giving and receiving genuine love. How large is this? Some research in group dynamics suggests that five may be the optimum number. But often groups of eight or twelve are suggested for church fellowship groups, and this range seems to have many advantages, as we shall discover later.

Simply putting eight or twelve Christians together does not make them a group. Nor will it, in itself, ensure that they will develop healthy group life. Members may, over a span of many meetings, remain strangers who share nothing more significant than what each thinks the others want to hear. A small group, which functions as the church, needs to know how to develop group life. Without initial guidance and help, or without an understanding of how the group can become an authentic Christian fellowship, a small group may move far off course.

There are **three reasons** which compel us **to take seriously the potential of small groups** in bringing new life to the individual and to the corporate life of those who are committed to be the kind of Christian disciple Christ intended us to be. These are: the example of Christ in his strategy for ministry, the example of the early church and the history of renewal in the church.

CHRIST USED A SMALL GROUP STRATEGY

At the heart of Christ's strategy was a dynamic small group. The genius of Christ's ministry was that he devoted himself primarily to a few People rather than the masses, in order that the masses could be more effectively reached with the gospel. Jesus deliberately concentrated his ministry on a very small number of people. Mark records, 'he appointed twelve to be with him, and to be sent out to preach and have authority to cast out demons'. (Mark 3:14,15)

With the short time at his disposal, he was not given to gathering a large following with uncertain commitment. He chose to build, into the lives of a few, solid foundations that would form the basis of his kingdom and withstand the storms which would assail them. With a whole world to save he spent most of his ministry, it would seem, in private with this little group. He set out to teach those men to love one another and to pass on the good news of God's love to others. One cannot miss the significance of the twelve, in searching for ways to vitalise the church of our day.

Our Lord gathered together a diverse and most unlikely group. It was an amazing synthesis of humanly irreconcilable elements—Simon the Zealot, the fiery nationalist; Matthew, servant of the establishment; Peter, all energy and impetuosity; John, thoughtful and prayerful; Andrew, a man of shining and untroubled faith; and Thomas, the reluctant believer. The very composition of that first group of twelve is a mighty witness to the universality of Christ. This diverse group found their strange union in Jesus Christ. It was a microcosm of the diversity of character of the church that was in the making.

In the eyes of the world, they were very ordinary people. They were not among the outstanding people in society. Christ chose the most unlikely people. He was more concerned about availability than ability. Not that he neglects outstanding people. But the message of the first small group was that Christ does not overlook ordinary people, and some emerged as significant leaders.

It is surprising that most of the apostles were probably in their twenties, John most likely a teenager, when they were with Christ. Here was a group full of the idealism and enthusiasm of youth. Christianity began as a young people's movement.

He called this group 'to be with him'. The time which Jesus invested in these few disciples was so much more by comparison to that given to others, that it can only be regarded as deliberate strategy. He ate, talked, slept, walked, sailed, fished and prayed with them. He spent more time with them than with anyone else in the world.

'To be with him' suggests a number of things. Firstly, on the human side of his nature, Jesus felt the need of human fellowship and support. 'For we do not have a high priest who is unable to sympathise with our weaknesses, but we have one who has been tempted in every way, just as we are—yet was without sin'. (Hebrews 4:15)

'And often when the world outside had been showing itself callous and hostile and contemptuous, he would turn back at nightfall with a great relief to these twelve men who, for all their faults and bungling, did love him and did believe in him. As Jesus himself expressed it, one day when the end was near, "It is you who have stood by me through my trials".' (Luke 22:28, Moffatt)

'It was not only that the Saviour felt the need of human

love and sympathy. It was also his purpose to train these men by fellowship with himself. Living with him every day, watching him in all kinds of situations, listening to his private talk, being admitted to his dreams and aspirations and hopes, they would gradually come to see things with his eyes and be fired with his own authentic fire. Intimacy with Jesus is the best of all teachers.'[2]

He maintained a constant ministry to his disciples by having them with him. They were thus getting the benefit of everything he said and did to others, plus their own personal explanation and counsel.

His strategy for educating his disciples was learning by association. He used an apprenticeship model. This was his simple methodology right from the beginning. The truth was embodied in Christ. He was the way, the truth and the life. He was the gospel. Essentially what he said and did was his own school and curriculum. Spiritual reality was incarnate in him. He was the living lecture.

'And to be sent out to preach and have authority to cast out demons.' Jesus did not keep the work of evangelism in his own hands. He chose to share his ministry with others, not delegating in order to help him cope with the growing demands, but to develop future leaders.

Christ's life and ministry teaches us that finding and training people to reach people must have priority. Christ concentrated his efforts on a small group; training them by word and example, encouraging them, trusting them, permitting them to take risks and at times allowing them to fail, in order to develop a small group to revolutionise the religion of their day and turn the world upside down!

Many who have changed the course of history have worked on the basis that lasting change comes through dedicated small groups. Undisciplined mobs achieve little.

Fidel Castro said, 'I began my revolution with 82 men. If I had to do it again, I would do it with 10 or 15 men and absolute faith. It does not matter how small you are, providing you have faith and a plan of action'.

But at the heart of the group of twelve was a core group. Three cameos in the New Testament make us aware that Jesus was giving special attention to Peter, James and John. Only these three were present on the Mount of Transfiguration (Matthew 17:1–9) and were with Jesus and the parents when Jairus' daughter was raised from the dead (Mark 5:37). Again these alone were present in the garden when, in great agony of spirit, he surrendered to the Father's will (Matthew 26:37). These were key leaders in the making,

taken into the inner sanctum of Christ's deeper thoughts and emotions and experiencing a greater revelation of Christ than any of the others.

Christ's ministry was more focused than most Christian ministry today. At the centre of Christ's strategy were two dynamic small groups. He committed himself to disciple a few and to do it well! Followers of Christ are discovering again the wisdom of that strategy and allowing it to guide them in continuing his ministry in growing the church, both in quality and quantity.

SMALL GROUPS IN THE EARLY CHURCH

The second reason which compels us to take seriously the potential of small groups is the example of the New Testament church. The early church followed the model the Lord gave to them. In its infancy, the church was a small group in which believers gathered to support each other in growing in Christ and in witnessing to their Lord.

Luke, in the book of Acts, gives two important glimpses of the life of the early church which depict the early Christian community having two focal points for its gathered life, the temple and the home. 'With one mind they kept up their daily attendance at the temple and, breaking bread in private houses, shared their meals with unaffected joy, as they praised God and enjoyed the favour of the whole people.' (Acts 2:46–47)

'And every day they went steadily on with their teaching in the temple and in private houses, telling the good news of Jesus the Messiah.' (Acts 5:42)

The whole Christian community daily went to the temple to pray (Acts 2:46; 3: 1–10). Here also was the centre of their ministry of preaching (Acts 2:14ff; 3:11ff) and teaching (Acts 4:2; 5:20–21). But from their inception, the early Christians placed the private home alongside the temple, as a focus for their fellowship together.

As the story of the early Church continues to unfold, private homes are depicted as becoming increasingly centres of worship and hospitality, of Christian teaching and missionary proclamation. Luke describes homes being used for 'prayer meetings' (Acts 12:12); for an evening of Christian fellowship (Acts 21:7); for Holy Communion services (Acts 2:46); for a whole night of prayer, worship and instruction (Acts 20:7); for impromptu evangelistic gatherings (Acts 16:32); for planned meetings in order to hear the Christian gospel (Acts 10:22); for following up enquiries (Acts 18:26); and for organized instruction (Acts 5:42).[3]

What is happening in Acts is that as the Church's missionary activity takes it outwards away from Jerusalem, spurred on in this direction by persecution at the centre, the focal point of its activity becomes, increasingly, private houses. By the time Luke has undertaken to write his two volumes, Jerusalem and the temple have been destroyed and the Christian church has spread throughout the Gentile world, meeting everywhere in the houses of its members.[4]

Peter's ministry in Cornelius' house in Caesarea is one of the great turning points in the story of the early church, as the gospel is directed to the Gentiles (the Graeco-Roman world) with great effect (Acts 10).

The house and the household have become the basis for evangelistic activity in the early church . . . A similar situation is revealed in the story of the Philippian gaoler, where Paul and Silas spoke 'the word of the Lord to him and to all that were in his house', so that 'all the household believed in God' and were baptized (Acts 16:25ff).

A different situation is seen, however, in the description of events following the beheading of James and arrest of Peter. We are told that Peter was rescued from Herod's clutches and that 'he made for the house of Mary, the mother of John Mark, where a large company were at prayer' (Acts 12:12). The house and the household had also become the centre of liturgical activity in the early church.

A further development may be seen when Paul's evangelistic activity took him to Europe. In Philippi, where he preached on European soil for the first time, he stayed in the home of Lydia who had been baptized, with her household, after 'the Lord had opened her heart' (Acts 16:11ff). During his time in Corinth, Paul lodged with Priscilla and Aquila and worked with them in their trade of tentmaking (Acts 18:1ff). Later, he sent greetings to the 'church in their house' (Romans 16:5). The church and the household were the centre of hospitality and fellowship in the early church.[5]

There are numerous references to households in the book of Acts and Paul's letters. The households of the gaoler and Lydia in Philippi, Priscilla and Aquila in Corinth and to Cornelius in Caesarea are referred to above. To these can be added that of Crispus, the ruler of the synagogue, and Stephanus in Corinth.

Paul sent greetings in his letters to household churches in the homes of Priscilla and Aquila (Romans 16:5) and Nympha (Colossians 4:15).

Paul's letter to Philemon, though primarily private correspondence, was addressed nonetheless to 'Philemon, our beloved fellow worker and Apphia our sister and Archippus our fellow soldier, and the church in your house'. A similar situation is probably to be inferred in Romans 16:15: 'Greet Philologus, Julia, Nereus and his sister, and Olympas, and all the saints who are with them'.[6]

It is almost certain that every mention of a local church or of a church meeting, whether for worship or fellowship, is in actual fact a reference to a church meeting in a house.

Primitive Christianity structured its congregations in families, groups and 'houses'. The house was both a fellowship and a place of meeting . . . The house and family are the smallest natural groups in the total structure of the congregation.[7]

Since the Good News abolished all artificial distinctions based on race, sex and class, the Christian household became the communal unit at its best. Master and slave, husband and wife, Jew and Gentile, and parents and children became a unity in Christ (cf. Galatians 3:28; Ephesians 2). This new-found unity of the communal unit formed the nucleus of the earliest Christian communities.

Public proclamation and household worship and instruction were integral parts of the dynamics of the early Christian mission, with the new unity of the extended family forming the nucleus of the community.

The early church followed their Lord's example in building one another up in the faith as they gathered in small intimate fellowships. This they balanced with witness to their communities in word and deed.

SMALL GROUPS IN THE HISTORY OF THE CHURCH

A third reason for us to seriously consider the role of small groups in enriching the life and witness of the church today is the place they had in the history of renewal in the church.

In the intervening history of the church, new spiritual life has been marked by the emergence of small groups. In the Middle Ages, amidst a church which had grown fat and short of breath through prosperity and muscle-bound by over-organisation, dynamic Christians such as St Francis of Assisi gathered in small groups for prayer and study, and training and service. They kept a flame burning amidst the darkness of a decaying ecclesiasticism. Various sections of the Anabaptist movement in Europe formed dynamic house-centred groups. The Hutterites in Moravia, Southern Germany, lived out a New Testament-style community life, which had a far-reaching impact. George Fox brought fresh power to the church through the clusters of small groups which became known as the Religious Society of Friends. The Lutherans also used cells for nurturing.

From among the many vivid examples of clusters which could be identified, one movement stands alone. Its influence appears to far outshine any other single cell model. Literally hundreds of thousands of people participated. The groups are those which were at the heart of the Methodist revival.

Small Groups in the Methodist Revival

The first cell structure in Methodism was known as the **Bands**. Having seen their effective use by the Moravians, Wesley introduced them to provide opportunity for mutual confession to one another (based on the scriptural injunction of James 5:16), and to give encouragement and support in overcoming temptation and developing a Christian style of life. These weekly groups averaged about six members and generally were divided by age, sex and marital status. Their open sharing focused on known sins committed, temptations met and dealt with and defining which thoughts, words and behaviour constituted sin or not.

Only about twenty per cent of Methodists belonged to these groups. A more intimate and searching fellowship for those who were making significant progress were the **select bands** or **select societies**.

While membership of bands was optional, all Methodists were required to be members of a Class Meeting, which built them into an on-going system of pastoral care. These were the core groups—the keystone of the movement. 'The class meetings were not designed merely as Christian growth groups, however, or primarily as cells for koinonia, although in fact they did serve that

function. Their primary purpose was discipline.'[8] Each group consisted of ten to twelve people from the same neighbourhood, coming together weekly for an hour or so.

'The leaders were lay people—some were men, but the majority were women—selected because of their high moral and spiritual character and common sense.'[9] The leaders were accountable to the preacher. Leaders regularly reported concerning the sick and the progress, or otherwise, of each member of their groups.

'The classes normally met one evening each week for an hour or so. Each person reported on his or her spiritual progress, or on particular needs or problems, and received the support and prayers of the others.'[10]

They had a clear evangelistic function, as people were converted during the meetings and those who had lapsed renewed their commitment to Christ. Wesley 'wisely discerned that the beginnings of faith in a man's heart could be incubated into saving faith more effectively in the warm Christian atmosphere of the society than in the chill of the world'.[11]

These cells also served the purpose of collecting funds for work amongst the poor and to support the travelling preachers.

The class meetings brought many into the kingdom and established them in the faith, in an open fellowship of firm discipline balanced with grace and love. They provided a network across England, conserving the fruits of evangelism and consolidating a movement which was able to make a deep impact on the nation. The same system spread around the world providing a similar role of evangelism and nurture in many countries.

'Wesley discovered biblical equilibrium in at least four vital doctrines:

The acceptance of voluntary and corporate disciplines.

Mutual accountability.

Total commitment to the Lord for growth into holiness.

An emphasis on the living relationships of believers to one another.'[12]

Writers such as Howard A Snyder (*The Radical Wesley*, Zondervan) and A Skevington Wood (*The Burning Heart*, Paternoster Press), David Lowes Watson (*Accountable Discipleship* and *The Early Methodist Class Meeting*, both Discipleship Resources) and models like the Covenant/Discipleship groups of the United Methodists in the USA, based on the class meeting, are helping people rediscover the genius of the early Methodist renewal groups.

> The Methodist system shows the need for something more than merely prayer or study groups. It reveals the need for covenant, discipline and accountability of the group to the larger church body. It shows that some sort of committed small group structure needs to be practised for the continual renewal and vitality of the corporate church.[13]

Here then are three compelling reasons for looking again at the role small groups can play in being a significant means for the Holy Spirit to renew those who take their Christian discipleship seriously, bring new life into the corporate life of believers and empower them to be agents of change and healing in a world which has largely lost its way.

THE BASIC PURPOSES OF A CHRISTIAN GROUP

While we have learnt much about group process and techniques from the behavioural sciences and the specialists in group dynamics and the human potential movement, we need always to be aware that small groups which meet in the name of Christ will have goals which in many ways are quite different and distinctive. Frequently there will be similar purposes to those groups without a specific Christian orientation, but the means and the motivation of achieving them will be different. It is well to keep before a Christian group its basic purposes. In evaluating its shared life these can be a helpful objective criteria against which its life can measure.

To worship and obey Christ
The prime purpose of all Christian community is to honour our Lord and God. 'Where two or three are gathered together in my name, there am I in the midst' (Matthew 18:20). Christ is central to each group—not to create a pleasant atmosphere or to increase the therapeutic qualities of the group, nor even to be a vague unifying factor in the fellowship. He is not there to be used, but to be worshipped and obeyed.

Our primary function is not to serve each other but to serve God. The church is not a collection of folk associated because they share a common interest in religion, but the fellowship of those whom God called into 'koinonia' (fellowship) with himself and with one another, through Christ. 'Koinonia' is a horizontal reference simply and solely because it has a vertical one.

The Lord's Prayer is a prayer for a group. Each request uses the plural, 'our'. Well we might pray when we come to 'hallowed be thy Name', 'may your Name be honoured, made holy, in the midst of our small group and through us, collectively and individually, in our community'.

Paul's prayer for the Christians in the young church in Ephesus is a prayer for the leader of every Christian group to pray, '. . . that Christ may dwell in your hearts through faith; that you, being rooted and grounded in love, may have power to comprehend with all the saints what is the breadth and length and height and depth, and to know the love of Christ which surpasses knowledge, that you may be filled with all the fullness of God'. (Ephesians 3:14–21)

The unique characteristic of a Christian fellowship should be the centrality of Jesus Christ. '. . . we are to grow up in every way into him who is the head. . .' (Ephesians 4:15)

To live under the authority of God's Word
'The Bible is the soil from which all Christian faith grows . . . Christ meets us and speaks to us in the Bible . . . Christians come from the Bible.'[14]

A prime purpose of Christian groups is to use all the means at their disposal to hear what the Bible is actually saying, in order to seek to discover the specific ways it applies to each individual's own situation and to support one another in helping that become a reality.

Lawrence Richards, in his discussion of such change in people, quotes from the *Handbook of Small Group Research* by A Paul Hore (p. 287):

> A whole series of studies shows that if one wishes to change attitudes and the subsequent behaviour of a group, discussion and decision where all members participate as directly as possible tends to be more effective than 'enlightenment' or 'persuasion' by the lecture method.

Lawrence Richards goes on to say:

In giving this vital role to the small group I am not in the least suggesting we diminish the role of Scripture. Rather we place Scripture as central to the life of the small group. I do point out, however, that our normal method of teaching God's Word (by sermon) has both communication limitations and also serious limitations on life-impact. Certainly I do not deny that the Holy Spirit uses the preached Word. I only insist that He is much freer to use the Word in a small group where it is studied and discussed together, and that this is one of God's purposes in creating the church. [15]

The whole gathered life of the group will also be lived out under the authority of the Word of God. We need to seek to enrich the relationships within the group by obedience to what is learnt to be God's intention for his people as a community of faith.

Biblical data is primary for a Christian group but it is never sufficient by itself. Belief needs to be tied into experience. This book seeks to lead groups to develop sound knowledge and understanding of the Bible, but it also provides ways of helping that which is learnt to result in change.

To be havens of hope

Being structures of hope is a significant purpose of the small group. The great uncertainty of the future, at all levels of life, has produced an underlying anxiety. Thoughtful people are asking: 'Is there hope for humanity?' This is met by the cynicism of pessimists, with a defeatist 'No!' But what of the Christian?

Gordon Cosby says:

. . . we must face the present situation and seek solutions in new global structures. As we live through the anxiety bordering on panic we must be aware of the temptations of sitting it out or to conform as much as possible or to withdraw from deep involvement with those who suffer. As Christians we can exude hope as we remain close to our Lord. We must build structures of hope.

The social climate in which the Methodist small groups were born, in England, was characterised by loneliness, isolation, despair, alienation, changes in family patterns and rapid advances in technology. The class meetings provided refuges in which people could discover together the 'God of hope' and a new confidence and strength to become 'apostles of hope' to their cheerless contemporaries. Our present day social climate, with its great similarities to that of eighteenth century England, provides fertile soil for similar disciplined Christian cells to again plant faith, hope and love. Small groups can be modern-day 'cities of refuge' (Numbers 35:6–28) to which the traumatised can flee to find a listening ear, an open door of acceptance and understanding, the security of a genuine caring community and a word of hope, as people explore the Scriptures with openness and expectancy in the presence and power of the living Christ.

To foster fellowship

Human beings are made for community and togetherness. However what we are concerned about here is something special, namely that extraordinary fellowship that is spoken of and sometimes reflected in the New Testament. The Greek word commonly rendered as fellowship is 'koinonia'. It literally means the state of sharing, of being partners, of having common or mutual interests. Christians share together in Christ, in God's love through Christ and together partake of the Holy Spirit. Because Christians participate by faith in Christ as their Lord and Saviour they are then, through the Holy Spirit who dwells in them individually and collectively, empowered to participate in each other's lives in a deep, intimate, caring way through the benevolent, outgoing love which the Holy Spirit engenders in their lives.

This deep commitment to love each other is what Christ had in mind when he said, 'By this all will know that you are my disciples, if you have love for one another'. (John 13:25)

This distinguishing mark of true Christian fellowship will most likely not be rediscovered in large meetings, where the participants seldom have more intimate gatherings to complement these experiences. For in such situations the numbers gathered and the physical aspects of the building and seating arrangements prevent us from truly knowing each other. We cannot truly love in these gatherings in more than a relatively superficial manner because we are not able to be involved in each other's lives. In large congregations most must remain strangers. Few have opportunity to share themselves or feel free to be truly honest.

Lawrence Richards writes:

> To learn to trust, and to become trustworthy—to learn to love, and to become loving—we must become deeply involved in the lives of others, to whom we commit ourselves in Christ. To develop this kind of relationship we need to share ourselves with others, and they need to share themselves with us. All of this demands time. More than this, it requires a face-to-face relationship. A relationship we can have only with a few others at one time. And thus a church is forced to move to a small group structure. [16]

We must reject solo Christianity as a rare exception rather than the rule. We are called to live out our Christian life in community.

> It is as individuals that we enter into a permanent relationship with Christ ... this personal relationship is lived out in fellowship with others; 'all of us are the parts of one body' (Ephesians 4:35 NEB). Group membership is not an optional extra for God's people. When a person responds in faith to Jesus Christ he is brought into relationship with others of God's people in that locality—he becomes a group member. This group, community, congregation or assembly of God's people, as it is conceived in the Old and New Testaments is thus not viewed simply as a sociological phenomenon, for it is thought of primarily in terms of God's call. [17]

We are called into a special relationship with each other with privileges and responsibilities (Galatians 6:16; 1 Corinthians 16:1; Colossians 3:12–17). Mutual dependence and influence upon, and respect for, each other are required of those in 'the body of Christ'. And each small group is seen by Paul as being 'the body of Christ'. The writer of the Epistle to the Hebrews exhorts each believer not to avoid these opportunities for Christian nurture and worship.

> ... and let us think of one another and how we can encourage each other to love and to do good deeds. And let us not hold aloof from our church meetings, as some do. Let us do all we can to help one another's faith, and this the more earnestly as we see the final day drawing nearer. (Hebrews 10:24,25, J B Phillips)

We are not saved in an isolated and individualistic fashion. Salvation brings us into close relationship with each other.

Browne Barr, in his lively and entertaining book *High Flying Geese* [18]), uses a flock of geese in flight as an unusual, yet apt, metaphor of what the church ought to be. He tells how Canadian Blue Geese have been observed to fly 17 000 miles in 60 hours non-stop. Part of the key to these remarkable flights is the formation flight of the birds, which improves their aerodynamic efficiency. Theoretically, 25 birds could have an increase of 70% as compared with a single goose trying to do its own thing. Geese fly much faster in formation. It increases distance, speed and endurance.

In a framework of interdependent, supporting, caring relationships, greater degrees of achievement are possible. The Indonesian phrase *Gotong Royong*, 'carrying the load together', expresses well the aim of Christian fellowship.

To bring people to a living faith in Christ

Small groups are playing an important role in awakening and reawakening people to their need of Christ, and helping them make an unhurried, thoughtful, life transforming response to the gospel. The small, house-centred, neighbourhood group is bringing warmth and intimacy to evangelism, which was absent in most larger evangelistic gatherings in the past.

The sensitive small group committed to bringing people to faith in Christ can treat the hearers as persons, respect their integrity, meet them at their point of present understanding, be involved long term with them and incorporate them into the group, to both give to and receive from the fellowship.

This book gives many practical suggestions, arising out of wide experience in the use of small groups for evangelism.

One way many groups keep continually before them their evangelistic purpose is through having an empty chair as an ever-present reminder that there are many as yet outside who are being prepared by the Holy Spirit to hear and respond in faith to the call of Christ. The group pray and work towards having people fill that empty chair.

The Prayer Triplet strategy, which was used with such success in the Mission England evangelism outreach, has now spread to many countries around the world. It involves three Christians meeting together regularly to pray for three of each of their unsaved friends. The aim of these Prayer Triplets is entirely evangelistic. However, as people come to faith in Christ, it also provides the framework to care for new Christians born through this intentional prayerful outreach.

To minister to each other

When the New Testament speaks of ministry in a local church, it is a ministry of all believers to each other. In the passage quoted earlier from Hebrews chapter 10, the exhortation is not to avoid gathering together, because we have a responsibility to minister to each other. When 'two or three' or more disciples are gathered, Christ is there ministering through each to the other, encouraging one another's faith. Each is potentially a minister, as well as one who also must be prepared to be ministered to by others in the group. Each is potentially a stimulator of the faith of the others, as well as a learner.

 Every true Christian believer is indwelt by the Holy Spirit. Peter's great Pentecost sermon climaxed with, 'Repent and be baptized every one of you in the name of Jesus Christ for the forgiveness of your sins; and you shall receive the gift of the Holy Spirit.' (Acts 2:38) Amongst the many aspects of the Holy Spirit's ministry, in and through each Christian, is the formation of a Christlike character ('fruits') and the equipping for ministry ('gifts'). Every true follower of Christ has at least one spiritual gift. In such passages as 1 Peter 4:9f; 1 Corinthians chapters 12 to 14 (12:4 to 31, 14:26) and Romans 12:4–8, the key features of ministry are that each Christian disciple has a gift, a special ability from God. There are varied gifts and accompanying ministries. These gifts are to be used for 'the common good'.

Spiritual gifts are given for ministry—to build fellow Christians up in Christ, to serve others and to bring them to faith in Christ. The Christian growth groups plan an important role in helping members discover their gifts, to affirm these gifts as a group and to help in the development and use of these gifts.

Small groups provide situations in which mutual ministry can take place. Only a small number can minister in a large gathering and then only in a fairly superficial manner to each individual. The majority are denied an opportunity to exercise their ministry to the gathered church.

As we are each affirmed, instructed and encouraged in our respective ministries, we become agents of the grace of God within the fellowship of other Christians and out in a hurting world which has lost its way. Enabling each other's spiritual growth is an essential aspect of each Christian's ministry within the body. Spiritual growth is concerned with change in ideas and in belief systems. But rightly understood, it is essentially concerned with character change— transformation of attitudes, of values and of personality; and these are socially anchored. They are learned through associating with others. They cannot be developed in isolation. For this new set of attitudes, values and behaviour, Christian disciples need a social anchor. They need a viable, authentic, supportive, accepting group in which the Word of God is studied and lived out by its members, individually and collectively.

An aspect of a small group's function in enabling ministry to each other is corporate accountability. This, as we have seen, was an essential dimension of all the small groups in early Methodism. Wesley believed all Christians need to counterbalance each other (in practical ways) with instruction, support, encouragement and accountability. Many contemporary groups, to varying degrees, now have agreed covenants. Some are simple; others have exacting expectations. (We deal with this in more detail later.) Some kind of accountability is mandatory if growth is to take place. Where there is no stated expectation of growth, it is unlikely to occur. Spiritual growth is more likely to take place where there is wise and balanced instruction, encouragement, prayerful support, exhortation and rebuke, all exercised in a framework of mercy and grace.

A distinctive new emphasis in small groups today is not upon each person using the group to meet his or her own personal needs, but to make oneself accessible and available to God and to the members of one's group. That is having our gifts set free by God, to minister to the needs of the other person and the world.

To prepare each other for mission in the world

The final dimension of group function is the preparation of its members for mission in the world. A group can become ingrown. It can become exclusive rather than inclusive. One of the common criticisms of small groups is that they can so easily become 'holy huddles', 'self-righteous cliques' or 'self-improvement societies'. The group experience can be so absorbing that the needs of others are neglected. A group which is alive in the Spirit will seek together to live God's Word, resulting in an overflow of love to others.

'To neglect the social is to be more ''spiritual'' than Jesus Christ had been . . . The core of the Gospel was not that the Word became Spirit, but that the Word became flesh and this meant that the Gospel had to be expressed in very human terms, in terms of social action, in terms of flesh and blood. Words alone were not enough.'[19]

As Elizabeth O'Connor puts it so well, we need to be engaged at the same time in both 'an inward and an outward journey'. The inward journey is marked by a sense of holy obedience and openness to the fresh instruction of Christ each time the group gathers. The outward journey is marked by an increasing sensitivity to suffering and to an intelligent effort to eliminate as much as is humanly possible.

The devotional experience and the social concern of the group, far from being in conflict, actually require each other in order to produce a healthy, balanced fellowship. 'Our love should not be just words and talk; it must be true love, which shows itself in action.' (1 John 3:18) As James says, 'My brothers! What good is it for man to say, ''I have faith'', if his actions do not prove it? Can that faith save him? Suppose there are brothers or sisters who need clothes and don't have enough to eat. What good is there in saying to them, ''God bless you! Keep warm and eat well!'', if you don't give them the necessities of life? This is how it is with faith: if it is alone and has no actions with it, then it is dead.' (James 2:14–17)

All too often groups can replay the roles of the priest and the Levite in the parable of the Good Samaritan, limiting their primary interest to personal salvation and personal holiness.

Small groups can play an important role in helping each other hear and respond in practical ways to the cry of our suffering brothers and sisters in our alienated, hurting world.

Serious reflection at depth on social issues, both in the immediate community and on a global level, linked with thoughtful action and accountability, is an essential part of true spirituality. An unhealthy imbalance creeps into a group when either the local or the world aspects of human need are neglected.

Groups in which I have been involved lived out their mission by planned regular visitation of the sick and shut-in, and providing accommodation for the homeless, refugees and those in crisis. Others were available to undertake special projects for their local church by becoming core groups, facilitating day-care centres and an outreach coffee shop.

One parish in a new housing area had all of its groups organised to provide neighbourhood support, irrespective of religious affiliation. They welcomed newcomers who moved into their area by providing a few meals while they unpacked, and then helped them get oriented to the area. They also kept alert to special needs, due to sickness or bereavement, providing back-up in practical ways.

Some headed up re-cycling programmes. Others organised charity door-knock appeals for their areas. Some raised funds to support an orphan or needy child in other countries.

Field trips were made by some groups, accompanied by a person in the caring professions, to poverty areas in their own communities and centres caring for drug addicts, alcoholics and those who were homeless. They linked this with a reflective and action-oriented process.

But this local concern needs to be balanced with the global dimension of human need. Groups provide ideal situations to wrestle with the problems of injustice, poverty, the arms build-up, responsible use of our resources, and the other deep issues which cause suffering and threaten our very existence.

Some groups build into their programmes times to view videos of some of these issues or hear guest speakers. Two members of one group going overseas for vacation carefully planned into their itineraries (with the help of Christian aid agencies) visits to developing countries, to observe human suffering first hand. On their return, the group struggled with the issues and their role in making adequate responses.

Small groups represent a tremendous potential in the kingdom of our God. The modern small group movement is no longer in its infancy—it is coming of age.

Christians are rediscovering the important place of small

groups in growing the church in both quantity and quality. In small groups, people are experiencing something of the intimacy and challenge of the band of young men who responded to Christ's call to share his life and ministry.

It is my prayer that the following chapters will give some practical help to those who are open to the new quiet movement of the Holy Spirit, in which Christ-centred small groups are playing a major role in bringing new life to the church and faith and hope to the world.

References

(1) Samuel S Shoemaker, *With the Holy Spirit and With Fire* (Harper and Row, New York and Evanston, 1960), p. 110.
(2) J S Stewart, *The Life and Teachings of Jesus Christ* (The Saint Andrew Press).
(3) Michael Green, *Evangelism in the Early Church* (Hodder & Stoughton, London, 1971).
(4) Athol Gill, contributor of the chapter 'Small Groups in the Christian Church', in *Building Small Groups in the Christian Community* (Renewal), by the author.
(5) Ibid.
(6) Ibid.
(7) O Michel, *Theological Dictionary of the New Testament* (Eerdmans, Eds, Kittal and Friedrich).
(8) Taken from *The Radical Wesley* by Howard a Snyder. Copyright © 1980 by Howard A Snyder. Used by permission of Zondervan Publishing House.
(9) James A Davies, Article in *Christian Education Journal*, Vol. V, No 2.
(10) Taken from *The Radical Wesley* by Howard a Snyder. Copyright © 1980 by Howard A Snyder. Used by permission of Zondervan Publishing House.
(11) Ibid.
(12) James A Davies, Article in *Christian Education Journal*, Vol. V, No 2.
(13) Ibid.
(14) Emil Brunner, *Our Faith* (SCM Press).
(15) Taken from *A New Face for the Church* by Lawrence O Richards. Copyright © 1970 by Zondervan Publishing House. Used by permission.
(16) Ibid.
(17) John Kleinig, *The Group—Its Nature and Role* (ANZEA, Sydney,1974), p. 7.
(18) Browne Barr, *High Flying Geese*. Copyright © 1983 by Browne Barr. Used by permission from Harper & Row, Publishers, Inc., San Francisco.
(19) Bruce Kendrick, *Come out of the Wilderness* (Collins, 1973).

Chapter 2
The Range of Small Groups

A group finds validity in its ability to meet the needs of the persons involved.

There are many kinds of small groups that function within the Christian church. In the main, if they are in any way vital they have one common factor: they exist to meet the needs of the people involved. Because individual needs differ greatly so do the range of groups which have emerged to meet these needs. In a real sense they cannot be ranked in order of importance. A group finds validity in its ability to meet the needs of the persons involved.

AN OVERVIEW OF TYPES OF SMALL GROUPS

Some of the more common categories of small groups found in the Christian church are given here. In practice they have their own unique characteristics.

Task groups
These groups have a specific function to fulfil which does

not necessarily involve the personal needs of its members. They are usually set up to undertake some task, e.g. a committee set up to plan, oversee or initiate an activity.

Friendship groups
Designed to establish relationships in an unstructured setting, these groups set their own pace and type of activity. Generally they are self-selective and meet for fun and pleasure. They are self-supportive in a social way.

Interest groups
People meet in these groups who have a common interest in developing manual, relational, educational or social skills.

Discussion groups
These may be short or long-term programmes. Generally books that consider Biblical, historical, theological, socio-logical, psychological and other current affairs are studied to use as a starting point for discussion.

Bible study groups
Along with the traditional 'prayer meetings', these groups were common in the church prior to the emergence of the present small-group movements in the last few decades. Unfortunately many of them became purely academic in their approach, often not seeking to explore the relevance of the Scriptures for real-life situations. The form of Bible study group proposed in this book is entirely different to most of these old style groups which generally used a didactic approach, the leader giving a lecture with little or no participation by the members.

Personal development groups
These take many different forms, but there is essentially a clear contract entered into among members and deep levels of trust and openness required. Some Yoke-Fellow groups are a good example, where individual self-evaluation forms are completed then evaluated by a clinical psychologist. This information then becomes the basis for the individual's work within the supportive framework of the group.

Support groups
These are usually for people who are experiencing high levels of stress. Pressures, doubts, fears, successes, failures, etc. are shared with others who care enough to listen and offer sensitive feedback and support.

Koinonia groups
The name comes from the Greek word for fellowship or oneness, so these groups are concerned with developing authentic Christian community, where a Christian lifestyle can develop. They usually incorporate prayer, study, sharing, personal growth and outreach. Their level of depth will vary greatly. This type of group goes under many other names, such as Home Bible Fellowships, Discipleship groups, Covenant groups and Class Meetings. More recently there are developing Covenant Discipleship groups of deeply committed people prepared to submit themselves to be accountable with a demanding covenant relationship.

Evangelism groups
These groups use a variety of strategies to present the gospel and give people an opportunity to come to a personal faith in Christ. They are often part of a wider programme.

Prayer groups
These have intercessory prayer as their main ministry. Well before the present extensive use of small groups the mid-week prayer meeting was commonplace in many churches. Unfortunately many of those were ingrown or stereotyped, but that does not mean that all of them were ineffective.

Mission groups
These exist to serve the church and outside community in a specific way. There is a commitment to maintenance of the group life and meeting personal needs, but with the purpose of making the group more effective in coming to grips with urgent issues, with which the group becomes deeply involved.

SOME GENERAL DISTINCTIONS
Groups form and operate in many different ways. It helps to be aware of this.

Spontaneous groups
These groups commence as two or more people become aware that they have a common need and decide to meet together to help each other address that need. A number of groups to which I have belonged commenced this way. A group of clergy, with whom I have met over an extended time, began because one day one of the present members

shared with me the struggle he was having in his ministry. My response was: 'I'm walking a similar road; let us walk together'. Over a period we discovered others who felt the same way, and we have now continued to meet over a number of years with some change-over of membership.

Single cells

The above groups, which form spontaneously, generally remain isolated cells, frequently with no official link to church structures. While this allows for greater flexibility, because of lack of accountability to a broader body they can develop in an unhealthy way, becoming introverted, isolated and having an inadequate understanding of Christian faith and practice. However this is by no means the case with all such separate groups as many have rescued those who have become disillusioned, overlooked or rejected by the established church.

Multi-cell networks

Clusters of groups linked together by a common purpose and loyalty are generally associated with a local church, parish or an organisation formed to provide an association of groups with common goals. In my own parishes we formed different networks of cells for youth and adults. I shared my vision with the congregations and more particularly with a small group of deeply committed people. This small group and I then took the initiative to awaken a sense of need and discovered those who were aware of their needs. We next took steps to develop an overall plan, select and train leaders and then gather people into a network of groups.

Covenant groups

These groups are for those with a serious commitment to the goals of the group. While the degree and extent of the covenants may vary, underlying each is a willingness to operate under spiritual disciplines which facilitate a deeper level of involvement and accountability to each other. The Bible study growth group, which is a special focus of this book, usually has an agreed covenant (see Chapter 3, pages 27, 28, 29 for more about covenants).

Non-covenant groups

These groups have no in-depth expectation of their members and are not governed by a covenant. There may be an agreement to meet regularly and to contribute to the group's life in some way but not with the same expectations of covenant groups. The friendship and social groups are examples of this type of group.

BASIC GROUPS FOR CHURCH GROWTH AND RENEWAL

This book is concerned principally with a small number of inter-related types of groups, which are proving to be foundational for the emergence of the new church in the latter half of this century.

I have itemised seven basic groups, though the Bible study growth group often fulfils the functions of many of these other groups.

Frequency and life

The Contact and Evangelism groups I have used have usually been one-meeting groups held from time to time. The Nurture groups are short-term, usually covering a six-week period. Bible study growth groups meet over an extended period, usually weekly, by terms, and dividing when an agreed number is exceeded. The intercessory prayer cells prove to be most regular and long term, meeting weekly in most cases for up to forty or more weeks per year.

Stages of spiritual growth

In diagram No. 1, the upper series of boxes represent the

stages of physical life. The first, the pre-natal period from conception to birth, and the second stage, the birth experience, is followed by the short-term care in the hospital nursery. The final box relates to on-going growth, ideally in the supportive context of a caring family.

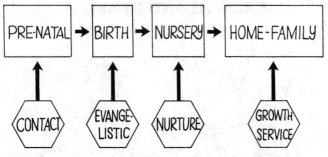

Diagram Nº1 · Groups for Different Stages of Spiritual Life.

This diagram can also represent the stages of spiritual life, the first being the 'pre-evangelism' stage when friendships are formed with unbelievers, during which availability and caring concern are some of the characteristics of the relationship. In addition there will be a modelling of the faith to them through a Christian lifestyle, a sensitive verbalising of the gospel at appropriate times and a genuine love, which all help the person begin to become aware of God and to take him seriously. The second refers to the evangelism stage, where people have the gospel clearly presented to them and are called to repentance and faith. Those who respond experience the 're-birth' of the Spirit. These new 'babes in Christ' need special nurture to become established in their relationship to God and to the community of faith. Continuing growth in Christ then takes place within the fellowship of other believers.

Four basic groups which relate to these phases in spiritual life are shown in diagram No. 1. The first two are bridge groups into an 'owned' faith experience, and the others provide orientation and continuing growth once a person has made a commitment to Christ.

Contact Groups
Contact groups seek to develop deeper relationships usually with unbelievers who are contacted on a regular or irregular basis, such as neighbours, people at work and other contacts within the community. They are low-key informal groups, for the purpose of getting to know others better. The number attending should not exceed sixteen, although more

may need to be invited to attain this number. They are essentially bridge groups to offer friendship, with no strings attached. Each meeting is complete in itself, with no planned further meetings. Usually they are organised by a couple in their own home, or two or three individuals.

The emphasis is upon informality with plenty of time for unstructured conversation. Most groups use a simple non-threatening get-acquainted game, such as the game of Interviews (see Appendix A), during the meeting. Anything which may make uncommitted guests feel uneasy, such as prayer, planned discussion of Christian matters or religious background music, are avoided. However, one needs to be prepared to be surprised by the issues which may arise naturally in the dialogue throughout the evening, which could lead to the related talk of things of God and opportunities for personal witness.

The groups have been held mostly in the evening with supper (coffee/tea and dessert) being served. Leaders need to be alert for expressions of interest in spiritual matters which can be followed up. More than once there has been an expressed desire to meet again, which has resulted in a continuing group exploring subjects raised during the original meeting. (See Contact Groups in Chapter 8 on page 75.)

These 'pre-evangelism' groups can be a stepping stone to the next type of group, with the whole group, or those who have shown an openness, being invited.

Evangelism Groups
These can be isolated groups organised by two or three people, or part of a wider programme. Again they meet in homes but are more intentional, being designed to permit a clear presentation of the gospel, either in the form of a brief address or two lay people sharing their faith story. In both cases the input is followed by discussion, an illustrated explanation of how to make a commitment to Christ and opportunity to respond. (See Chapter 8, 'Sharing the Good News Together', for practical ideas we have proved to be effective in these groups.)

Nurture Groups
Initial help for beginners in the Christian life to reorientate their lives to a Christian style of living is provided through Nurture groups which meet for six to eight weeks. These are the kindergarten groups of the Christian community, aiming to make the members feel accepted and loved, celebrating

together their new found faith, assisting them to understand their new commitment to Christ and giving them some basic help in surviving and beginning to 'grow up into Christ'. (See Chapter 9, 'Caring for New Christians Together'.)

Bible Study Growth Groups

I use the name Bible Study Growth Groups because of the significant place given to the exploration of the meaning and relevance of the Bible for everyday living, individually and collectively, and the concern to grow mature, dynamic followers of Jesus Christ.

This type of group covers a broad spectrum of groups which study the Scriptures, have similar goals and have different degrees of commitment. They are variously known as Koinonia (fellowship) Groups, Growth Groups, Covenant Groups, Home Bible Fellowships, Discipleship Cells. Some small house churches also fit into this category.

Some operate outside church structures, but often develop loose links with similar groups. These, despite disillusionment with the church, are committed to its renewal and loyally minister through their local churches.

They have varying degrees of commitment to developing spiritual gifts and leadership skills of their members, through involving all in different leadership roles within the group. These groups, on the whole, see themselves as 'playing coaches' and are not solo-performers. They play a facilitating role, are resource persons with a degree of maturity and are open to learn from and with the group.

Covenants generally play an important role in these groups, being an indication of serious commitment to the group, its goals and the common disciplines it believes will enable the members to meet these goals (see Chapter 3, 'Keys for Effective Small Groups').

The following are also found with different levels of emphasis:

Praise and creative worship.
The development of active listening and in-depth relationships.
Growth in Christian discipline.
Intercession for each other and people and situations outside the group.
A desire to see people won to Christ through the group and personal witness.
A new openness to the supernatural through the work of the Holy Spirit.
Pastoral care for one another between meetings.

Availability for various forms of service within the local church.
Concern for social issues.

The ones that are playing a significant role in church growth have a clear growth to the point where they divide, usually in a twelve-month period.

These Growth Groups provide the cutting edge of a Christian community. Usually the dynamics for evangelistic and social concern and care come from them and they are generally the seed-beds for personnel, for leadership and for all the actions in the name of Christ which occur in that locality. The staff for the Contact, Nurture and Mission Groups will be drawn from these types of groups. In communistic terms, these are the *cadres* of the Christian church. They provide the potential to develop to the point where they are comprised of disciplined, dedicated, trained people, who will provide the cutting edge for the mission of Christ in the world.

Most of the keys in Chapter 3 apply to this type of group.

Growth Group Leaders' cell

Where there is a network of Growth Groups, this leaders' cell is the key to keeping the groups dynamic. While the highest goal for the Growth groups is for them to grow to the point where they become true in-depth Christian cadres, the leaders' group should model this depth of commitment to Christ and the continuous extension of his kingdom.

This cell is the hub of a Christian community. It will involve leaders of all the Growth Groups and possibly other leaders as well.

Where there are more than twelve leaders, they should meet in smaller groups but organise times for all of the leaders to meet to build a sense of unity. Frequency of the meetings varies, but most find it necessary to meet monthly, especially in the early stages of a multi-cell programme. (See Chapter 3, pages 32, 33 and Chapter 17, pages 139 and 140 for more on leaders' groups.)

Prayer Groups

While many old style prayer meetings were dull, stereotyped experiences, today there has emerged new vital prayer cells, where people are taught to pray, creative methods are used and short prayers and a positive spirit are encouraged. In many there is a new understanding of the role of the Holy Spirit and a dependence upon his empowering. (See Chapter 13, 'Praying Together'.)

A relatively new and most effective form of prayer cell is known as:

Prayer Triplets

Prayer Triplets is a prayer strategy which was one of the most significant factors in the success for Mission England in

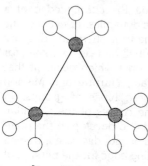

Diagram Nº2 · Prayer Triplets.

1984–85. Brian Mills shares his vision of this simple, flexible scheme in his book *Three Times Three Equals Twelve* (Kingsway), which is available in Australia as *Prayer Triplets* (Anzea).

Prayer Triplets involves Christians getting together into groups of three to pray for a total of nine of their non-Christian neighbours and friends.

By the time Billy Graham arrived for his three-month preaching tour in England, an estimated 30 000 triplet groups had been formed, praying by name for a staggering 279 000 people. Triplets met in colleges and schools, in places of work and in institutions. Some were neighbourhood based, others were church based. All ages were involved. It is reported that three eight-year-old boys formed a Prayer Triplet! Those involved became part of the answer to their own prayers, as they felt encouraged and supported to share their faith with those for whom their whole group prayed regularly. Many of these prayer groups turned into nurture groups, as those won to Christ found those who had prayed for them their first point of reference.

Amongst the factors which contributed to the effectiveness of Prayer Triplets, Brian Mills lists:

The praying is outgoing rather than inward looking.

Prayer is specific. People are prayed for by name; day to day needs are upheld with a special focus upon them becoming Christians.

Those praying feel motivated and supported to share their faith with those for whom they pray.

Relationships deepen, confidence grows, faith is strengthened, spiritual growth takes place and a close bond develops. The group provides an effective framework for sharing, mutual support, encouragement and warm accountability.

Expectancy levels begin to rise as faith deepens, understanding of the meaning of prayer takes place, and the strong help the weak.

It is biblical. Matthew 18:19–20 is acted upon: 'If two of you on earth agree about anything, it will be done for you by my Father in heaven. For where two or three come together in my name, there am I with them.'

The Prayer Triplet strategy is now being used extensively in evangelistic outreach around the world.

FOUR OTHER SIGNIFICANT GROUPS

These groups will indirectly affect church growth and renewal so I have listed them separately.

Support Groups

While members will experience significant care in Bible Study Growth Groups, some may feel the need to meet with others who are peers or experiencing similar pressures. Bible study will play a role in these groups but the group's main attention is upon open sharing, discussion of problems being encountered by prayer and pastoring of one another, usually in pairs between group meetings.

Christians seeking to live out a Christian witness in their professions, in various forms of public office, in unions and in their work place are often at risk and would benefit from the opportunity to share the pressures they experience in a small supportive group, where they are able to struggle together with issues and find personal and spiritual support. For a number of years I belonged to such a group of businessmen and politicians which was part of a world network. One of the questions which these groups constantly struggle with is: 'What will it involve for me to live under the lordship of Jesus Christ in every area of my life (family—daily occupation—church—leisure—"neighbours")?'

The Pittsburgh Experiment in the USA, commenced by Bishop Sam Shoemaker, has a long successful track record in facilitating these groups for businessmen and women, the unemployed and those in a variety of other situations.

Clergy, their spouses and others in full time Christian ministry are in vulnerable, fairly isolated situations, where they may need opportunities to meet, especially with peers, to share and pray together. This type of continuing group plays a major role in my own life and witness. Our group finds it has helped us clarify ideas, given wise counsel, pastored us through some difficult situations, encouraged and constantly upheld each of us in prayer. The group comes together to uphold a member in special need. In Newcastle, the Steel City north of Sydney where from my parish we established a city-wide detached youth work ministry to work mainly on the streets with disadvantaged and anti-social youth, our workers were very vulnerable. Two support groups were established. One met weekly to provide personal, emotional and spiritual support. The other comprised a group from various professions to provide expert advice and help when required.

Support groups have been formed for people rehabilitating after treatment for emotional problems, those affected by various forms of grief and also the unemployed. As they have enabled each other to better understand and adjust to their situation, members have found new hope. These groups include a capable leader and some who have successfully worked through these problems, as well as others still struggling to cope.

Mission/Action Groups

A group of people with a common concern for issues within the church or community bind together to study the issue, alert others to the need, explore solutions and take appropriate action. Community issues often include injustice, hardship and environmental matters. These groups work on the basis that there is strength in numbers. Amongst the common projects that such groups in my parishes have set up are: a mobile domiciliary nursing service, language classes for migrants, a drug advisory service, senior citizens' club, a pre-school kindergarten, an aged care hostel, and the city wide youth service described above.

'At Home' Groups

This is a strategy my wife and I developed in our parish ministry to help build a deeper sense of community within our congregations. Different people were invited in small clusters to our home over an extended period, in an effort to foster deeper relationships in the congregations. These groups were also used on a continuing basis to help orient newcomers. More detail on these groups and how to organise them is given in Chapter 16 entitled ' "At Home" Groups'.

Committee Sub-groups

The efficiency of committees can be improved by dividing members into smaller sub-groups to deal with difficult issues. In my parishes I found this strategy involved the total group more effectively in the decision-making process and resulted in greater commitment to decisions made. The process was facilitated by the executive meeting held well in advance to formulate the agenda and identify issues which needed careful thought. Information on each issue was compiled and distributed well beforehand. When these issues came up in the course of the meeting, we divided into groups of three or four for ten minutes or more, answered any questions at the conclusion of the period, then took a vote without any further debate. The one or two who objected initially were those who normally dominated any debates!

While chairing our annual State Synod meetings, during a difficult protracted debate I suspended the discussion and asked the 650 members to discuss the issue with two or three around them. The assembly quickly came to a decision after that exercise.

Professor Roberta Hestens from the USA has improved the efficiency and quality of life in smaller committees by replacing the 'opening devotional' with a sharing and prayer time around these two questions: 'What is your own greatest personal need that we could pray for?' and 'What is the greatest need in your ministry that we could pray for?' (An audio cassette of her address 'Turning Committees into Communities' is available from Fuller Theological Seminary, Pasadena, California, 91182 USA, or Serendipity Christian Resources, GPO Box 1944, Adelaide 5001, South Aust., Australia.)

Chapter 3
Keys for Effective Small Groups

As we have seen, there are a wide variety of small groups. Their purpose differs according to the specific needs of the individuals involved. It is virtually impossible to give a list of guidelines which apply to all groups, so we shall consider in this chapter some applicable to a number of the most common types of small groups found within the Christian church, especially those concerned with making disciples and growing the church.

Here are a few suggestions with more in other chapters which have not been repeated here.

Determine the aim of the group
Group life suffers and some groups never get off the ground because goals and expectations of the individual members are either never defined or are too diverse for the group to work together in unity. Any healthy organisation usually has a clear statement of purpose and an agreed-upon method of pursuing that purpose. Goals must be specific, achievable and measurable. Groups firstly must determine clearly their ultimate (long range) aims or goals. These spell out *why* the group is meeting, and its overall purpose. Having done this, action or intermediate (short range) goals should be set to give direction to specific periods in the life of the group, thus enabling it to move towards its ultimate purpose.  Short range goals are concerned with *how* and *when* the group moves towards its goals and determine the group's programme. These goals may be say for six weeks or six months, and spell out clearly specific things to be achieved. With a clear statement of purpose, both the ultimate and intermediate goals also provide objective criteria, against

which the accomplishments of the group can be measured at different stages.

Although a mere setting of goals does not ensure their realisation or the consequent effectiveness of the group, small groups acting in the name of Christ which we are considering exist as part of the life and mission of the Christian church. Therefore goals should be consistent with the overall nature and purpose of the wider Christian community.

During the first meeting of most types of group, members should be given time to express their hopes and expectations of the group. Each writes answers to such questions as: 'What are you hoping this group will achieve?' and 'What do you expect of this group?' These are summarised on a board, or the like, and an aim formulated. Some groups keep a journal (not a 'minute book'!) of some of the happenings in their group, which they want to be able to recall from time to time to track their progress. The aim could be one of the first entries in that record.

Having done this, one or two may feel this does not meet their hopes, and if their expectations cannot be incorporated in the aim to everyone's satisfaction, they may feel this is not the group for them. This can avoid future frustration and conflict for both them and the group.

All the activities will be built around this aim. Study programmes, sharing, worship, prayer, evangelism and service will seek to move the group to reaching its stated objective. The goal areas for a group to consider include fellowship, worship, learning, prayer, sharing, service and outreach.

Groups committed to **church growth goals** will focus on facilitating quality of lifestyle and witness, growing together as a community of the Holy Spirit, and increasing numerically. Development which is authentic will avoid a preoccupation with numerical growth, with only superficial attention to these other facets. Indeed the growth which will last, and best reflect God's intention for the body of Christ in this world, is a work of the Holy Spirit. It will grow from a disciplined life together, arising out of a sustained and earnest encounter with God's Word, expressing itself in a continuous involvement in Christ's mission in the world.

Plan to grow

One of the soundest strategies for church growth is based on the establishment and expansion of small groups. A church which is committed to growth can experience both quality and quantity growth through a small group strategy, without the strains associated with some forms of church growth being propagated today.

Small groups that are committed to be midwives of the Holy Spirit in bringing new life to both those inside and outside the Christian fellowship will set themselves clear goals to grow to the point where they have to divide.

There are simple principles to follow in moving towards this objective. First, **begin with a small group of two or more** who are committed to win people to Christ and to care for these new Christians. The **Prayer Triplet plan** (outlined in Chapter 2 on types of small groups) could be followed, but with a Bible study and worship dimension incorporated into it. Let the the goal be to grow to 10 or 12 members by the end of the first year. They could take a grain of wheat as their symbol, based on Christ's words, 'Unless the grain of wheat falls into the earth and dies, it remains alone; but if it dies, it bears much fruit.' (John 12:24) (The great paradox of the Christian life is that by 'losing life we find it'!) This becomes the group's motivation for their life together—to grow to the point where they lose their original identity by dividing at the end of twelve months, to become the basis for two more groups with the same goal. As this process is repeated, so the redemptive fellowship of the original small group is multiplied.

On this basis, if four groups of three people decided to commit themselves to this strategy and keep up this process over a ten-year period, the incredible result would be 2 048 groups with 20 480 members! Most of us are usually not impressed by such calculations, for there are too many variables to take into consideration. However, the exercise at least serves to show the potential in small groups, provided those involved catch the vision and commit themselves to it, and seek the Holy Spirit to work through such a strategy.

Secondly, plan to meet for **three or four terms each year**. No new members are added during each 6–8 week term, as this usually disrupts the growth and relationships of the group. New members are therefore added only at the commencement of each term. However during the term an empty chair is placed in the group as a reminder of the group's evangelistic purpose. Some who are unbelievers will fill the chair; others will be believers at different stages in their spiritual growth. (Of course the empty chair will also remind the members of the ever-present Christ, who brings

both consolation and a continuous call to his mission in the world.) New members are presented with this philosophy and encouraged to become part of this great dream by being on the look-out for others to link up with the group.

Thirdly, make preparations for the dividing of the group well in advance. Potential leaders should be identified and given opportunity to develop their gifts by sharing some aspects of the leadership. They will be encouraged to expand their knowledge through reading books on small group leadership, such as this one, and attending appropriate training programmes. In the third or fourth term, they may be invited to attend the leaders' group and the annual planning and training conference.

In the last term, **prepare the group for its division**. This can be done by conducting the study segment in two sub-groups meeting in different rooms, and then coming together for the closing exercise. The second last session for the year could be held in different homes, but with all joined for the last session. The final step is to commence the new year with separate groups. Two members of the original group may form a leadership team to head up each new group if individuals are not sufficiently confident to lead a group on their own.

It is important to be aware that a group which has grown close together in fellowship over the year will experience grief through the division. Groups which are not prepared for this could fragment. Grief will be experienced by most for some time, despite the steps taken to ease them into the parting and the celebration associated with achieving the growth goal. For this reason, build into at least the first term of the next year a few opportunities for the groups to come together, either for a normal meeting or a social gathering.

For this programme to work effectively not only the philosophy needs to be understood by the believers in the group, but they will also need training in witnessing to others and then how to disciple those who join. Help will need to be given in how to invite others, e.g. guidance in how to tell others about the value of the group fellowship in their own personal faith journey.

Some committed to this plan for church growth will feel the need to belong to two groups: one for outreach, as described, and another for in-depth personal and spiritual growth. With frequent additions to the groups, the level of spirituality reached may not satisfy the more deeply committed members. In such cases, additional groups are often formed which remain closed for 12-month periods or more to enable the development of deeper spirituality.

Even if a group does not wish to commit itself to this growth plan, the principle of dividing groups before a group grows too large remains. The size of the group reaches an upper limit, beyond which meaningful interpersonal relationships become less possible at any depth. If a group increases to over 12 it should divide, just to ensure that it exists as a viable group. Acquainting the group with this principle from its inception will ease the trauma associated with the division.

Plan optimistically

If we have faith in the power of God to produce change, then we can be optimistic about the possibilities of renewal through small groups. We ourselves need to be thoroughly convinced that small groups are a viable method for new life in the church. Our enthusiasm and optimism will rub off onto others.

It is often the one who may seem to be the least likely person who will be interested in joining a group. Do not prejudge potential interest in a group. I am frequently surprised that some whom I thought would not be interested, willingly link up with a group and become active members. The majority will become involved because they have been personally invited.

Train leaders

Ideally, training for leadership of a small group should involve both pre-service and in-service training.

Before each of the small group multi-cell programmes

commenced in three of the parishes in which I have served, basic leadership training was given. This varied. At Port Kembla the leadership of the groups grew out of a larger study/fellowship group, which met for over two years preceding the decision to commence the small group programme. Training in the content of the Christian faith was accompanied by the demonstration of various methods of study and leadership techniques. Honesty, openness, growth in relationships and experience-centred learning, were some of the characteristics of training. A short, intensive, pre-service programme dealing specifically with small group leadership skills

then sought to prepare the new leaders for their specific tasks. On other occasions, the period of preparation for potential leaders was much shorter, and for this reason I felt the leadership in some cases was not as rich as in the Port Kembla groups.

The development of skills in group dynamics will be balanced with training in Bible study, theology, church history and discipleship if our small groups are to avoid being superficial and deteriorating into a sharing of ignorance. Each leader should be expected to have the basic texts in the kit of books listed in Chapter 11 on Bible study and be given help in how to use them.

Leaders who are relatively immature spiritually can be effective, provided there is continuing pastoral support and ongoing educational opportunities. In one of my parishes a number of the small group leaders had been Christians for only a short period. However, they proved to be capable leaders despite their inexperience, because of the in-service training and support provided through the regular cell-leaders' meetings (see later in this chapter) and the encouragement and guidance I was able to give. An annual evaluation and planning event for the small group programme, also mentioned in this chapter, further enhanced their leadership.

Use informal situations

For most small groups, it is generally more beneficial to meet away from the church building. This need not be a home—it could be an office, or a special room set aside in a church. Church facilities do not always provide ideal situations for natural interaction between people in small groups. Also, where groups are committed to reaching those not associated with a church, it could be a deterrent initially to invite people to a church building.

The intimacy and comfort of a home situation makes it easier to put people at ease and facilitate close relationships. Meeting in homes also allows greater flexibility for churches committed to church growth. As the groups increase, more homes are enlisted. Alternatively, if the groups decrease, the church is not left with expensive empty buildings, as has been the case where special

facilities were developed on the church site to accommodate groups.

If possible, use the same location for each term. People are apt to get confused and cease attending if the meeting is held in a different home each meeting night, especially if a person misses a meeting or loses their roster list. The people in whose home the group is held need to be warm and friendly in order to make people feel welcome and relaxed.

Refreshments after the group can be useful, in that it can be a relaxing time for informal fellowship. However, most people are more concerned about having a well-run meeting and getting home, though single people may want to stay on. The element of competition can so easily creep in, where somebody wants to put on a better spread of snacks than somebody else. The hosts and hostesses can be given some pointers, such as not busying themselves during the meeting with preparation of refreshments to be served at the conclusion.

Determine the size of the group

'What is the ideal number to have in a small group?' There is no one simple answer to that question. It depends on the purpose of the group and the background, maturity and resourcefulness of the members, along with other variables. However, some upper limits can be set. Changes in beliefs and attitudes of persons are more likely to take place where there is opportunity for all to be involved with interaction in the clarification and expansion of ideas. The amount of interaction possible between people in a small group is determined by its size.

There is a simple equation which expresses the number of relations possible among people in various sized groups: $R = N(N-1)$. This is based on the fact that if one person communicates with another and is satisfactorily received, a relationship has been formed. When the reverse takes place, another relationship is established between the two people.

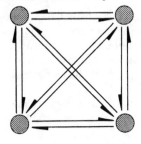

The number of relationships, R, equals the number of persons in the group. N, multiplied by one less than the number of persons in the group, $N-1$.

As shown in the diagram, when four people are involved in dialogue there is a pattern of twelve interpersonal relationships. The number increases steeply as only a few extra are added to the group.

Diagram Nº3 : Possible Relationship in a Group of Four.

For a group of 6 (6×5) 30 relationships
For a group of 8 (8×7) 56 relationships
For a group of 10 (10×9) 90 relationships
For a group of 12 (12×11) 132 relationships
For a group of 15 (15×14) 210 relationships
For a group of 20 (20×19) 380 relationships

It is evident that the larger the group, the less possibility there is of deep interpersonal relationships among the participants. It is generally agreed that the upper limit for a small group, in which members are able to participate meaningfully, is twelve. Beyond that number the group tends to be dominated by a few aggressive members.

However, the upper limit for deep relationships is not the only factor which determines the size of the small group. For growth groups and some other types of small groups dealt with in this book, six to eight is a good number to aim at.

Twelve not only sets the upper limit for meaningful relationships, but provides a non-threatening situation for those who are new to small group experiences. This allows involvement of the participants to the degree they desire. It helps them exercise their individual right of dissent, to stay out of involvement in the group to any real depth without being obvious.

It is significant that Jesus chose twelve men to be in his group. His radical message required deep interaction with himself and each member of the group, but the size of the group allowed each to determine his own level of involvement while growing to a point of total commitment to Christ.

Don't overlook odd times to hold meetings

Often people's immediate reaction when they are asked to join a small group is 'I haven't got a spare night'. Giving the impression that the Holy Spirit only operates between 7.30 pm and 9.30 pm on week-nights, with some variations to his schedule on Sundays, should be avoided!

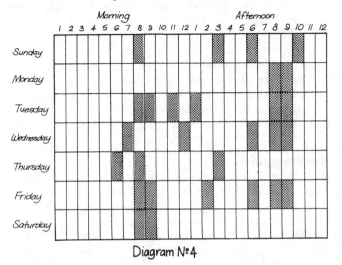

Diagram Nº4

Everyone has numerous time slots in the week which are possibilities for small group meeting times. The chart dividing a week into one-hour time slots serves to show a variety of possible times for small groups to meet. The shaded segments indicate the time slots used by groups in my parish experiences and because successfully adopted deserve comment.

Less obvious times:

(i) A number of young mothers tried meeting during the day, but were frustrated by the natural disturbance of their small children. To find quietness to study and relate at depth, they chose to meet from 5.00 am to 6.30 am weekly—not a popular time by any means, but for this group a rich growing experience eventuated which lasted for a number of years. A deep sense of need will motivate people to consider more unusual times.

(ii) A group of teenagers, another of businessmen and community leaders, and in another instance clergy, met over breakfast; which for some meant starting at 6.00 am and others up to 7.00 am. The host ate before the group arrived in order to be free to serve the group. Study and sharing took place during the meal, which was always kept simple.

(iii) A frontier youth workers' support group met at 7.30 am in a regional centre, where the participants did not have far to travel to work after the meeting.

(iv) Groups of businessmen and women and tradesmen held meetings during their lunch hours; mostly meeting in office or committee rooms, sometimes in a corner of a workshop, and one met in a secluded corner of a greasy boiler-house!

(v) Students gathered for their group meetings over supper, after an evening of study.

(vi) Periods before and after church worship have been popular times for busy people.

(vii) Senior folk often preferred to meet in the afternoon rather than in the evenings.

Meet regularly

Frequency of small group meetings will vary from group to group. Certain types of groups will need to meet more regularly than others to maintain the group life and achieve the agreed goals, though meeting weekly generally provides the desirable frequency in most situations. Some groups will find a fortnightly meeting adequate and the only possibility under their circumstances. Meeting less than bi-weekly usually lacks continuity but I belonged to a group for a number of years whose members all

travelled extensively. So we met whenever we were all available, which sometimes meant four weeks between meeting, yet it was a very helpful group.

Meet by terms

If a group is heavily study oriented, it is helpful to meet by terms of 6 to 8 weeks, roughly following the pattern of school terms. In our adult groups we generally commenced the first term mid-February. The final term ran to late November, closing before the heavy Advent preparations in December. After running a small group programme for three years which met for 52 weeks in the year, we found this a sensible variation well received by the participants.

Meeting by terms has many advantages:

It avoids both busy and slack periods such as Easter, Christmas, school vacations and school and university examinations.

Each term a new study unit can be accomplished. This helps hold interest and provides a range of subjects.

The fresh start to the groups throughout the year encourages enlistment of new members who otherwise may be reluctant to break into a group which has been functioning for a period.

The breaks between the terms give opportunity to make alterations to the groups in terms of leadership or membership.

A different home can be used for each term, providing a variety of venues without the confusion which can arise when a different home is used each week.

Each term can be commenced and concluded with a combined gathering of all the groups, which is an advantage in preventing isolation.

The conclusion of the term provides a natural opportunity to undertake evaluation, sometimes overlooked in a group which meets throughout the year.

The period between the terms provides a welcome break for the group without feeling guilty about missing a meeting.

Some leaders have used the recess to visit drop-outs or potential members.

The term system seems to best fit the groups with a heavy study content but some other types of groups also follow this practice. However, some growth groups find it more effective to meet regularly with a recess over the summer holiday period.

Limit the length of each meeting

The length of meetings varies with the amount of time available and the work to be done. Breakfast and lunch-hour groups may be limited to 45 minutes; evening groups from one hour and a half to two hours.

Regularity and punctuality are of great importance. In any effective group, faithfulness in attendance is essential. Most small group covenants list it as the first commitment the group member is asked to make. It is therefore a reasonable

26

expectation that meetings will be held as scheduled, and that they begin and close at the hours agreed upon. Other responsibilities of the members should be respected; from keeping business appointments to getting the baby sitter home on time.

If a group is involved in an absorbing sharing or discussion period which looks like taking the group over time, the leader should seek a group decision regarding exceeding the scheduled time for finishing. Those who may have to leave should be able to do so without being made to feel they are letting the group down.

Have a pattern for each meeting

Each group will need to create a particular pattern of meeting which serves its needs and situation.

There are certain elements which are common to most small groups in the Christian church: worship and praise; study—of the Bible, literature, books on the Christian faith, etc.; sharing—insights, problems, questions, judgements; prayer—of various kinds, and both silent and spoken.

A possible model which has been used, with the timing allowed for each segment during a two-hour group meeting, is:

Brief worship (10 mins)—including praise in song and possibly some simple form of liturgy. Hymns, psalms, Scripture passages and most church hymnals provide resources for simple responsive reading. One group member could be assigned the task of preparing and leading this segment.

Brief prayer (3 mins)—silent or spoken to recognise the presence of Christ in the group.

Feed-back segment (15 mins)—in which people report on their research of issues raised in the previous meeting. Certain persons may have been assigned this task, or the leader may have been wise enough not to muddle through a difficult question raised previously and may be prepared now with an adequate answer. This period may also be used to recapitulate on the previous study, especially if it is part of a unit. Time may be given for sharing on the reflection of the members on the previous week's experience, and how they sought to relate it to their life situations during the week.

Study (50 mins)—linked with a discussion/sharing and hopefully some creative group work, using some of the methods suggested in other chapters.

Prayer as a response to hearing the Word of God through the study period (10 mins). Chapter 14 on prayer methods suggests a variety of ideas to use: silent, written, spoken, conversational prayer, etc. This period of prayer will focus on petition, confession and thanksgiving.

Intercessory prayer may follow (20 mins) for persons and situations raised by the group. This will be an important part of a group which has a wide vision of its mission in the world expressing care and concern which is wider than the needs of the immediate group.

Praise segment (10 mins). This may be included at another point in the session as well as, or instead of, at the conclusion. Wherever God's people gather, the spirit of joyful praise should be apparent.

The format and timing can be varied to suit the aims of the group and time available.

Make a covenant with each other

Elizabeth O'Connor has some pertinent things to share when making comments about the place of discipline in the Mission groups at the Church of the Savior, Washington, D.C.

As members of a mission group we need to be disciplined and we need to be willing to require a discipline of those who would be on mission with us. No person or group or movement has vigor and power unless it is disciplined. Are we willing to be disciplined ourselves and to require it of others when it means that we will be the target of the hostilities and the pressures of many who do not see the necessity? The chances are that we will give in unless we know that this 'giving in' means that our mission group will have no hard sharp cutting edge, and will in time peter out.[1]

Group life suffers and some groups never get off the ground, because goals and expectations of the individual members are too diverse for the group to work together in unity. Any healthy organisation usually has a clear statement of purpose and an agreed-upon method of pursuing that purpose.

In forming a covenant, questions the group will need to answer are: 'What is the purpose of the group? To what discipline or tasks will each participating member need to commit themselves to achieve the stated goals of the group?' Differentiation will need to be made between maintenance goals (those which concern the life within the group) and the goals which have to do with the work undertaken by the group.

It is important that the covenant be a group decision and not superimposed by the leader. Even in a situation where a number of groups are formed to operate under the same covenant to help in the achievement of an overall agreed goal (such as in some networks of covenant/discipleship groups), each group is generally given the option to commit itself to only a number of the aspects of the agreed covenant at the commencement, with others being introduced as each group develops.

For some new Christians an extensive covenant can be too daunting to begin with. It is better to let the commitment grow rather than over-burden them with too high an expectation at first.

When a single group is considering a covenant the leader may submit a model such as that used by the Covenant Groups at the National Presbyterian Church in Washington, D.C. But the group should negotiate this and come to a group decision, to ensure a full commitment.

It is imperative that covenants be administered in a spirit of grace and not law. While it is reasonable to have high expectations of people who thoughtfully and prayerfully commit themselves to such a covenant, we must avoid creating a legalistic spirit in the group. A lazy or undisciplined person will need to be nudged. A healthy Christian fellowship embodies exhortation and rebuke, but this always must take place in a pastoral atmosphere of love and patience. Essentially, covenants in Christian groups are about 'watching over one another in love'.

However, don't water down the expectations of a highly motivated group to the point where the group life rises little higher than the superficiality and lack of discipline so common in many sections of the church. Our Lord said to those who would be his disciples, '. . . let him deny himself and take up his cross daily and follow me'.

Most group covenants have these common features:
> regular attendance
> ordered personal devotional life
> prayer, and pastoral support for each member of the group
> practice of Christian stewardship
> involvement in regular worship of the gathered church
> availability for service.

Louis Evans Jnr, senior pastor at National Presbyterian Church in Washington, D.C., gives some guidelines followed by the groups attached to his church. He stresses they are principles and not legalisms.

Covenant groups are an expression of our life in Christ and cannot reach their potential unless He is an active member of the group. Our life and strength flow from Him; therefore we can take joy in His presence and express what He is accomplishing in our group as a member of it. His Word is our guide to all of life and therefore it should be used as the groups feel the need. It is out of His Word that we identify the following covenant dynamics:

1. **The covenant of Affirmation** (unconditional love, agape love) There is nothing you have done, or will do that will make me stop loving you. I may not agree with your actions, but I will love you as a person and do all I can to hold you up in God's affirming love.

2. **The covenant of Availability** Anything I have—time, energy, insight, possessions—are all at your disposal if you need them. I give these to you in a priority of covenant over non-covenant demands. As part of this availability I pledge regularity of time, whether in prayer or in agreed upon meeting time.

3. **The covenant of Prayer** I covenant to pray for you in some regular fashion, believing that our caring Father wishes His children to pray for one another and ask Him for the blessings they need.

4. **The covenant of Openness** I promise to strive to become a more open person, disclosing my feelings, my struggles, my joys and my hurts to you as well as I am able.

The degree to which I do so implies that I cannot make it without you, that I trust you with my needs and that I need you. This is to affirm your worth to me as a person. In other words, I need you!

5. **The covenant of Sensitivity** Even as I desire to be known and understood by you, I covenant to be sensitive to you and to your needs to the best of my ability. I will try to hear you, see you and feel where you are, to draw you out of the pit of discouragement or withdrawal.

6. **The covenant of Honesty** I will try to 'mirror back' to you what I am hearing you say and feel. If this means risking pain for either of us I will trust our relationship enough to take that risk, realising it is in 'speaking the truth in love, that we grow up in every way into Christ who is the Head'. I will try to express this honesty, to 'meter it', according to what I perceive the circumstances to be.

7. **The covenant of Confidentiality** I consider that the gifts God has given me for the common good should be liberated for your benefit. If I should discover areas of my life that are under bondage, 'hung up' or truncated by my own misdoings or by the scars inflicted by others, I will seek Christ's liberating power through my covenant partners so that I might give to you more of myself. I am accountable to you to 'become what God has designed me to be in His loving creation'. [Used with permission.]

The Yokefellow Movement

is a vigorous effort to give depth and direction to a full participation in the cause of Christianity by any Christian who wishes to share the 'yoke of Christ'. The Yokefellow card sets the disciplines out in this way:

'As one who seeks to submit his will to the will of Christ, I humbly undertake to wear His yoke in the following ways:

1. **The Discipline of Prayer.** To pray daily, preferably in the morning with a minimum goal of 30 minutes for the devotional period.

2. **The Discipline of Scripture.** To read, reverently and thoughtfully, every day, a portion of Scripture, following a definite plan.

3. **The Discipline of Worship.** To participate each week in the worship, work and fellowship of a local church.

4. **The Discipline of Money.** To give a definite portion of my annual income for the promotion of the Christian cause.

5. **The Discipline of Time.** To employ my time in such a way that I do not waste God's gift, but make a daily Christian witness, particularly in my regular work.

6. **The Discipline of Study.** To develop my understanding and insight by the regular study of serious Christian books.

7. **The Discipline of a Group Experience.** To attend weekly meetings of a Yokefellow Group, and give priority to the meetings and the daily devotional period.' [Used with permission.]

The Serendipity relational Bible study resources covenant

has enabled the development of caring groups which reach out to others with the Good News of Christ, while making unexpected discoveries in encountering the Word of God together.

Lyman Coleman says:

Insist on the Covenant. In the push to transform the church overnight into a network of Bible study and growth groups, the temptation will be to cut corners—especially on the requirements for membership in groups. Don't do it!

If a person is unwilling to sign the Covenant, you should ask this person to wait until a later time when he/she is able to give him/herself to the common disciplines. [2]

The Serendipity Covenant is:

1. **Attendance:** Priority is given to the group meetings. Except in cases of emergency, you will be present and on time.

2. **Participation:** The purpose of the first 6 sessions is to get acquainted and build up a sense of oneness, or 'koinonia', in your group. This is accomplished by letting each group member 'tell his or her spiritual story' to the group. To be in a group, you must be willing to let the group hear 'your story'.

3. **Confidentiality:** Anything that is shared in the group is kept in strict confidence. This is not a therapy group, but information will be shared from time to time that should not be repeated outside the group.

4. **Accountability:** At the close of every session, an opportunity is given for you to share new goals you want to set for your life. When you state a goal and ask the others in the group to 'support' you in these goals, you are giving permission to the group to 'hold you accountable'.

5. **Accessibility:** The group is for people who know they are weak and need the help of others to overcome temptation, spiritual depression and chronic weakness. In asking to be in a group, you are admitting you need support . . . and that you are willing to support others in the same condition.

To be in a group, you are giving others permission to call on you for spiritual help—even at three o'clock in the morning—and you are asking for the same permission from others.

6. **Evangelism:** The group is willing and ready at any time to adopt new people who need the support and correction of your group. In forming a group, you also agree to 'keep an empty chair' for anyone who needs your help and is willing to agree to these minimum disciplines. [3]

Make all study relevant

A common criticism of some small groups in the church has been that they are dull, uninteresting, their studies are irrelevant and rather than produce change, they reinforce limited thinking and experience. Instead of helping people grow, they stunt growth.

One of the reasons for this criticism is that the topics studied in many cases have not grown out of the expressed needs of the participants. The particular interests of each member have not been explored. Instead the subjects have frequently been imposed by the leader or without adequate opportunity for the group to plan together its own syllabus.

The methods of study have been another area contributing to this irrelevance and ineffectiveness. Generally, an authoritarian leadership style results in a didactic, lecture type of presentation with little or no opportunity for the group to think through the issues raised. The inductive method, on the other hand, makes for relevance as it involves the whole group in the learning. It draws upon the individual experiences of each member, reflects upon and analyses these, and sets lines of action which will affect their life situation. Chapter 10 on 'Learning Together' develops this further.

The study of the Bible has been often little more than an academic or intellectual exercise. Minds have been filled with information but opportunity has not been given to apply this to the stage the learners have reached in their personal and corporate life. The Bible is the vehicle through which God reveals his will to humankind. It is meant to foster change. It is intended to help people realign their lives

to God's intention for them in their everyday situations. Time must be taken to let this happen in other than a superficial manner. Methods, like those set out in Chapter 12 on Bible Study methods, should be used to enable people to wrestle with the relevance of the Scriptures to their inner life, every aspect of their relationships, their home, their work or study situation, their leisure and the world in which they live. And that takes time, it involves honesty, is somewhat risky and there will be agony of mind on occasions. But unless we make all study relevant, small groups can become part of the problem rather than part of the answer.

Provide opportunities for worship and celebrating the Lord's Supper

Praise should have a prominent place when God's children gather together. It brings pleasure to God and joy to those who sing from the heart. But the worship segment should be varied. Instead of 30 minutes of singing, the worship session could include, along with some singing, an affirmation of faith, said together; or a poem, or a psalm. The worship segment should focus on God, affirm his love and mercy, and set the tone for the meeting. On occasions the whole meeting could follow the pattern of praise, confession, thanksgiving, petition and intercession, interspersed with singing and the reading and study of the Word of God.

There are certain orders of service which could be adapted for small groups, e.g. an agape feast, or a Shalom meal.

An early account of the agape meal is thought to be described in a 2nd century document called the Didache. The people gathered for supper and brought with them offerings of food. After this supper, the food was shared in what is now called the Mass, or communion, and the leftover food was given to the poor. Gradually the meal fell into disuse because of the problem of control, and because congregations became too large for such informal meetings. . .

Today the agape meal is becoming a popular form of worship and celebration in ecumenical church gatherings because it makes possible a form of 'breaking bread together' which is outside the confessional rules and regulations and can be celebrated by laity of all confessions.[4]

Worship Now (published by The Saint Andrew Press, Edinburgh, 1972) contains an order of service for the celebration of the Lord's Supper in a small group. It has been well received by groups in which I have been involved though it is rather lengthy. Some segments could be omitted. We have reproduced it with permission in Appendix C.

The celebration of this sacrament has proved to be an enriching experience for combined gatherings of small groups, especially to conclude a term or yearly programme. Often we have done it in creative ways while still keeping to the order. After the reading from John's Gospel relating to Christ's washing of the disciples' feet, we have washed either each other's feet or hands.

Pastor each other between meetings

Where deep relationships are developed in a group, the care and concern expressed for one another when together will continue between meetings. In some groups the leaders contact each member at least once weekly. Other groups appoint one or two members with pastoral gifts to keep in touch with the members who have expressed special needs. In most groups, however, this is done informally, growing out of a genuine concern for one another.

Concern has been expressed through personal visits, by telephone or a short note. What an encouragement to have an unexpected call to say, 'I'm just ringing to let you know I will be praying for you as you face that big responsibility today,' or 'I'm just checking you are O.K. I've been remembering you in prayer since you shared so openly. Is there anything I can do to help?'

Our groups have often expressed concern in practical ways: by minding a young mother's children to enable her to cope, assisting with shopping and housework, providing meals, helping a family move house and a host of other means of support.

Avoid isolation

Isolation can produce real problems in small group life. It is easy for a group to become inward looking and degenerate into a 'holy huddle' or 'bless-me-club'. This is always a risk in groups where there is much sharing of personal thoughts, feelings and experiences. The high degree of subjectivity can cause the group to deteriorate, unless it is balanced with more objective experiences. This can be done by introducing more objective content into a group study, making frequent opportunities to serve as a group and through widening the fellowship by meeting occasionally with other groups having a similar purpose.

These enlarged group events help broaden the group life. New ideas and experiences are introduced and new leadership styles encountered. This is reasonably simple to organise where a number of groups are involved in the same cell programme. In most of the groups in which I have been involved which operated by terms, we sought to avoid isolation in one of three ways.

1. For the first meeting of a term the groups gathered together in the local church or hall to launch the term. Each group was assigned a task in the programme, which varied from leading the praise segments to preparing and serving drinks and refreshments at the conclusion. A film or specialist resource person was frequently used to introduce the theme for the term.

2. Midway through an 8–10 week-term, all the groups met in pairs. The leadership and venues were pre-arranged and the programme was similar to an ordinary meeting.

3. At the conclusion of each term the groups converged on the local church. The programme included a sharing time in which a chosen representative of each group recounted the most helpful aspects of the group life during the term. A panel often dealt with questions raised in the groups, but not answered during the term. Sometimes small group work was done in the hall, with each person meeting with people other than those in their regular group. On occasions the Lord's Supper

would be celebrated together. These were enriching experiences which helped avoid the problems associated with isolation.

Small groups which are not linked with a network of cells can seek out similar groups in their own or other denominations in the district and suggest combining for a meeting. Occasional open meetings to which spouses and children or neighbours and/or friends are invited will help keep the group alive. Possibly other times than those on which the groups meet may need to be considered for these special events. Times when the group as a whole becomes involved in outreach and service will also help to avoid the group becoming introspective.

Serve to live

The Christian church is 'the servant church of the servant Lord'. We are called to serve. Where a Christian community exists for itself it soon deteriorates and expires.

Busy group members who are involved in their church and community will often by-pass this principle of serving to live by asserting that they are already serving individually. However, there is real advantage in serving as a group, at least on occasions. Some of the richest times in groups for me personally have been while working alongside other members, especially in situations of need in the community.

In one small group programme we used a regular meeting night mid-term to reach out. The groups assembled in their usual meeting place a little earlier than normal for a brief worship session. The groups divided into pairs, each receiving two or three assignments to visit shut-ins, drop outs from the local church or those only loosely associated. They regrouped again at 9.00 pm, shared their experiences, prayed for those visited and had refreshments. All agreed these nights were some of the highest points of the groups' activities.

Many churches organise their groups to be responsible for different aspects of the local church programme. In one church I observed, every group was responsible for keeping contact with a section of both the active and inactive families on the church roll. They gave pastoral oversight, distributed church publications and kept them in touch with both the regular and special aspects of the church activities.

In another church every group was required to have a 'mission' task to which it felt called. Some groups were responsible for launching and maintaining a coffee shop to reach the unchurched. Others provided services for socially disadvantaged people. The worship and fellowship activities were the responsibility of other groups. Two groups headed up the educational dimension of the church life.

Frequently a conference I have led for a local church has been organised by one of the groups linked with that fellowship.

Groups with a service dimension keep dynamic. They are blessed when they gather for fellowship, but share that blessing with others. They practise the great Christian paradox, that it is in losing our life for Christ's sake that we find it! (Matthew 10:39)

Prayer is one of the most important aspects of our call to servanthood. An intercessory prayer group which keeps its prayer life vital is operating on the frontiers of service. However, such a group will keep itself available to be a channel through which its prayers are answered. It will be willing to put legs under its prayers to provide tangible expressions of its love and concern for others.

Hold regular leaders' meetings

This obviously applies to a situation where a number of small groups are associated with each other in some way— usually linked with a local church. The leaders' meeting played a vital role in all our small group programmes for a number of reasons.

(i) It is the **key to co-ordination** and the maintenance of some **sense of common direction**. Curricula, study resource, basic and in-service training programmes, service and outreach, combined meetings and finance were all given oversight by this meeting. The leaders would pool the feed-back, gathered verbally or from questionnaires, concerning most of the above items.

(ii) **Regular evaluation** was facilitated by the leaders getting together. It took place informally as the leaders shared. More formal evaluation took place as discussion was guided by a leaders' meeting check list covering each facet of the small groups programme. The findings from questionnaires distributed to the group members further facilitated evaluation.

(iii) An **in-service training** segment was provided in each session. Generally a chapter of a suitable book was discussed or new skills developed in brief workshops. Problems encountered in leadership were discussed and there was a sharing of ideas, skills, resources and new insights gained while leading their groups.

(iv) It also had a **clear pastoral purpose**. The leaders found it to be personally supportive. Problems were shared and there was ready support and affirmation for those who were discouraged. These leaders did not suffer from the isolation that most leaders of individual cells experience. There was always a listening ear, prayerful concern and encouragement, plus training and new resources to help them in their ministry.

The pastoral aspect extended to group members. The problems of members which surfaced during the regular meetings of the group were shared in confidence, ways of providing help were discussed and planned; all was specifically remembered in prayer. Other leaders frequently offered to provide care for the member, in addition to that given by the leader of the group. Where it was reported that a member was not fitting into a group, this would be discussed and, if necessary, another more appropriate group found.

In some leaders' meetings with which I have been involved, each group was represented by its leader and one or two members who were seen to be potential leaders.

A leaders' meeting check list used in some networks of small groups is found in Appendix D.

Evaluate regularly

'The unexamined group life is not worth living.'[5] The importance of evaluation to the life of a small group cannot be over-estimated. It is absolutely necessary if the group is to function as a vital activity in which: members find fulfilment, significant growth takes place and goals are achieved.

Evaluation will take place whether it is planned or not. Too often evaluation takes place after the meeting by one or two people sharing their frustrations or grievances. The group cannot profit from these private judgements. Only when a group member's critical or reflective comments are heard by the group can something be done about them.

Evaluation of small group life is concerned with understanding what each person is experiencing in that situation. It involves an understanding of the relationships which are taking place—the interaction between the participants.

Group process is a major area which needs to be constantly evaluated. This involves what is actually going on within and between the group members, the series of actions or changes and how the group is operating. Based on this evaluation, a judgement of what is good and bad can be made. The good can be affirmed, the bad faced, and action planned to avoid continuance.

Sara Little suggests **four areas in which evaluation should take place** at the same time or at different times.

'Purpose—did we achieve our purpose?
Content—what did we learn?
Group Process—how well did we work together?
Personal Growth—what happened to us as individuals?'[6]

The following list is not exhaustive, but fairly representative. It gives another slant on the kind of evaluation necessary:

1. Clarity of goals.
2. Agreement on major and minor goals.
3. Agreement on methods of attaining the goals.
4. Support of group activities.
5. Co-ordination of activities in group tasks.
6. Availability of resources necessary for task accomplishment.
7. Effectiveness of communication.
8. Competence of leadership.

9. Clarity of lines of authority.
10. Participation in decision.[7]

This list may be used as a general standard by which to measure the effectiveness of most groups. Sara Little's list and this further listing could be used as the basis for making your own evaluation form, or as items for a group to discuss its effectiveness.

Evaluation by the group can be done at some stages during the session. But it is generally undertaken after the session, when time is set aside to reflect and determine what experiences have been helpful and what could have been improved.

Occasionally a whole meeting should be given over to do a more thorough evaluation than is possible after most regular meetings. Where a group has met for an experimental period, an unhurried time should be allowed for evaluation.

If a **leaders' meeting** is held where there is a network of groups, time should be taken out to do some evaluation in each meeting. The outcome of individual group evaluation can be shared, especially if unresolved problems have been encountered. In my own experience, leaders have found this to be a supportive experience, especially for relatively unskilled leaders.

It is also valuable to hold **an annual evaluation and planning retreat** for multi-cell programmes, in which members and leaders participate. Evaluation forms should be completed and collated beforehand to form the basis of much of the work undertaken. The presence of a skilled resource person to help reflect upon and interpret the data adds an important dimension.

Leaders will be involved in **informal evaluation** continuously. They will observe group members' actions and attitudes to discover anxiety or dissatisfaction. When a member stops attending, the leader will follow up to discover why and not be easily put off by evasive explanations. The behaviour of members in the group clearly reveals disinterest or disagreement. A question to the persons concerned, during or after the group, can bring to the surface issues which the whole group can evaluate.

A natural way to evaluate, which doesn't give the appearance of a structured evaluation, is simply to ask the group at the end of the meeting:

What did you like best about the session?
What did you like least about the session?
What will be most useful to you?
What did you learn from the session today?
What specific things came up today that you would have liked to explore further?
How would you suggest the session could have been improved?

This method of general discussion within the group seems to be a low-key approach but can result in some in-depth assessment. The leader will need to be a free person, who is willing and able to accept suggestions without becoming defensive.

There are a number of more **formal ways** to undertake evaluation. A common one is to use reaction sheets which are prepared beforehand, using questions, often with multiple choice answers or columns in which to indicate degrees of positive or negative response. These usually cover the areas suggested earlier.

Sometimes **an observer**, usually not a group member, is used to observe the group. Often this person will follow a check list and then report findings to the group.

We have found the following use of an observer very worthwhile in helping members to evaluate their participation in the group. The observer places a large piece of chart

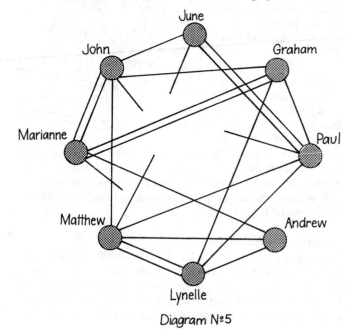

Diagram No5

34

paper in the centre of the group, and each person draws a small circle on the chart to represent their position, writing their name next to it. We find this 'personalises' the chart. The observer then sits outside the circle and charts the interaction by drawing a line from the name of the speakers to the names of the ones to whom they seem to be speaking. Remarks addressed to the group in general go to the centre of the circle. As the lines accumulate, they will show who speaks the most, and silent members will stand out clearly. The drawing could look something like Diagram No. 5 shown on page 34.

During the report segment, the chart is placed in the centre of the group, in the same position as it was previously. Discussion could centre around these questions:

How do the group members feel about the amount of their participation?

Has anyone dominated the discussion?

How do people feel about getting, or not getting, attention?

What can be done to gain wider participation?

More time-consuming methods involve the **audio or video recording** of a group meeting. This method is entirely unselective, whereas human observers bring prejudices and limitations to their work.

Appoint an 'overseer' for multi-cell programmes

We found it beneficial, where there were a number of associated groups with similar goals in a parish, to appoint a person to act as 'pastor' of

these groups. The 'pastor' or 'overseer' was kept free from permanent commitments as a leader of any one group though in some cases, especially in small networks, this person did lead a leaders' cell. The 'overseer's' task was to keep a finger on the pulse of the programme, act as an enabler and resource person to the leaders and convene leaders' meetings. A different group would be attended each week, and the 'overseer' would usually participate as a group member.

Occasionally a group might be led by the 'overseer' if the leader wanted to observe a new style of leadership. In some groups where there were problem members, a leader appreciated seeing how another person handled them. In most small group ventures in which I have been involved, this was a role played by myself (the minister); in other instances it was effectively fulfilled by another.

Be loyal to your local church

Small groups can become a divisive force within a local church fellowship. For this reason criticism is often directed towards the small group movement. Loyalty should be characteristic of a healthy group. This will extend to the wider Christian community of which they are a part, and its appointed leader.

I have frequently counselled frustrated and discouraged people who, having caught the vision of the possibilities of renewal through small groups at one of my conferences, have returned with high hopes and renewed enthusiasm to their local church, only to have the new insights rejected out of hand by their local minister and church leaders. There are reasons for this reaction.

Sometimes previous groups have been badly handled and become divisive, either through a 'holier than thou' attitude or poor strategy and impatience in seeking to produce change in the church.

Alternatively, ministers or other church leaders can be autocratic and feel that unless they are running everything their authority is threatened. Happily, not many are like this, but unfortunately some do dominate a church and cannot let people grow.

Some ministers feel that heresy or doctrinal unsoundness will creep into the church unless they are leading most, if not all, of the teaching dimension of the local church. Certainly some leaders have had to cope with people in their churches who have propagated grossly inadequate or wrong beliefs and practices. As leaders, they are commissioned to uphold the good order of the church and, when this is threatened, they can rightly be expected to respond accordingly. My plea here is for patience and understanding. From my broad experience, I have found very few instances of church leaders resisting the formation of small groups if the group leaders are godly, balanced, loving people, committed to maintaining the unity of Christ's body.

We are required as Christian disciples to be faithful. Loyalty is closely aligned with faithfulness. We need to be loyal to our group, our church (its members and leaders), but above all to our Lord Jesus. If you have a small group meeting in your home, it is courteous to inform the minister and leaders, but you don't have to ask him to attend all the meetings, nor are you obliged to let him lead.

As a group, maintain a warm, caring attitude, keep uncritical in a negative way, be available to serve when possible and be open to others. Then your leaders will see modelled the kind of dynamic groups that we are advocating.

Plan some leisure events

Opportunities should be provided, in addition to the regular group meetings, for informal socialising and leisure activities. Occasional outings for recreation, relaxed meals together or a weekend away, all help develop relationships in an informal atmosphere and provide for restoration. These also can include spouses, friends and families on occasions, providing a way of interesting potential new members.

When a member moves away

Once people have experienced the depth of care and concern and growth possible in a vital small group, they will generally never again be completely satisfied with trying to be a Christian alone. The small group should be aware of its continuing ministry to those who leave their groups because they have to move out of the district. A leader with the heart of a pastor will try to find details about cells meeting in the district to which the member is moving. The group should together continue to give support through prayer and personal contact.

A copy of this and other appropriate books could be given to help in the formation of a new group by the departing member. A sharing of resources and ideas could be offered to help the new group become established.

Depend upon divine grace

In seeking to establish worthwhile groups, we must not depend only upon some of the insights gained from this and other similar books, or our own experience, education, personality and natural gifts. I continually remind myself that what I do will only count for eternity if I take the time to unhurriedly listen to what God would have me say and do; then, having some idea of what is God's intention, I plan and work in a spirit of dependence upon God's enabling grace.

We can 'make ready . . . but the victory belongs to the Lord'. (Proverbs 21:31)

References

(1) Elizabeth O'Connor, *Call to Commitment* (Harper and Row).
(2) Lyman Coleman, *Serendipity Basic Series*—Leader's Guide (ANZEA/JBCE).
(3) Ibid.
(4) Letty M Russel, *Ferment of Freedom* (National Board, YWCA of the USA, 1972), p. 61. (See pp. 59–67 for a description of a Shalom meal.)
(5) Philip A Anderson, *Church Meetings That Matter* (United Church Press), p. 58.
(6) Sara Little, *Learning Together in the Christian Fellowship* (John Knox Press, 1956), p. 60.
(7) D Cartwright and A Zander, *Group Dynamics Research and Theory* (Row, Peterson and Company).

Chapter 4
Effective Leadership

'The "good news" must always be incarnate. The lives of Christian leaders are the gospel of their followers.'

The fundamental qualities for the task of leading a small Christian group do not need to be those of an exceptional person. It is not necessary to have sophisticated skills in group dynamics nor great knowledge of the Bible, nor to be a mature Christian. Most effective small group leaders feel inadequate for their role. But what is essential for any leadership role in the church is a life touched and renewed by Jesus Christ. Then ordinary abilities become extraordinary.

Some of the best small group leaders I have worked with over the years have had very little formal training and a number were immature spiritually, having been Christians only a few years. However, they were highly motivated to learn and serve and approached all they did with a deep sense of dependency upon God.

> When we think of leadership in Christ's terms, the normal connotations must be put behind us. Christ only is Head of His church. Leadership in the church is not related to self-aggrandisement: the leader is to be like Christ, the servant of all. For a man to wear the mantle of leadership humbly, and to lose himself in service to others, his **character** will be far more important than his accomplishments.[1]

The New Testament model is a person who *lives* the truth—others believe and follow. This is the key issue—credibility and integrity. 'The "good news" must always be incarnate. The lives of Christian leaders are the gospel of their followers.' Paul was so credible he was even able to say 'do as I do', 'copy me'. If he were simply an egotist demanding adulation he would have been disregarded.

Our ultimate model and example is Jesus Christ. Our credibility and effectiveness stem, not from having 'arrived' spiritually, but from a willingness to admit we have not, but are still in the process of becoming, in the power of the Holy Spirit.

A SMALL GROUP LEADER IS ONE WHO . . .

Sees each person as having worth and dignity in his/her own right.

Respects people enough not to intrude upon their privacy.

Does not force people to speak.

Does not tell others to participate but creates a situation in which they can participate.

Helps people to really communicate with one another.

Believes each member of the group has something to say that is worth hearing.

Is a good listener and one who encourages others not just to hear, but to listen carefully to what others are trying to say.

Is patient and gently draws people out and assists them in becoming articulate.

Does not manipulate the members of a group to agree with his/her ideas.

Is not self-seeking.

Is flexible, but not casual; sensitive to the mood and expressed needs of the group.

Is the servant of the people in the group and not the master.

Has warmth, understanding and an easy manner.

Makes all his/her life available to the group.

Does not expect to be a perfect leader.

Remembers most of these fundamental guides in this chapter and tries to use them as a basis.

CHOOSING LEADERS—WHAT TO LOOK FOR

Frequently God calls the most unlikely person to a position of leadership. People who would usually be overlooked receive God's call. Availability, commitment and high motivation to learn and serve have enabled many to achieve far more than others who are more richly endowed.

'For consider your call, brethren; not many of you were wise according to worldly standards, not many were powerful, not many were of noble birth; but God chose what is foolish in the world to shame the wise, God chose what is weak in the world to shame the strong, God chose what is low and despised in the world, even things that are not, to bring to nothing things that are, so that no human being might boast in the presence of God. He is the source of your life in Christ Jesus, whom God made our wisdom, our right-eousness and sanctification and redemption; therefore, as it is written, "Let him who boasts, boast of the Lord".' (1 Corinthians 2:26–31, RSV)

For many years the most common approach to the study of leadership concentrated on leadership traits per se, suggesting that there were certain characteristics, such as physical energy or friendliness, that were essential for effective leadership . . . Since all individuals did not have these qualities, only those who had them would be considered potential leaders.

A review of the research literature using this trait approach to leadership has revealed few significant findings. As Eugene E Jennings concluded, 'Fifty years of study have failed to produce one personality trait or set of qualities that can be used to discriminate leaders and nonleaders.'[2]

A careful study of all the characteristics listed by Paul as requirements for leadership in the church reveals that they are those that he expected of every Christian. These leadership qualities are the outworking of the indwelling Holy Spirit—'the fruit of the Spirit'.

While teaching for a short time at Rahronga Theological College in Papua New Guinea, I asked a group of senior students what they would look for in choosing a small group leader. Here is what they listed.

A person who loves Jesus. One who is continually growing like Jesus through praying and reading the Bible regularly, and seeking to obey him.

A person who loves people and shows this through his/her patience, willingness to listen, care and concern, availability and servanthood.

A person who loves Christ's church shown through being loyal, seeking to maintain the church's unity and working for its growth in numbers and quality.

I find it difficult to improve on this list when I am asked what I would look for in a small group leader.

HOW TO CHOOSE LEADERS

The right Christian leaders are chosen by God. Our task is to discern on whom God has placed his hand.

Three of the critical functions of a congregation are: first, to ensure all understand about spiritual gifts; secondly, to be able to discern the different gifts of the Holy Spirit given to its members; thirdly, to develop structures that function to train and develop these gifts. Many congregations now have these structures in place, having undertaken serious study of the New Testament teaching on spiritual gifts, along with books by authors such as: Peter Wagner (*Your Spiritual Gifts Can Help Your Church Grow*, Regal, USA), Robert Hillman (*Twenty-seven Spiritual Gifts*, Joint Board of Christian Education, Melbourne), Donald Bridge and David Phypers (*Spiritual Gifts and the Church*, I.V.P.), Arnold Bittlinger (*Gifts and Ministries*, Hodder & Stoughton) and Michael Green (*I Believe in the Holy Spirit*, Eerdmans).

This teaching is often linked with the use of the Wagner-Modified Houts Questionnaire (Charles E Fuller Institute of Evangelism and Church Growth), which enables individuals to identify their own spiritual gifts. The majority of churches which educate their members concerning the New Testament teaching on spiritual gifts now understand what their gifts are, and individuals are called to ministry by the leaders accordingly.

A general appeal for someone to fill a vacancy is not a successful ploy in calling a person to a particular ministry. Many have found this outlined procedure to be effective:

Gather the elders or deacons, pray for guidance, list any names that come to mind, read slowly through the church rolls for more possibilities and be prepared to be surprised! Discuss the persons' gifts and suitability. Appoint two elders/deacons to approach individually those chosen and to make an appointment with the potential leader. A 'call' is issued on behalf of the church. The role and time commitment is clearly explained, along with the training and support to be given. An immediate response is not sought, but time is allowed for the person to pray and consider the call.

DEVELOPING NEW LEADERS

The identification and development of leaders should be an ongoing process in the local congregation. Group leaders should be helped to recognise those with leadership potential in their groups. These can, in addition to sharing in the leadership in the group, then be encouraged to attend training events, extend their reading in this area and be invited to participate in some of the activities especially for leaders.

THE ROLE OF THE PASTOR

The pastor plays a key role in a network of small groups in the local church. Indeed little of significance happens if the pastor doesn't have a commitment to the programme. The degree of the pastor's involvement will depend upon a number of factors, including his/her spiritual gifts, other commitments and whether the vision was his/hers initially.

A pastor with a strong teaching gift may lead an education programme for potential leaders, with others providing in-put in areas in which he/she is not skilled. Whether the pastor's gift is administration, or ability to help others catch the vision and move ahead in faith, the focus will be on that area, with others taking the lead in different aspects.

Where a pastor is a good small group leader (and not all are because their gifts lie in other areas), they may lead the initial group from which the future leaders emerge.

In networks of groups in my parishes I helped the congregation catch the vision and then played mainly the roles of trainer and pastor. I led the leaders' cell, providing in-service training and pastoral support for the leaders. I also kept myself free to visit the groups systematically and to act as a resource person.

LEADERSHIP STYLE

Leadership style is how we behave when we are trying to influence the performance of a group. The chart shows four common styles of leadership with the main characteristics of each.

(Diagram No. 6 source: Items 1 and 8 in each column, and all the items in the 'Authoritative' column are by Roberta Hestens.[3] The other items are taken from the author's book, *Building Small Groups in the Christian Community*, Renewal Publications, Australia, 1978.)

Leadership Styles

Autocratic (Domineering, dictatorial)	Authoritative (Definite yet responsive)	Democratic (Group-centred)	Laissez-faire (Permissive, passive)
1. Total control, with members as listeners and followers.	1. Strong control, with members actively involved in the discussions.	1. Shared control, with leader and members sharing functions and decisions.	1. Minimal control, with members directing.
2. Determines goals and policies and wants the group to choose the goal he or she has chosen.	2. Has a definite purpose and plan but is open to modification.	2. Shares leadership responsibility.	2. Doesn't prepare and lets things drift.
3. More interested in the subject matter (content) than with the people (process).	3. Active and energetic and seeks the activity of others.	3. Believes in other people.	3. Doesn't seem to care.
4. Makes decisions regardless of other viewpoints.	4. Prepared to give direction and support as needed.	4. Creates a sense of security and belonging in the group.	4. Causes the group to accomplish very little.
5. Talks too much.	5. Uses communication skills to involve others.	5. Ensures that other members have opportunity of leadership.	5. Encourages fragmentation through indiscipline and unreliability.
6. Focuses attention on himself or herself.	6. Takes responsibility until others can assume it.	6. The leader's withdrawal will not mean that the group will fall apart.	6. Makes no attempt to appraise or regulate the course of events.
7. Group members are almost puppets.	7. Uses personal power to empower others. Asks others to take functions.	7. All policies a matter of group discussion encouraged and assisted by leader.	7. Lacks courage in making decisive plans.

In a Bible study:

8. Asks and answers all questions.	8. Prepares and asks questions; members respond and discuss.	8. May ask other(s) to lead discussion; leadership may be passed around, using study guide.	8. Asks one vague or general question, then is silent.

№6

The small group leader needs to keep sensitive to what is happening in the group and respond with a style of leadership which is appropriate. This is sometimes referred to as **functional leadership**. The leader is flexible in order to respond to the needs of the group in fulfilling its task, maintaining good group relationships and meeting the needs of each individual.

Situational leadership is an approach to managing and motivating people developed by Paul Hersey and Ken Blanchard, and written about originally in their book *Management of Organisational Behaviour: Utilising Human Resources* (1969). Changes have been made to the original model and this now forms the basis of the popular One Minute Manager series. Although it is concerned with managing people in an organisation, there are principles here which are applicable to leadership in a small group setting. Blanchard talks about turning the common organisational model, often thought of in terms of a pyramid, upside down. He says, 'Managers should work for their staff . . . provide them with the resources and working conditions they need to accomplish the goals you've agreed to . . . help them win . . . if they win, you win.'[4] This sounds very familiar to what the New Testament says about mutual ministry, with the Christian leader equipping others to fulfil their own ministry. It gathers together the roles of teacher, servant, encourager and enabler.

The situational model of management accepts that 'people who are at different levels of development need to be treated differently'.[5] Blanchard teaches four ways of behaving when trying to influence the performance of someone else: 'Directing, Coaching, Supporting and Delegating BUT . . . THERE IS NO ONE BEST LEADERSHIP STYLE.'[6] The 'skill of diagnosing a situation before you act is the key to being a situational leader'.[7]

In using the situation leadership style in a small group, we recognise that group life is dynamic, always changing. If a serious conflict situation arises—such as a person being brutally put down by another, the group overlooking its task and getting side-tracked, or members not hearing each other in a heavy argument—a directive or autocratic role will be exercised to rescue the person being hurt, get back on the track again or improve communication. But the use of that particular style may be needed for only a brief period of the meeting.

If during a learning segment the leader keeps asking questions to which none are prepared to respond, a laissez-faire style will be more appropriate. The leader will repeat the question, remain silent, use some eye contact with the group but essentially be passive. This can motivate group involvement.

In the early stages of a group, the leader will normally need to be more directive in helping the members begin to develop relationships, set directions and decide on an agreed programme. However, as the group grows generally, there will be more involvement of the members in the leadership.

The Situational Leadership Style recognises that group life is dynamic; it is full of variables. Small group leaders need to develop sensitivity and skills in identifying the clues in the situation, and adapt their leadership style to meet the changing demands of the group. There is no one best way to guide people when they cluster together.

All of us have natural styles of leadership. Some by nature are more directive; others are more passive. In growing as a leader we need to identify our natural style and then work on developing the other styles. Role playing in training sessions and practising different styles in a variety of informal situations can help us gain confidence in using other styles.

LEADING BY EXAMPLE

The adage goes: 'Christianity is caught not taught'. Modelling the fruits of the Spirit and a joyous Christian style of life will be a key role of the leader. Paul said, 'Be imitators of me as I am of Christ.' (1 Corinthians 11:1) The young church at Philippi were exhorted, '. . . what you have learned and received and heard and seen in me, do.' (Philippians 4:9)

A group usually learns to be open with each other when

the leader is one who doesn't pretend or live behind a mask.

Christ modelled servanthood by washing his disciples' feet, and in many other ways. The disciples not only heard Christ teach '. . . whoever would be great among you must be your servant' (Mark 10:43), they saw it regularly demonstrated and on one occasion followed by, 'I have given you an example, that you should do as I have done to you.' (John 13:15) Followers look to their leaders for evidence that the gospel really works. We are called to be 'living epistles' (2 Corinthians 3:3,4)—'letters from Christ' for all to read.

WHO SHOULD LEAD?

There is no such thing as a leaderless group. Even groups which claim to have no designated leader will have one or two people who unobtrusively facilitate the group. For a number of years I have belonged to a group of clergy who are all most capable in small group leadership. We have no one person to whom we refer as our leader, but one or two of us take the initiative in ensuring all know if there is a change of meeting place and in enabling the accomplishment of our informal sharing and prayer in the time allotted.

Many groups share the leadership on a roster basis. While having a different person or couple lead the group each meeting can relieve the preparation load, develop leadership and give variety, it can however result in lack of continuity and a degree of insecurity amongst the members. There is no one pattern to follow but from my experience the best way seems to be to have one designated leader, with others taking responsibility for different segments as the group matures. The one leader heads up the group for a term or a year at least.

In the early stages of the group's life, the leader will carry the full responsibility while playing an inductive role in enabling the group in its learning. All will be involved in the process but not initially in leadership roles.

As the group begins to cohere, different members can share various tasks. One may be responsible for preparing and leading the praise segment, another the intercessory prayer time, two or more may be responsible for aspects of the study period and one or two the refreshments. The designated leader will act as a guide and resource person to these people in the preparation, and be ready to support and encourage them in their leadership. The leader will also help them evaluate their presentations. The leader's degree of involvement will depend upon the capability of the members. Affirmation, availability and prayerful support will develop confidence and future leadership.

HELPING THE GROUP ACHIEVE ITS MAXIMUM POTENTIAL

In Chapter 6, 'Life Together', we deal with a variety of issues affecting group interaction. Here are a few techniques which the leader can use to help the group function more effectively.

Question Making
This is a tool the leader uses in order to stimulate talk and contributions from all members.

Use straight questions, not those which are weighted in one way or another, such as:

> Don't you think . . . ?
> You don't think, do you, . . . ?

Avoid questions with a simple yes/no answer.

To involve a person who has not contributed or those who could make a contribution to the discussion, ask:

> What do you think of this (name)?
> I'm interested in your opinion (name)?

Or ask a question of the whole group rather than to a particular person. Modify the above or ask:

> Does anyone have a contribution on this?
> What is the main point here?

To redirect. The leader must learn not to answer most of the questions asked but to redirect them to the group as a whole or to a specific person, by asking:

> What do other members of the group think about this?
> Let's hear what (name) thinks about this first. How would you answer this, (name)?

To clarify. Conversation can get confused and often lead to misunderstanding and conflict if people do not clearly understand what a person meant by what they said. Asking clarifying questions can also help the people develop their own thinking as well as get them a good hearing. Ask questions such as:

Could you put that another way for us?
What do you mean by saying that . . . ?
Why do you make that statement? What is your understanding of that? or Why did you use that?
Have you considered this . . . ?

To move on. The group could have talked out an issue or appear to be spending too much time on one item so the leader can ask:

Do you think we have covered that sufficiently?
Should we move on now?

Summarising. To help the group in their thinking or to reach a conclusion, leaders will give their summary of what they understand the group to be saying. Opportunity is then given for approval or amendment by asking:

Is that your understanding of what is being said . . . or the conclusions we have reached?

The summary can be attempted by the group in response to questions such as:

What have we agreed to so far?

Silences are a valued part of group process
Silences can give people space to reflect and think. Sometimes the silence will occur after a question is raised by the leader. The leader should not break the silence by asking: 'Doesn't anyone have an answer?' or by answering it him/herself. The silence can motivate individuals to get involved, as few can stay with silence very long.

Occasionally the leader may suggest a period of silence during a discussion to allow for individual consideration, or to seek to hear God's perspective.

Facilitating group participation
Leaders should seek to position themselves so they have eye contact with each member. This eye contact will make all conscious that the leader is aware of their presence, and even a casual eye contact can motivate a particular person to respond. The eye contact is also important to pick up non-verbal communication of each person.

Part of the leader's role is to enable each member to participate and seek to curb those who are dominating. Normally a leader will interfere with the flow of conversation as little as possible, letting it flow back and forth. It is not always routed through the leader.

The flow of conversation where either the leader is dominating the group or people are not comfortable enough to get into dialogue with each other is shown in Diagram No. 7.

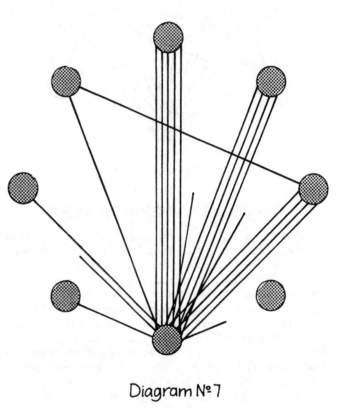

Diagram No 7

Group participation should be as shown in Diagram No. 8, where the leader is playing a good enabling role.

43

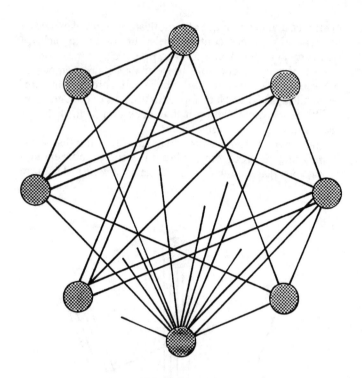

Diagram № 8

USING A LEADERSHIP TEAM

In certain situations it will be helpful to involve a number of members with you in the group leadership in ways other than those dealt with elsewhere in this chapter.

In my first experience in using clusters of small groups, because of the large number of people wanting to participate in the new small groups programme, we had to use many relatively new Christians who were inexperienced not only in matters of Christian discipleship but also in group leadership. These were teamed in pairs to share the leadership. The regular evaluation we kept undertaking, which included feed-back from the group members, indicated the effectiveness of this approach.

Another form of team leadership practised fairly widely is to **assign members' roles according to their spiritual gifts**, with the leader playing more of a co-ordinating, enabling role. One or two persons with the gift of **administration** take responsibility for arranging venues, making

rosters, ensuring all are informed of decisions made, making any changes to arrangements and organising special events. Those with the gift of **hospitality** are responsible for welcoming newcomers, facilitating the informal socialising before and after meetings, and organising get-togethers of a recreational nature. Follow-up of lapsed members and those who have special pastoral needs are undertaken between meetings with house or hospital calls, phone contacts and notes in the mail by those with **pastoral** gifts. These may also keep an attendance record.

Those with the gift of **teaching** share the preparation and leadership of the study segment. The prayer segments are led by those with special **prayer** gifts. They may keep the group prayer journal, recording prayer requests made at each meeting on one page and noting the answers on the blank page opposite, during future meetings. They may also come with a summary of current news items to include in the intercessory prayer time.

The serving dimension of the group is facilitated by those with gifts of **service**. They may follow through on needs in the local church or community, involving the whole group where necessary.

Those with gifts in leading **praise and worship** keep this aspect alive by ensuring variety and making it relevant to the topic being studied.

The **evangelist(s)** of the group will be on the lookout for new members and keep the group alert to the need for outreach and growth.

The **other many spiritual gifts** will surface as the group proceeds—some will be ongoing, others emerging from time to time as the Spirit sees appropriate.

Another way to use a leadership team is to draw from the group a **recorder**, a **reporter**, a **researcher**, a **timekeeper** and occasionally an **observer**. This form of team leadership is more appropriate for a conference setting, where small group experiences are  provided during the sessions as part of the learning process. However occasionally ongoing groups may benefit from using people in some of the roles listed here:

The recorder writes group findings on a visual aid such as a board (chalk, chart or white) or an overhead projector. These may be particular points as the discussion proceeds, so that they will not be forgotten. In this way it is useful in visualising thoughts, especially when the group is trying to formulate a statement or restate some points.

The reporter is most commonly used where there are a number of groups meeting in the one setting and the individual group work is followed by a plenary/report back segment. Key points are noted and checked out with the group before reporting.

In a continuing group, this role could take the form of keeping an attendance record for follow-up purposes, and possibly a group journal in which highlights of the sharing and discussion in each meeting are briefly recorded, along with prayer requests.

The timekeeper. This is a role which varies depending on the type of group. It is perhaps most useful in a conference session or a group seeking to follow a session plan divided into time segments.

Time segments for items to be covered are agreed upon at the commencement and the timekeeper gives gentle reminders of how the time is progressing. The group determines whether to stay with the original plan or extend aspects.

The researcher. Where more information is needed on an item raised in the discussion this person undertakes to dig out this information by consulting books or resource people and report to a future meeting. The person may also undertake to gather additional material in preparation for a meeting.

The observer. This role is used occasionally by groups wishing to improve their performance as a group. The person can be a group member or an outsider. The observer does not participate and does not normally sit within the group. The group interplay is observed: how frequently various people speak, how freely the discussion moves. A flow chart may be prepared. The observer notes whether one or two members monopolise the conversation, when things go off the track or when the discussion gets bogged down. The observer is as objective as possible in his/her assessment and comments. The information is then discussed by the group and areas for improvement and strengths noted.

David Watson wrote of the importance of leadership in cell groups in his church:

> However, the leadership of these groups and cells is all-important to healthy growth and expansion. In our church in York, we have found value in developing a 'support group' consisting of the leaders of a number of house groups in a given area. The leader of this support group will be an elder who has pastoral oversight of all the groups represented. In so far as this support group of leaders is able to be open to God and to each other, so that same openness is likely to happen in the groups they lead. Thus the reality of spiritual life in the support group is vital: worshipping, praying, sharing, studying, caring. If these and other ingredients are increasingly to be found, they are likely to be reproduced in the rest of the fellowship. In this way, there is the continuous training of leaders, comparable to the 'in-service' training so widely practised in the secular world. (8)

References

(1) Taken from *A New Face for the Church* by Lawrence O Richards, pp. 112–3. Copyright © 1970 by Zondervan Publishing House. Used by permission.
(2) Paul Hersey and Ken Blanchard, *Management of Organisational Behaviour* (Prentice Hall, 1969).
(3) Roberta Hestens, 'Using the Bible Series: In Groups' (Westminster Press, 1983).
(4) K Blanchard, P Zigarmi and D Zigarmi, *Leadership and the One Minute Manager* (Collins Willow).
(5) Ibid.
(6) Ibid.
(7) Ibid.
(8) David Watson, *Discipleship*, pp. 91–2 (Hodder & Stoughton, 1981).

Chapter 5

Understanding and Helping People in Small Groups

It is . . . within the church that a person might hope to experience koinonia, that fellowship, that sense of community binding Christians together— a fellowship which is, indeed, far more than a sense of 'groupness'. Baillie says that God's eternal purpose for man was that he might be a part of this fellowship, and that, through the fellowship, he might become what God intended him to be. [1]

GROUPS ARE FOR PEOPLE

Every group is made up of people, each bringing into the group experience, attitudes, prejudices, needs and expectations. If a sense of real fellowship is generated, members of a group will want each other's help and support. Worries, fears and doubts can be brought out into the open in an atmosphere of loving acceptance, and joy and hopes celebrated.

One of the most thrilling things that can happen to a group, as it becomes established and as masks are allowed to drop, is that God uses these times of closeness. As we share other people's hopes and fears and as we pray for each other, our spiritual and human discernment grows. You may find the group seeking each other out, apart from the meeting times, as it becomes a truly sharing-caring fellowship.

If practical help is offered this involves genuinely being available to people when they want us, not just when it is convenient for us.

GROUP NEEDS

Group needs are three in number:

(i) The need for a **task**;
(ii) The need of the **individual** members;
(iii) The need for group **maintenance**.

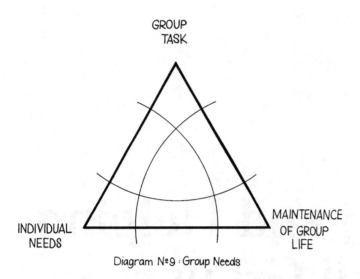

Diagram Nº9 : Group Needs

Every group must have **a task or purpose**. The **task** overlies the aim. If the interest and commitment of the members is to be maintained and their imagination captured, everyone needs to know what this task is and the consensus must be that it is worthwhile.

For example, a small group may form with a vague idea that it will be both a study and service group. Somewhere along the line the service idea may dissipate and some members may become restless and dissatisfied. 'We are always studying and never doing', they may say and they

Diagram Nº10 : Maslow's Heirachy of Needs

may drift away or openly rebel. If there is a profound misunderstanding about the aim or function of a group from the outset, then the group is doomed to dissolution.

Each member brings to the group situation the sum of their life experience to that point: their conditioning, their attitudes, prejudices, points of view, strengths and weaknesses. Each one brings **individual needs** to the group. These needs are not always admitted and will include the basic psychological needs indicated in Diagram No. 10 of Maslow's 'Hierarchy of Needs'. Spiritual needs will also be present, such as the need for forgiveness, assurance that they are acceptable to God, discovery of their role in the body of Christ, confidence in expressing their faith, and many more.

Most will bear wounds caused by themselves or others from their immediate situation—and some from their distant past. These individual needs must be recognised and accepted; they will inevitably affect a person's participation and task achievement. 'To understand people I must try to hear what they are not saying, what they perhaps will never be able to say.'[2]

One of the basic functions of the effective leader's role will be to spend time with people outside of the group meeting to understand these individual needs of members. Every symptom has a cause. Behind all disruptive behaviour there is a reason—often buried in the sub-conscious which, when surfaced and adequately dealt with, will bring freedom and the emergence of the real person.

Group maintenance is concerned with the need to preserve a free and healthy group life for it to retain its unity and purpose. Every member is committed to the maintenance of the group through active listening, ability to empathise, sensitivity, openness, development of trust and a willingness to both affirm and confront. Chapter 6, 'Life Together', opens up this subject more fully.

For the group to operate in a way which will bring fulfilment to the members and achieve the purpose for which it exists, the leader and the members will **need to keep these three needs in balance**. There will be times when the task will be seen to be dominating the group, to the exclusion of the needs of individual members or the total welfare of the group. At such times the group will need to pause to become more sensitive to each other. People matter more than goals or tasks. In one group a member said, 'My doctor told me yesterday I have been diagnosed as having cancer'. Immediately the set task for that night paled into insignificance, as the group provided the space for that

48

person to unburden their shock and disbelief. The group reached a high point in caring concern. To a lesser degree I have found there is seldom a meeting passes that one member does not surface a pressing concern, with the group giving more time to that person in that particular meeting.

At other times the group will get side-tracked and need to be brought back to its agreed task; otherwise many will become frustrated.

THE ROLES PEOPLE PLAY

Every group is comprised of a variety of individuals who will bring their own personalities, attitudes, values and behaviour to bear upon the group. Each will play different roles in the group. Not all those listed below will be found in the same group (hopefully!). How-ever, you will find some playing more than one of these roles.

Harmoniser
Attempts to reconcile disagreements. Minimises conflicts. A 'let us all be friends' approach reduces tension.

'Blessed are the peacemakers' but not if it means sweeping conflict under the rug! Conflict needs to be wisely confronted, not avoided or diffused.

Blocker
Interferes with progress of group. Keeps group from getting its work done. Goes off at a tangent. Reacts negatively to all suggestions. Cites personal experiences unrelated to problems.

As a leader you are responsible for keeping the group on the track to fulfil its task. Use your active listening skills to help this person hear how they are coming across to the group. Consciously 'act' towards this person rather than 'react'. Don't become defensive. Model a positive spirit yourself—our God is 'the God of hope'. Seek positive responses  from others in the group and explore possibilities with an expectation of the miraculous!!

Helper-Facilitator

Opens communication by encouraging others. Is warm and friendly, making it possible for others to make a contribution to the group. Clarifies issues.

Pray you may have at least one of these in your group! And, as leader, see this as an essential part of your own role.

Intellectualiser
Puts discussion on a high plane. Gives little lectures on theories. Talks about 'basic concepts' or 'it is known that . . .'

While this type of person can give an impression of being superior to most in the group and make others feel inferior and threatened, they can also lift the discussion above the superficial and get people thinking. They can be a useful resource person, however they can also be theoretical and fail to consider the relevance for everyday living. Encourage them to relate their input to real-life situations by asking: 'How do you see that working out in your own life?' Affirm the contributions of those who may suffer with a sense of inferiority for their own sake and to endeavour to help the intellectualiser appreciate the input of every member of the group.

Non-participant
Acts indifferent or passive. Doodler, daydreamer. Withdraws from group by using excessive formality. Can withdraw verbally, perhaps by whispering to others.

Not everyone feels like becoming deeply involved in every meeting. No one should be coerced into participating; all have the right of individual dissent. Sensitively ask quiet persons for their opinion without embarrassing them. If they are bored, check on the relevance of the discussion, the resources and the methods being used. Also check your own leadership style and whether you are enabling the fulfilment of the three needs of the group mentioned earlier. Shy people should be made to feel wanted, and that it is O.K. to be a silent member of the group.

Student

Relies on authority or sanction of others: 'My lecturer says that . . .' or 'Research indicates that . . .'

Affirm the desire to learn. Ask, 'But what do **you** think about . . .?' Learning involves **understanding** as well as knowledge.

Fighter

Aggressive. Works for status by blaming others. Deflates ego of others. Shows hostility against group or some individual.

If someone is getting hurt, the person causing the trouble needs to be confronted head-on. Rebuking this person within the group should be avoided if possible, but not at the expense of others being destroyed.

Initiator

Suggests new ideas. Proposes solutions. Makes new attack on problems. Definitive approach. Organises materials.

Also pray for one of these to be in your group! However, they may move the group along before it has adequately dealt with an issue. Don't let them control the group. Take notice of these people because, as a group member, they may be able to see the situation more objectively than

yourself. But trust your own hunches about direction and speed of the group.

Joker

Clowns. Jokes. Mimics others. Disrupts work of group.

This person can be either a hindrance or a help. They are a hindrance if they overplay this role, but can be a help in relieving tension. Clowning can be their way of avoiding some issue which may be threatening or drawing attention to themselves. Try to direct attention

away from them, or direct questions to them to try to get them to take the discussion seriously. If they persist, give them a task which will help them get attention without being disruptive.

Dominator

Interrupts others. Launches on long monologues. Tries to assert authority. Dogmatic.

A tough one, this! Like all difficult people, this person shows symptoms of deeper problems, such as a lack of recognition and affirmation, and a deep insecurity. Part of a leader's role is to control the flow of interaction so that each is given space to contribute. Draw others into the discussion through eye-contact or asking for their input. Having someone make a flow chart of the group's interaction may help the awareness of the dominating person. Affirm good and positive contributions and encourage them to be patient with others. God has not finished with any of us yet!

In terms of the group needs, we have already considered it may help to be aware of the functions of the above roles within the group. The 'Harmoniser' or 'Helper-Facilitator' will serve to keep the group functioning as a whole, thus maintaining its life. The group will be aided in the accomplishment of its task by the 'Initiator' and the 'Helper-Facilitator'. The 'Fighter', 'Joker', and 'Blocker' may hinder the group's progress as they seek to have their individual needs met. However, sometimes they can perform a useful function in drawing the group together to cope with the demands they make, or force the group to re-examination or to an exploration of new directions.

HELPING 'PROBLEM' MEMBERS

It is sobering to keep before us that we are all potential 'problem' group members. At times we may reveal aspects of these people we have considered. As leaders, we are also wounded people who need to be open to, and indeed to seek the help of the group in our growth in Christ-likeness and more effective leadership of the group.

> And above all these put on love, which binds everything in perfect harmony. And let the peace of Christ rule in your hearts, to which indeed you were called in the one body. And be thankful. Let the word of Christ dwell in you richly, as you teach and admonish one another in all wisdom . . . (Colossians 3:14–16)

It is all too easy to categorise and pigeon-hole people who do not see things our way, as 'difficult' or 'problems'. It is essential we do not rely on first impressions, nor cast people into stereotyped roles. We must be wary of projecting our own hang-ups on to other people. We may feel inadequate in one person's presence, or we may feel superior to others who don't conform and fit into the pattern we want.

Hopefully, you may not meet many problem people in your groups.

Much of a leader's handling of these situations will occur outside the group sessions, in a personal counselling relation. The confidentiality of this counselling is essential.

Occasionally someone will turn up with whom we are not equipped to deal, and we must seek help and specialised guidance. It is not wise to try to deal with this person yourself; be prepared to discuss the problem with another leader, your minister, a counsellor, a psychologist or a specialist in group dynamics.

We are dealing with people who have the same psychological needs (although to different degrees) and people with spiritual needs. All of the 'problem' people need the group and what it offers. The group also needs these people. Accepting them and working through their problems can be a means of growth for all concerned. Christian groups are part of God's mission in this world, to make individuals and society a new creation in Christ.

No matter how high our ideals and aims for the group, we must not manipulate it and organise it to our own satisfaction. We are not trying to mould everyone to our way of thinking or into a group of people indistinguishable from one another.

Some people may leave the group in anger or frustration. They may not be compatible with the group and sometimes it will be right not to persuade that person to rejoin.

We cannot expect every group meeting to be a happy experience for every member. Growth involves discipline and pain. Sometimes our growing will take place in stress situations.

John Powell warns:

> We must be very careful, extremely careful, in fact, that we do not assume the vocation of acquainting others with their delusions. We are all tempted to unmask others, to smash their defences, to leave them naked and blinking in the light of the illumination provided by our exposure. It could be tragic in its results. If the psychological pieces come unglued, who will pick them up and put poor Humpty Dumpty Human Being together again? Will you? Can you? (3)

Paul's letter to the Philippians embodies the thoughts of an ideal leader. Notice how he yearns over his people, his affection for them and what he expects of them.

> So if there is any encouragement in Christ, any incentive of love, and participation in the Spirit, any affection and sympathy,

complete my joy by being of the same mind, having the same love, being in full accord and of one mind. Do nothing from selfishness or conceit, but in humility count others better than yourselves.

Let each of you look not only to his own interests, but also to the interests of others. Have this mind among yourselves, which you have in Christ Jesus who, though he was in the form of God, did not count equality with God a thing to be grasped, but emptied himself taking the form of a servant (or slave), being born in the likeness of men. And being found in human form he humbled himself and became obedient unto death, even death on a cross. (Philippians 2:1–8)

If people are to meet God in the group and to grow into Jesus Christ, then the group must be receptive to the Holy Spirit and understand His work. The Holy Spirit is God's agent of growth and change in human beings at all levels of spiritual life—collective and individual. Christian groups must draw upon the supernatural resources of the Holy Spirit for wisdom, love and grace, so that each member may more fully discover the freedom that is in Christ and therefore bring glory to God.

But if any of you lacks wisdom, he should pray to God, who will give it to him; because God gives generously and graciously to all. (James 1:5)

References

(1) Sara K Little, *Learning together in the Christian Fellowship* (John Knox, Richmond, Va., 1956, p. 18).
(2) John Powell, S.J., *Why am I afraid to tell you who I am?* (Tabor, 1969, p. 113).
(3) Ibid.

Chapter 6
Life Together

Life is community and community is relationships and relationships die without communication.—
Bonhoeffer[6]

Small groups have a crucial role to play in the renewal of individuals and society. All the liberating forces of the small group, now recognised by the social sciences, have been inherent from the beginning in the church. When the divine power of the Holy Spirit, present in individuals, operates in conjunction with the natural power of group relationships, people can be set free to relate to each other and to God in new and deeper ways.

Relationships within the small group are a most important factor. Whatever the purpose of the group, what happens to the people involved is more important than group structure or work accomplished.

The group itself does not cause spiritual renewal. But the structure and the dynamics of a small group seeking God's leadership provide an atmosphere conducive to growth,

discovery of gifts, commitment and service. Renewal is a gift which God in his grace bestows upon those who genuinely

seek him and this is important to keep before us throughout this chapter. While drawing upon the insights of group dynamics, as a Christian group we must always be aware of the divine factor present in each group. Technical know-how provides the framework in which the Holy Spirit may or may not choose to work renewal.

THE FELLOWSHIP OF THE HOLY SPIRIT

The nature of the life Christians seek to experience when they gather is not just common human togetherness. It is something special, namely that extraordinary fellowship that is spoken of, and sometimes reflected, in the New Testament. How can it be defined?

Gordon Dicker writes:

> The New Testament word rendered as fellowship is koinonia. It is derived from the word koinos, which means common. This is the word used in Acts 2:44, where it is said that those who believed had all things in common. Koinonia literally means having something in common, being partners, or mates, in a venture, sharing together in a common project. It is this sharing together which is the foundation of fellowship. There are some things we all share in common, such as our humanity, and that alone may be the basis of fellowship, but normally we look for people with whom we share more particular things, such as work, hobbies, a particular outlook on life. Such things become the basis for fellowships such as business clubs, sporting clubs, and societies of various kinds. Christian fellowship is also based on the sharing of things; the difference is in what it is that Christians share. They are a fellowship because, whatever differences there may be, they are sharers in the love of God, sharers in Christ and in the gift of the Spirit.[1]

If you have experienced this deep fellowship with a group of other Christians, you will know just what Robert Raines is talking about when he defines koinonia.

> Koinonia is fellowship with the triune God. Koinonia is healing friendship in which we are converted. Koinonia requires personal participation and mutual sharing with others.
>
> Koinonia is God present with us in Christ. This is koinonia; that communion in which He abides in us and we in Him. This is the communion of the saints which partakes of eternity in the here and now. It is that communion in which conversion takes place.
>
> The Apostles' fellowship was a total sharing of life. It was a genuine family in Christ.
>
> Bible study, sharing of life, Communion, prayer: here are the ingredients which again and again are found to provide the

context for koinonia. They could almost be described as the conditions for koinonia.

In the context of Bible study and prayer, they entered into a new dimension of friendship, the fellowship of the Holy Spirit—koinonia.

The church must foster and sustain the conditions in which koinonia can be known. This cannot be done for most people simply through morning or evening worship. Worship is indispensable as the weekly meeting of the Christian community. But it is effective only as the total sharing of all the people of the friendship in Christ they have known between Sundays. There cannot be real first-hand koinonia among hundreds of people. The best evidence of this is the fact that hundreds of people in a given local church can worship faithfully for years without any appreciable change in quality of commitment or direction of life. Many of the same people, exposed to a breath or taste of koinonia in a small group, begin to change in a matter of months. The church is obligated to lead its people into small-group fellowship where the conditions for koinonia prevail.[2]

Gordon Dicker continues:

It is the Spirit himself who creates the community by creating the fellowship (koinonia in Greek) on which it is based. The creation of the koinonia was as much a direct work of Pentecost as the conversion of individuals. The two cannot be separated. The community is not just the result of the decisions of like-minded people to form a group together. It is created by God through the Holy Spirit. According to 1 Corinthians 12–14, this is what the charismatic work of the Spirit is all about.

This fellowship is always in danger of being disrupted by human sin. Even those who are justified by grace through faith still have sin remaining in them. Their selfishness and self-centredness must be broken again and again if they are not to offend one another, or be offended. This also is the work of the Spirit.

The fellowship is not an end in itself. It is not a holy huddle. It is called into being for a purpose, and that purpose is participation in God's mission. The Church exists by mission, just as a fire exists by burning—so wrote the Swiss theologian Emil Brunner many years ago.

The Church engages in mission basically in two ways: by its being and by its doing.

To be sure, mission involves doing, but it is always a doing that springs from, and is supported by, the Church's being. When the Church is genuinely a caring, supportive fellowship; when its members speak the truth in love, share each other's joys and sorrows, and participate in worship and sacraments with unaffected joy; and when the ecclesiastical institution is more concerned about justice and service than its own self-interest, then the Church points the way to Christ by its own life and character. Nevertheless the missionary task of the Church calls for action as well as being.[3]

The dynamic life of the group, which is the outworking of both the **fruit** and the **gifts** of the Holy Spirit, is to be entered into fully thus creating a sensitive, caring fellowship to enrich each member's life and the relationships in the group. But the end is to develop new life with the purpose of sharing the good news of Jesus Christ and expressing active, loving concern in an estranged, hurting world.

THE DYNAMICS OF THE GROUP

Groups are more than just a certain number of individuals together; more than just the sum total of their membership. In every group, whenever people come together, unique emotional pressures are at work. These pressures arise from the different relationships within the group, the group's relation to the outside world, and the different needs individuals bring to the group. These forces and pressures help shape the nature of each group. The feeling of 'team spirit' is released when a group is committed to a particular goal and to some extent to each other. But these forces are not only constructive. People will often change their behaviour or do things that they would not normally do as individuals when in a group. We refer to these forces as 'group dynamics'.

Group cohesion

One of these forces is known as group cohesion. This refers to those pressures which encourage the members to join and maintain their membership of the group. The individual will relate to a group to the degree that he/she sees it meeting some of his/her needs. And the extent to which the group can meet these needs of its different members will determine the degree of group cohesion. Leaders should be aware of the most common needs individuals bring to the group. These needs include:

A sense of belonging and love.
A sense of purpose and meaning.
To be able to share in planning.
To have a clear understanding of what is expected of themselves and the group (i.e. the group's goal).
To experience genuine responsibility and challenge.
To feel that progress is being made towards set goals; a sense of achievement.
An intense desire to be kept informed.
A desire for recognition when it is due.
A reasonable degree of security.

In addition to the positive forces (sometimes called **rewards**) listed above, which encourage group cohesiveness, there are also forces (**dis-rewards**) working against the maintenance of the group membership. Some of these could include:

Loss of free time.
The presence of 'problem' members in the group.
Ineffective leadership.
Lack of opportunity to 'do their own thing'.
Destructive competition among the group members.

While these may appear obvious, we often tend to think of a group from our own point of view, rather than that of the other members. Although we cannot make our groups appeal to everyone, we should be aware of the effects of both the rewards and dis-rewards from the members', or potential members', point of view.

People bring their own assumptions, attitudes, mental sets, values, etc. to the group. Feelings and prejudices are communicated through words, intonations, facial expressions, posture, etc. Be sure that you are at least aware of your own attitudes and feelings as they affect the group's life, for you can be sure that they will be communicated, either verbally or non-verbally, to the group and will affect the meaning the other members draw out.

Informal organisation

It is also necessary for the leader to be aware of the informal organisation within the group (i.e. the values, relationships, etc.) that may not be provided for by the official, formal group structure and organisation. The nature of the informal organisation within your group will depend on how your group sees itself and its purpose. This is one reason why goal clarification and periodic evaluation of the group life and task achievement is so important.

If your group is primarily 'task-oriented' (i.e. concerned above all with the achievement of the observable objective—e.g. planning a particular project), the informal organisation will favour those who are productive and helpful; if companionship oriented, then those who are companionable and friendly. However, to be really effective groups need to be efficient in performing their task, as well as effective in their interpersonal relationships.

Informal leadership

Informal organisation involves the aspect of informal leadership. In any group meeting, one or more people may naturally assume leadership roles at different stages of the meeting. Informal leaders further the real interest of the group; their behaviour comes closest to the group ideal; they are the group representatives. It is important then to recognise your informal leaders—don't feel threatened by them. It is not necessary to formally incorporate them into the leadership team, but it is essential to utilise them as a communication channel to the group. Recognise them as an asset and relate to them accordingly. Have them on side!

Communication

Proper and effective communication is the most strategic factor in motivating a group. But communication only takes place when the meaning (i.e. the facts plus the subjective interpretation of the facts) intended by the communicator coincides with the meaning interpreted by the group. For this to happen communication must be seen as a two way process. The communicator must listen to the group as well as talk. Indeed speaking and listening skills should be used to build a warm, accepting, friendly climate in which all members feel free to participate in relevant communication and discussion. The flow of communication is affected by the interpersonal relationships within the group and the relevance of information being communicated to the life and purpose of the group. As has already been indicated, the leader—through their knowledge of group dynamics, but more importantly through their love and concern for the members of their group—must facilitate this climate.

Helping people change and grow

It should be stressed here that, as Christians, we are not in the business of manipulating people towards either our views or the lifestyle we might believe they should follow. However, groups are concerned with the learning, growth and development of their individual members, and therefore we should be concerned with helping people change and grow. To influence the behaviour of individuals in a group we need to deal with the group as a unit, because the individuals are held in position by forces pressuring them to conform to the group's standards. So you need to 'unfreeze' the existing group standard through uninhibited discussion, free expression of views and feelings and perhaps changing the physical environment (e.g. a more relaxed physical setting), until the group as a whole accepts a higher standard. As Kurt Lewin, one of the leaders in the field of group dynamics has said, 'It is easier to change the ideology and social practice of a small group handled together than of single individuals'.

It is important then for group leaders to be aware of the forces below the surface in their groups and to be able to, in some degree, manage them. Jesus himself understood the importance of group dynamics and to some extent utilised those forces in his ministry. In the small group of twelve disciples, ideas, attitudes and behaviour were changed. Group dynamics is a very real tool that the Holy Spirit uses to minister to us and through us to each other.

FACTORS WHICH AFFECT OUR COMMUNICATION WITH OTHERS

One of the major influences upon group life is the quality of the communication which exists. There are at least five major factors which contribute to the way in which each person in the group will help facilitate good or poor communication: self-image, listening skills, ability to express themselves, conflict and the degree to which each is prepared to be open with others.

Self-image

Self-image is the concept we have of ourselves. It is the very centre of our being from which we see, hear, evaluate and understand everything else. A healthy, strong self-image is necessary for vital and satisfying interaction with others, for this helps people live fully and confidently and enjoy life and people.

A person with a poor self-image is insecure, lacks self-assurance, is over-concerned for what other people think, feels unworthy and inadequate. Because of this he/she feels that his/her ideas and thoughts are uninteresting and are not worth communicating. This person fears rejection, criticism and so has difficulty in relating to others in an open, honest way. 'I am afraid to tell you who I am, because if I tell you who I am, you may not like who I am, and it's all that I have.' John Powell continues by saying:

> . . . this thought reflects something of the imprisoning fears and self-doubt which cripple most of us and keep us from forward movement on the road to maturity, happiness and true love. [4]

As our self-image affects the way we communicate, so our communication with others shapes our concepts and the way we see ourselves. We derive a great deal of self-knowledge from our experiences with other human beings, particularly from the 'significant others' in our lives—parents, family, peer group and those we love. If a person is to have a strong self-image, he or she needs the assurance of the love, respect and acceptance of those who are the 'significant others' in his or her life. In a supportive small group, members may have these needs met in a way which will enable growth and acceptance of themselves which has never previously been possible. They can also discover there is a divine inner capacity which can enable them to be more than they are.

Listening

A great deal of our failure to communicate stems from the fact that we do not listen properly. Creative, sensitive, accurate, non-judgemental listening is vitally important in a meaningful relationship. Growth takes place within us when we can offer this kind of listening to another and also when we have been the recipients of this kind of listening.

Carl R Rogers says:

> I can testify that when you are in a psychological distress and someone really hears you without passing judgment on you, without trying to take responsibility for, without trying to mould you, it feels doubly good. At these times it has relaxed tension in me. It has permitted me to bring out the frightening feelings, the guilt, the despair, the confusion that have been part of my experience. When I have been listened to and when I have been heard, I am able to re-perceive my world in a new way and to go on. I have deeply appreciated the times that I have experienced this sensitive empathetic, concentrated listening. [5]

Most of Christ's parables conclude with 'He who has ears to hear, let him hear'. Each of the letters to the seven churches in the book of Revelation end with 'He who has an ear to hear let him hear what the Spirit says'. God's complaint in Psalm 81 is 'O, that my people would listen to me'. In his epistle, James exhorts, ' . . . let everyone be quick to listen and slow to speak'. (James 1:19) Christ in his explanation of the parable of the sower emphasises that each seed which failed stood for someone who had not listened properly, and therefore did not grow.

Listening does not only mean the physical process of hearing with the ears—it involves an intellectual and emotional process as well, when one's whole being strives to understand and hear the thoughts, feelings and meanings behind the words being uttered. It requires patience, sensitivity, understanding, acceptance and alertness.

Clarity of expression

Communication is often hindered because some have difficulty in translating their thoughts into the words which express what they really mean, or feel.

A sensitive group, committed to the full participation and growth of each member, will help develop each other's thoughts by feeding back what is received and asking appropriate questions to draw out and help people develop their thoughts.

Use 'I' Messages

Communication in the group improves when members are willing to take responsibility for their own ideas and feelings and use the personal pronoun 'I' when it is appropriate. All too often people say something like this, 'After studying this we should take this seriously', rather than indicating that they personally have gained new insights and challenge by saying, 'After studying this I'm convinced I should take this seriously'.

The leader should model for the group in his/her communication a willingness to share directly what he/she feels or thinks by saying 'I', 'my', 'mine', rather than talking about others or hiding behind the generalities or vagueness of 'People say . . .', 'You will want to . . .'.

Using personal pronouns to express personal feelings or thoughts directly can deepen the level of communication in the group, avoid indirect or vague messages and develop relationships through greater openness.

Conflict

Many people find conflict unbearable. They would rather smooth over a situation than let feelings of hostility or anger be displayed. This inability to deal with conflict frequently results in a breakdown in communication. Feelings of resentment and hostility are repressed and may only surface when triggered off by perhaps some totally irrelevant incident.

Sometimes conflict can be fruitful. We reveal our innermost feelings and, if we are in a group, the group can channel healing to us.

Christians are expected to get angry about evil in all its ugly forms. However we must separate righteous indignation from petty spite, or annoyance because something has inconvenienced us. Righteous indignation, which is not prolonged to the point of turning a person sour, can be constructive. Paul wrote to the Ephesians:

> Throw off falsehood; speak only the truth to each other, for all of us are the parts of one body. If you are angry, do not let anger lead you into sin; do not let sunset find you still nursing it; leave no loop-hole for the devil. (Ephesians 4:25–26, NEB)

Christ did not suppress his anger with those who were robbing the pilgrims visiting the temple, or with the religious leaders who were more concerned about religious observances than the healing of the man with the deformity.

Conflict handled wisely can help a group draw closer together. There may be some cost involved, but there usually is when growth is taking place.

Self-disclosure

Self-disclosure in a group is a mutual process. The more we know about each other, the more effective and efficient our communication will be. Mask-wearing, pretence and play acting all hinder the life of a group. Many sit week after week in a group, never feeling able to be open about a deep hurt or their doubts and fears. We cannot bear each other's burdens if we do not know what they are.

Carl R Rogers talks about 'communicating the real person', telling it like it is. James' injunction, 'Confess your sins to one another and pray for one another that you may be healed' (James 4:16) encourages an openness beyond what is found in most groups today. Unfortunately many groups do not encourage such openness. To be accepted in some, one has to appear to always be succeeding. To discover a real sinner in their midst would be intolerable!

The self-disclosure envisaged here has been a characteristic of the great movements of the Holy Spirit. In those situations it happened quite spontaneously with no manipulation by those present. The lesson here is that no one should be coerced into self-disclosure.

As the group develops deeper levels of trust; as a caring, relaxed, accepting, open spirit arises; and as the leader sensitively models greater openness, members will gradually feel freer to let themselves unfold.

These elements make interpersonal communication enriching and enhancing.

HOW TO LISTEN TO OTHERS

Dietrich Bonhoeffer writes:

> Many people are looking for an ear that will listen. They do not find it among most people they meet, not even amongst their close friends. But he who can no longer listen to another has lost contact with life. For life is community and community is relationships and relationships die without communication. One who cannot listen long and patiently will presently be talking beside the point and never be really speaking to others; unfortunately, he will not be conscious of it. [6]

Some active listening skills

One of the ways to improve our communication skills is to work at active listening. Active listening means more than simply concentrating on what the other person is saying, although that is part of it. It includes letting the other person know that you have heard what he/she has said.

Very often in conversation, we assume we know what the other person means by a statement, that is, that we understand what the other person intended by his or her remarks.

This may be the case, but often we may be missing an

58

important element in the person's communication to us. It is often useful to check to see if we have heard what he really intended to communicate.

1. Paraphrasing

The basic skill involved in active listening is paraphrasing or putting into your own words what the other person seems to be communicating to you. This gives him/her a way to know whether you have missed his/her point and further clarification is needed. Paraphrasing is letting the other person know the meaning his/her words have for you in order to test whether or not you have heard what he/she intended to communicate to you.

Here are some examples:

Ted: There's nothing in church for me any more. None of it makes any sense.
Ned: Church no longer has any meaning for you.
Ted: I wish it did, but I can't believe in God any more.
Ned: You mean the real problem with church is that God doesn't seem real.

Jane: I can't stand the remarks my father makes about my friends! He thinks they're all irresponsible idiots.
Anne: You're angry with him because he doesn't like the friends you choose.
Jane: It's more that he jumps to all the wrong conclusions without making any effort to understand them.
Anne: You wish he didn't write them off so quickly.

To paraphrase is not to make a judgement about the other person, who is the only one who knows what he or she really meant. Paraphrasing is a way of testing your understanding of what the other person meant and is always open to being changed. It may not be in the form of a question, but a question mark is always implied. Paraphrasing does not mean approving or agreeing with what the person says, nor is it seeking to reassure, or to probe, or to argue. It is simply letting the other person know they have been heard.

Obviously, paraphrasing is not your only response in a lively conversation. The examples above may seem one-sided, because they do not include any feelings or opinions from the person who is responding, as you would expect in a typical conversation (this is often a neglected element). However, this kind of active listening can greatly facilitate good communication.

There are added benefits from paraphrasing. It lets the other person know you are really interested in what they are saying. It shows you want to know what they mean. If the other person feels you can understand their point of view, they are more likely to want to hear your point of view. Paraphrasing can also be useful to the other person in helping them to clarify their own thoughts or feelings by seeing them more objectively or in a different perspective.

2. Reflecting feelings

Paraphrasing may respond to two dimensions of a communication: the information or content in the communication, and what the person feels about the information or content. Sometimes the feeling level will be the real message and at other times almost no feeling at all will be involved. Effective paraphrasing will seek to pick up what the person is really intending.

Paraphrasing words tests whether or not the listener has heard what the speaker intended to communicate. In a similar way, reflecting the feelings which the listener perceives to be communicated gives opportunity for the speaker to confirm, deny or clarify. Feelings are expressed directly or in metaphor, e.g. 'I'm angry', 'I feel accepted', 'I'm confused' are direct expressions of feelings. 'I feel as though I'm being treated as a child', 'I feel like something the dog dragged in' are feelings expressed in metaphor.

Being able to recognise and describe the feeling clearly is important if it is to be reflected properly. The label given needs to be clear in meaning—love, anger, attraction, boredom, curiosity, fear, frustration, hope, hurt, joy, rejection, relief, embarrassment.

The feelings being communicated through these statements are obvious:

'Will you stop that!' 'That was a wonderful evening.'
'Can't you ever get home on time?' 'This is a thoughtful group to belong to.'

Here is an example of feeling reflections:

John: 'I have had it with that son of mine!'
Stephen: 'You sound very angry with your son.'
Another example:

Jill: 'The way you said that just now gives me the impression that you are bored.'
Mary: 'No! I'm not bored. I had little sleep last night and I'm very tired. I'm finding it hard to remain alert.'

3. **Perception check**

These are responses you can make to ensure you are not making false assumptions. Express your own idea of the other person's statement. You may say, 'Is that what you meant?' 'I feel that you are disturbed. Did my last statement bother you?' 'I believe we are agreed to meet at the Post Office corner at five o'clock. Is that correct?'

4. **Behaviour description**

This involves reporting the specific acts of another to check on your own interpretation of their behaviour and to give opportunity for confirmation or correction by the other person. 'I saw you closing your eyes for a moment. Are you very tired?' 'I saw you jump. Were you startled?' 'I saw your smile turn into a frown. Are you displeased?' 'I saw you waver and sit down. Are you feeling ill?'

5. **Direct questions**

This involves asking questions without any evaluative judgemental words.

6. **Describing your own feelings**

'I feel warm about your helping me in this way.' 'I am sad to hear about that.' 'I am very anxious about your trip tomorrow.' 'I am very upset with you.' 'After discussing this together, I feel very hopeful.'

Listening, **questioning** and **observing** are three major categories of communicating.

Some More Hints for Better Listening

Resist distractions—noises, views, people—and focus on the speaker. You may need to change your position, move to another location or ask permission to turn off a television or radio. Try to take control of the situation, which is an unselfish act, to help you respond adequately to the speaker.

Listen with expectancy, so as to evoke the fullest reality and capacity of the person speaking. You can show this with your seating position, your facial expressions and adequate eye contact.

Listen so as to be involved in what the person is relating. Ask appropriate questions. Make non-verbal responses such as moving your head and/or using your hands. Use linking words such as 'and then', 'so', 'but', 'you felt . . .' and 'really'.

Listen with care and concern, though such listening is never cheap. It costs listeners something of themselves. Ask for clarification. Express concern in your facial expressions and by two or three word responses such as, 'that's tough', 'how exciting', 'that must have hurt', 'great!'

Be honest. If you are finding it hard to concentrate because of things on your mind, sickness or personal discomfort, tell the speaker and ask their help in enabling you to listen.

Allow time to reflect upon content and to search for meaning. Do not avoid times for silence. Pauses can be productive. You may need to suggest a time of brief silence to think about what has been said.

Wait before responding to the speaker—too prompt a response reduces listening effectiveness.

Listen beyond the outer layer of the spoken word. There must be a capacity to hear through many wrappings. Sometimes we hear not only the words but also the thought, the depth of feeling, the personal meaning, even the meaning that is below the conscious intent of the speaker— sometimes we hear the deep cry of human need.

Be aware of the possible barriers to the meaning the speaker is trying to convey. Nearly all people have a fear of being rejected, ridiculed or misunderstood, so they 'test the water' by entering into superficial conversation or by presenting a need which is not the real need, until they feel accepted and confident in the listener.

Guard against trying to impose upon the other person a detailed account of your own experience. Many listeners almost immediately turn the spotlight on themselves by saying 'I had an experience like that; it happened when . . .' or 'I have that trouble too, I . . .' This effectively blocks off the speaker and leads to frustration and disillusionment. There may be an opportunity to briefly tell your story, but at an appropriate time later.

Openly and honestly engage in a discussion of the concerns that arise.

Remember the speaker has a 'spectator listener'. It has been said that 'within each of us there is a "spectator listener" who is aware if the other person is listening in depth. When the sensitive spectator is not being heard as a person then the 'spectator listener' within each of us signals us not to fully reveal ourselves. We with-hold or water down what we really think and feel, because we know that no one is really listening.'[7]

Know when to stop. If you can't pick the non-verbal signals of the speaker or if the person does not indicate their wish to finish, ask, 'Do you want to keep on talking about this?' or 'Shall we continue this later?'

NON-VERBAL COMMUNICATION

Research into face to face communication between human beings has found that the *verbal* dimension (words spoken) provides only about 7% of the total impact of a message. The *vocal* dimension is the way a person speaks those words (the tone of voice, where the emphasis is placed and inflection), together with other sounds which are not actually words, contributes 38% to the message a person actually receives. However, the *non-verbal* aspect, a person's facial expressions and body language (movement and position), contributes 55%. Some researchers set this non-verbal figure in excess of 65%.

The techniques regarding verbal communication already described in this chapter will significantly improve the verbal dimension. But even using these skills will not improve the impact nearly as much as that of the vocal and non-verbal aspects.

A number of well written books are available on non-verbal communication. *Body Language* by Allan Peace (Camel) is easy to follow and well illustrated.

I have only touched on some aspects of non-verbal communication, hopefully to stimulate you to read more on the subject.

Always keep in mind that non-verbal communication is complex. You should be warned against taking one cue in isolation. Usually a number of cues need to be taken into account before drawing a conclusion concerning what a person is involuntarily communicating.

Walking style

This relates to how people carry their bodies, whether they swish, amble or stamp. Observe how people arrive at the group. Their movements could convey expectancy, confidence, purpose, caution, heaviness of spirit, joy, etc.

Touching

This is probably the most powerful non-verbal communication form. We can communicate interest, trust, tenderness, warmth, anger, rejection and a variety of other emotions through touch. People differ in their willingness to touch and be touched. Some give out non-verbal signals that say they do not wish to be touched. Different cultures respond in different ways to touching. We need to be sensitive to this in groups of mixed racial backgrounds.

Eye contact

People tend to size each other up in terms of trustworthiness, through reactions to each other's eye contact. Counsellors know that eye contact is an important way of creating

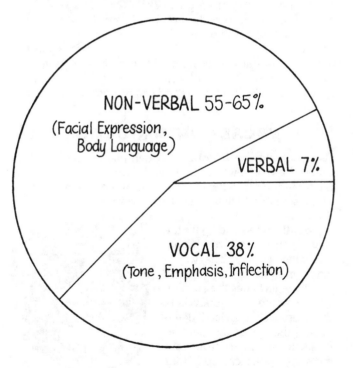

NON-VERBAL 55-65%
(Facial Expression, Body Language)

VERBAL 7%

VOCAL 38%
(Tone, Emphasis, Inflection)

Diagram Nº 11 : Dimensions of Face to Face Contact.

understanding and acceptance but, again, we need to keep in mind that some cultures give less eye contact than others.

When seeking to get people involved in discussion, a general question can be followed up by a brief look at one or more in the group to invite their involvement, or a fleeting glance around the whole group to seek anyone's response.

Posturing

How people position their bodies when seated or standing constitutes a set of potential signals that may communicate how one is experiencing his or her environment. People who fold their arms and cross their legs are often said to be on the defensive. It is sometimes observed that a person under severe psychological threat will assume the body position of a foetus. A person slouched in a seat may be bored, feeling relaxed or showing disagreement.

Mannerisms or tics

The involuntary nervous spasms of the body can be a key when a person feels threatened, not in agreement, or irritated. The continuous or even casual movement of a foot or the fingers can indicate disagreement or impatience with what another is saying. These mannerisms can be easily misinterpreted.

Distancing

Each person is said to have a psychological space around them. If someone invades that space they may become tense, alert, defensive. We tend to place distance between ourselves and others according to the kinds of relationship that we have and what our motives are toward each other.

Some people who have had a traumatic experience with another person, especially in early life, will find it disturbing to have another person stand close to them. This needs to be kept in mind when leading a small group. Most will be very relaxed about sitting close to one another, whereas others may want to keep some space around them until they feel comfortable in the group, and for some that may require an extended period of meetings.

Gesturing

Gestures (the way we use our hands and arms) carry a great deal of meaning but do not mean the same things to all people. Again, these need to be interpreted against a person's cultural background. Gestures give emphasis to our words and often clarify our meanings. They often are expressive of deep emotions and can be both threatening or accepting.

VOCAL COMMUNICATION

As has already been indicated, when people speak to each other, the way in which they say the words that they speak contributes 38% to the effectiveness of the communication. Other sounds which are not strictly words also contribute to this aspect.

Vocalism has to do with the way we pronounce or emphasise what we say. The way a word or sentence is packaged vocally determines the signal it gives to another person. Where the emphasis is placed determines the meaning another is likely to infer from our message. As an example, take the sentence, 'I love my son.' Shifting the emphasis to a different word each time it is spoken can give an entirely different message. For example, if the emphasis is upon the first word, '*I* love my son,' the implication is that others do not, or it could be defensive against an accusation that the speaker does not love his son. If the emphasis is upon the second word, it could be given to deny neglect or emphasise the depth of the relationship. By emphasising 'my', the implication is that someone else's children do not receive the same affection. Whereas to emphasise the word 'son' could mean there are other members of the family who are not held in the same regard.

My wife and I most times call each other 'darling', but that word gets packaged in different ways. When we are feeling warm towards each other it expresses a closeness and deep love. If we are being inconsiderate or disagreeing with one another, the same word comes over as less than accepting and affirming!

Sub-vocals are the sounds uttered when trying to find words, e.g. uh, um, er. We use a number of non-word expressions in order to carry a meaning to another person. We hum, grunt, groan, and so on. These are not words, purely noise, but they do carry meaning, saying: 'I agree', 'I understand', 'I'm impatient, get on with it', 'When you have finished', 'I have something to say', 'I do not agree', 'Surely not', 'You can't be serious!'

HANDLING CONFLICT CREATIVELY

Jesus lived a life of authentic person to person encounter in which he creatively confronted and used human conflict. He did not avoid conflict with the Pharisees and the religious authorities.

Conflict and tension can never be avoided by the Christian. It is part and parcel of our call to discipleship. It is interesting too that the behavioural scientists affirm that conflict and tension are vital for human growth and maturity. Unfortunately many tend to think of conflict as always being something negative.

Responding to conflict

We can classify our strategy for handling conflict into three categories: **avoidance**, **defusion** and **confrontation**. We have already stated that avoiding the conflict is no answer. Ignoring the 'stirrer' in a group or pretending that people 'don't really mean what they say' in the heat of an argument helps no one and gets nowhere. If that conflict is not squarely faced and properly handled it will simmer below the surface and pollute the relationships within the group.

Some people think that conflict is like a bomb. If you can't avoid it then defuse it! But defusion is a delaying tactic. Invariably defusion results in feelings of dissatisfaction and frustration towards the leader, 'problem' person or the group as a whole, and anxiety about the future and one's own image.

The third way of responding to conflict is by an actual confrontation between the conflicting issues or people. But confrontation itself can be further subdivided into **power** strategies and **negotiation** strategies. Power strategies mean the use of physical force; bribery (e.g. gifts, favours); punishment (e.g. withholding love, money); and exercising one's authority, 'pulling rank', to settle the conflict. From the point of view of the 'winner' such tactics are often quite effective. Unfortunately, hostility, anxiety, resentment and physical retaliation are generally the 'loser's' reactions to these win-lose power tactics. And such reactions are totally destructive not only regarding the relationship between 'winner' and 'loser' but for the entire group.

On the other hand, with negotiation strategies both sides can win. The aim of negotiation is to resolve the conflict with a compromise or a solution which all the parties involved would find acceptable and satisfying. Therefore negotiation is regarded as the most positive conflict management strategy.

The conflict management process

Successful conflict management requires the knowledge and practice of necessary negotiation skills.

Diagnosis of the nature of the conflict. In this first step the important thing is to determine whether the conflict is a 'value' conflict (i.e. one arising out of different life attitudes and values) or a 'real' (tangible) conflict, or a combination of both.

'Value' conflicts are very difficult to resolve. However, a difference in values is only really significant when our opposing views affect us in some real or tangible way. It is not necessary for either of us to change our values in order for us and the whole task group to come to a mutually agreeable position.

If it is a conflict in differing personal values that in no way affects the life of the group, then we should respect one another's rights to differ, and leave it at that. However, most conflict situations in small groups are 'real' conflicts that do affect the life of the group and its different members, and as such need to be resolved.

Effectiveness in initiating and confronting a conflict. The most effective way to approach the situation is to state the actual effect the conflict has on you personally, or on the group. If the conflict directly affects the whole group, invite other members to check out how they are affected.

Hearing the other's point of view. It is vital to listen to and really hear what the other party is saying. He or she may react with a defensive counter argument or a hard-line approach. Avoid making argument-provoking replies. Do not try to defend yourself; do not explain your position, and do not make threats or demands. Instead listen to, and reflect back to, the other person, in your own words, what he or she is feeling and saying.

Showing that you have listened to your opponents and checking out their position will lower their defences. You have indicated that you have made an effort to begin to understand their viewpoint. As a result, they will be more ready to hear your point of view. Only then should you present your position. In this way, not only is the road opened for a resolution of the immediate conflict, but you are starting to build a bridge of understanding between yourself and the other person that will lead to improved relationships and greater honesty within the group.

Problem solving. The final skill needed to resolve a conflict is the use of the problem solving process by the group to reach a decision that is agreeable to all. This involves clarifying the problem using the skills already outlined. The group should consider: 'What is the real issue or concern here that affects us; what is its real cause; and how does each of us stand concerning the issue?'

The group should then explore possible solutions and then select what they consider to be the most appropriate.

A clear plan to do something about what has been decided, including a deadline to work towards, should have built into it an opportunity to reflect on the effectiveness of what is planned and the option to re-think if it isn't working out.

A final word for group leaders

It goes without saying that the role of the group leader in conflict management is especially important. In addition to acquiring the above skills the leader should be aware that, in the initial stages of a conflict, the group members must feel that the leader is strong, competent and personally secure enough to be able to stand in the middle of an aggressive confrontation. Furthermore, the climate in the group needs to be an open one with evident trust, if a resolution is to be reached. Members must be encouraged to accept their own feelings, hold their own values, and strengthen those ideas which seem to be most helpful to them.

References

(1) Gordon Dicker, *Faith With Understanding* (Joint Board of Christian Education, Melbourne).
(2) Robert A Raines, *New Life in the Church* (Harper and Row, New York).
(3) Gordon Dicker, *Faith With Understanding* (JBCE, Melb).
(4) John Powell S. J., *Why am I afraid to tell you who I am?* (Tabor).
(5) Carl R Rogers, *Some Elements of Effective Communication* (A Transcript of talks given at the California Institute of Technology, Pasadena, CA, USA).
(6) Dietrich Bonhoeffer, *Life Together* (SCM Press).
(7) Carl A Rogers, *Some Elements of Effective Communication* (A Transcript of talks given at the California Institute of Technology, Pasadena, CA, USA).

Other sources:
The section on 'Handling Conflict' is based on material prepared by Graham Beattie, used originally in the author's book *Building Small Groups in the Christian Community*.

A number of roneoed resource sheets and short articles have been drawn upon which were received from the Yokefellow Institute, Richmond, Indiana and the Program Council of the Iowa United Methodist Conference, Des Moines, Iowa. Unfortunately, the authors' names were not indicated.

Material in a number of Annual Handbooks for Group Facilitators, by Pfeiffer and Jones (University Associates, California), has also been adapted for use in this chapter.

Chapter 7

Getting Started

One never knows where the Holy Spirit may come into a relationship or a company and give it his own stamp of meaning and power. Perhaps the first question is not whether we want to start a group, but whether God does? If he does, he must ordinarily find someone who is open to such direction and leadership. It does not take great saints, else none of us would be used; but it takes people with spiritual purpose and the beginnings of spiritual experience. If the will and intention are there, and prayer, God can use you.[1]

There is no magical formula, no set pattern to follow when commencing a small group. The history of small groups in the church shows that they commence in a variety of ways. It is helpful to know how other groups commenced. Some guidelines will emerge if we study how people have been drawn together. We need, however, to ensure and preserve flexibility, for the way your group commences may have some similarity or it may be entirely different.

HOW SOME GROUPS BEGAN

In my small groups conferences, I have asked participants how the small groups with which they have been associated began—what was the initial motivation. Here is a collection of the answers given, some of which give the reason why a particular individual joined a group.

I was not achieving and felt I wanted fellowship with others to help me grow.

There was a lack of depth in the fellowship available in my church.

After a house-party experience we felt a deep desire to extend the depth of fellowship and learning which took place over that weekend.

I wanted to improve a skill.

It was a tradition in our church to work through small groups. They had been successful in helping people grow so I wanted to join one.

I had a need for self-acceptance which I felt could be met in a group.

I was lonely and insecure.

A number of us felt we wanted a continuing situation in which we could be encouraged, supported, affirmed and loved. (Repeated.)

I had a deep desire to share with others where I stood spiritually.

I wanted to be honest. I wanted to learn more.

We wanted to break down the barriers which exist between age groups.

A number of us wanted to show concern for others outside the church. (Repeated.)

My problem was communication with others — this led me to seek out a group.

Someone invited me to join the group to which they belonged.

A group which had grown too large divided.

I liked the informality of a group in contrast to the formal fellowship in rigid worship services.

One person was the driving force. (Repeated.)

It was commenced as a follow-up to an outreach programme.

As a couple we wanted to meet with other couples who were experiencing similar problems.

In the main these groups commenced because:

(i) There was a common interest.
(ii) There was a deep sense of need.
(iii) One person had initiative and vision.

These generalisations were supported from further feed-in at these conferences after groups had read sections of books dealing with experiences of new life in the church, in which small groups played a major role. After seeking to learn from each writer about how small groups commence, the groups reported:

The initiator shared honestly and openly a deep sense of need with others.

The group began in an informal manner.

One person took the initiative to seek out others who felt the same way.

The witness of others helped motivate the need.

There was a willingness to 'give it a go'.

They all needed each other.

There was a convergence of events which drew the group together.

One insignificant person gave himself wholly to God.

It doesn't take a saint to start a group!!

People can not be coerced into joining a group.

Often the least likely person will want to join.

The Holy Spirit was the key factor.

Having found others with a common need, they did not procrastinate: a definite time and place was set.

The leader did not have all the answers but he was prepared to search for them.

The Holy Spirit directed but he needed individuals who were responsive and available but not necessarily with great ability.

There was a hunger for knowledge and a gripping sense of need for purpose and meaning in their lives—for something better. (Repeated.)

There was a willingness to be open and take risks in sharing their own lives.

The group started as a response to a call from God, not as a gimmick.

There was a need to share a vision in order not to lose it.

From these observations we can deduce that:

A common interest and sense of need were necessary prerequisites.

The significant role played by an inadequate person, who was nevertheless open and available, is established.

The need to make definite plans to get together once a number feel drawn together is imperative if the initial vision and motivation is not to be lost in vagueness and indecision.

The prime role of the Holy Spirit in awakening the sense of need, giving a vision of how this need can be met and enabling the initiator and participants is a deep insight which should always be kept in mind.

John L Casteel sums up these findings:

Groups come into being when the hunger, faith and determination of concerned persons are matched with the leading and empowerment of the Holy Spirit. [2]

HELPING OTHERS CATCH THE VISION

Gaining a vision of what it is like to belong to a caring, concerned, redeeming small community of people as a necessary first step in implementing groups is vital. 'Unless there be a consciousness of the significance of groups and their possibilities, leaders are not likely to improve those now existing or to set up new ones to fill new purposes.' [3] Potential members will also need to be helped to gain such a vision of the role the small group experience can be expected to play in meeting their needs and those of others.

People sharing their experience of being in groups can be valuable in helping people see the potential of the small group. A living witness always helps motivate the sceptic who needs 'proof'. A small group of lay people whose lives have been touched by this process can be a strong encouragement to others. Individual members from two of my parishes, where we had networks of small groups, would often be asked to share their experience of the value of the small group with churches in other areas. I made cassette recordings of some testimonies which I took with me when called in to consult with parishes about this means of renewal. Whenever we conducted a Lay Witness Weekend, most of the team would be members of our small groups and inevitably spontaneous sharing about the value of the small group experience would take place during the supper groups. Frequently new groups have been formed after these events.

A team from a church or parish with successful small groups has often conducted a conference or series of special meetings to help another church or parish to see the possibilities of small groups through the team's rich first-hand experiences. The overflow of lives enriched by small groups is a powerful means of helping others catch the vision.

The media available to us in a local parish is another channel through which the message can be communicated. Articles in the parish paper giving the rationale for small groups, reports of successful groups and testimonies of individuals who have been enriched through such experiences all heighten interest. A number of suitable films are available which could be used at appropriate times.

Preaching on related subjects is another way. In one of my parishes in the period between the leaders catching the vision at a Church Life Conference and the planned commencement of the small group programme, I preached a series of sermons on the early church, looking at the quality of its life and witness. Other sermons focused on the ministry of Jesus, his calling of the twelve and their life together.

Books and articles of the experiences of people helped through being in small groups will be helpful. Articles appear in Christian magazines and papers from time to time, telling of significant small group work. There are many books on the market today linked with the small group movement, telling of the search for spiritual renewal which found fulfilment in a small group experience. Others treat the subject directly and show how new life came into local parishes through small groups. These are helpful to put into the hands of thoughtful people. I made it a policy in parish work to keep books circulating amongst my people which had helped me catch a new vision for various facets of our ministry. Then it was not a superimposed programme from on top, but a moving forward together.

Use recorded resources. There are a number of prerecorded audio and video cassettes, which you could lend to people, on the value of small groups. Recorded lectures by leaders in the small group movement are also available.

Enable personal discovery. A variety of methods can be used to help people discover for themselves the value of small groups. There are a number of worksheets available which are useful for this task, or they can be designed to meet the local situation without requiring special skills. On page 12 of his book, *69 Ways to Start a Study Group and Keep it Growing*, Lawrence Richards O lists some dimensions of relationships of which the Bible speaks. Next to each he provides a graded check line to help individuals check out their own life and decide if perhaps they need to become involved in a group. This could be varied in a number of ways to cover the characteristics of a Christian community or aspects of a Christian style of life which are developed in relation to others. Against these lists people measure their individual and collective Christian life. It could help awaken a sense of need for the growth which is possible in a small group.

Special learning events. On two occasions in my parish work, the local membership caught the vision during a Church Life Conference. We considered the New Testament pattern and characteristics of church life. Against this model we evaluated our existing life within the local community of faith. Alternative styles were considered. Out of this reflection by the members grew significant networks of groups for youth and adults. In both cases I circulated a variety of books for thoughtful individuals to read in the three and four months prior to each conference.

Use a weekend away. Most church camps or retreats provide a variety of small groups experiences which introduce people to the quality of fellowship possible in the small group. In some retreats participants are formed into small groups for the entire period. Study, worship, recreation, kitchen duties and the like have all been undertaken in the small group, with only occasional combined activity. Following such events some have extended the small group experience or formed new groups.

Other ways of leading people to see the potential of small groups were given by participants in our training conferences during brain-storming sessions:

Use the individual approach.

Share your own sense of need for a group.

Use the small group method in as many aspects of your leadership as possible until people see their value, e.g. in teaching, planning, evaluating and in meetings of larger groups.

Learn to depend on the Holy Spirit to lead you to people who have the same need; then share how the small group can help.

Personal enthusiasm will play an important role in inspiring others.

Listen to people.

Have an open home to which people will feel free to come and informally experience care in a small group.

Share with others resources and experiences gained at a Small Groups Conference.

Invite others to accompany you to Small Group Training Conferences.

Use small groups in church services such as getting people to discuss or share in pairs.

Pray until you are convinced about sharing your need with a person.

Talk about small groups, how others have been helped and what they have meant to you.

Demonstrate the value of small groups through your own growth.

Provide opportunities for people to think about the best methods for the church to fulfil its work and witness.

Introduce them to small groups as a viable method.

TWO WAYS TO BEGIN

Start small and let it grow. Many groups have been started because just one or two people felt the need for them. Two or three motivated persons who have a desire to grow in fellowship and faith are enough to begin a group.

It is better to begin to develop a group with a small number of well-intentioned persons who can relate to one another at some depth because of their sense of need for such an experience, than to begin with a large number who come with reservations. From a small but sound beginning the group can pray that God will either send to them or send them to people who should be in their group. Lyman Coleman says, 'One person with a genuine hunger is enough to start a group. One group is enough to penetrate a community. The question is not one of quantity, but quality,'[4]

Start big and let it consolidate. Some have been guided to gather a large number for a period in a seminar-type teaching programme which later provided a foundation for small groups. Work in small groups was undertaken in the large meeting, helping participants become used to the process. This meeting then divided to form the nucleus of a number of house-centred cells.

COMMENCING A SINGLE CELL

As we have observed, there is no one way to commence a small group. Each group is unique. No two small group experiences are exactly the same. We consider here some possible alternatives for commencing a single cell.

Check your motives. The Faith at Work small group movement recommends that we begin with a period of self-examination in which we ask ourselves two questions: 'Why do I want to start a small group?' and 'Why do I need a small group?' The suggestion that answers be written down and considered will help us to clarify our motives and the expectations we have and will assist us in our approach to others.

We will be better able to express our hopes and aspirations for the group when talking to them.

Decide what kind of small group you want. Having considered motives and expectations, the type of group which will best meet these needs will be clearer.

Listen for expressed needs which can be met in small groups. In taking the initiative we need to do so with sensitivity to people who are aching for this type of experience yet are not communicating it verbally, at least in direct terms. I remember the advice Professor Ross Snyder of Chicago gave to a number of us in this regard at a National Conference of Christian Educators in the United States. He led us in a variety of small groups experiences over a number of days and thoroughly whetted our appetites for an ongoing group experience when we returned home again. At the conclusion he advised us not to rush into drawing a group together. 'Take time to really listen to people. Seek to recognise their inner stirrings. Listen between the words they use for veiled expressions of a deep heartfelt need which can be met in a small group. Some will be crying out to you from the depth of their inner being, "I want to belong. I long to be wanted. I desperately want to grow", without so much as using any of these words.' When I returned home I put this advice into practice and it worked! My first experience of sharing openly and honestly in a small group was an unforgettable freeing and renewing experi-

ence. It was made up of the most unlikely people drawn from a broad cross-section of the community. That group came together because of this method of seeking to be sensitive to expressed needs.

Listening is an art which requires time and practice. Hearing people express the desire to belong to a group will often occur when we least expect it. We will be best tuned in to people when we are tuned in to God. Sensitivity to spiritual need is a gift of divine grace.

Take the initiative yourself. Sometimes God will guide us to be more direct in approaching others. In some situations it will be right for us not to wait for others to make the first move, but to make the effort to do all we can to encourage the formation of a group. By taking the initiative we may awaken a sense of need, or help some to articulate deep desires for a more authentic life.

Test interest by giving a book to a selected group of people. Pray about who could be invited to link up with a group. Select a book which fits in with the expectations you have for the group. Buy a few paperback copies and distribute them to those to whom you feel drawn. Say you would like them to read it and meet together in a few weeks to share their reaction. Some may have already communicated an interest in linking up with a small group. It may be wise not to mention at this stage that you are hoping to start a continuing group. This method tests people's sense of need. Give a precise period for reading, and set a date for a get-together. Keep the meeting informal and let the Spirit move in the way he wishes. Each should be given opportunity to share their thoughts and feelings about the book. Openly receive both negative and positive responses.

At the conclusion of the group some may spontaneously express the desire to meet again to discuss the same book more fully, possibly taking a chapter at a time over a number of meetings. The wish may be to take another book and deal with it in the same way. Don't expect everyone to continue with the group. From such an experience a continuing small group could begin. It tests interest without initial specific commitment to an ongoing group. The once-up meeting can be of value in itself even if it doesn't result in the formation of a group.

Provide 'sample' small group experiences. People can be given a one-time small group experience to help them see the potential of belonging to a small group. This is similar to the previous point but without the requirement for preparation prior to the group. Chapter 8, 'Sharing the

Good News Together', and Chapter 16, ' "At Home" Groups', give some suggestions for this type of experience. The group should be kept informal. Some relationship games which provide a completely non-threatening experience could be used. At the conclusion, a test of their readiness to go on into a continuing group could be made by simply asking, 'Would you like to meet again?' A series of these low-key groups may be needed before the group decides to be an on-going group. We have also used this method to help a whole congregation grasp the potential for small groups. A series of four low-key meetings were held with the emphasis upon getting to know each other and undertaking some simple, related Bible studies.

Treat early group experiences as experimental. Most of us hesitate to commit ourselves to new experiences that do not have a clear cut-off point. For this reason, suggest a specific number of meetings in a set period of time when the group decides to be on-going. Six to eight meetings on a weekly or bi-weekly basis is a reasonable period of an experimental quality which encourages a definite commitment. At the end of the time the experience can be assessed and a decision made whether or not to continue.

Pray about it. The setting up of small groups in the name of Jesus Christ is essentially God's work. Our task is basically that of co-operating with what God is already doing in his world. In prayer, we acknowledge this, make ourselves available to God, check on our motives, develop the right attitude, listen to God's leading and seek to make God's timing our timing. As we pray, God can strengthen our desire and resolve to start a group, or he can make it clear that we should wait for some other opportunity.

Paul Everett, director of the Pittsburgh Experiment which facilitates hundreds of small groups in that great city and elsewhere in the USA, advises those wishing to commence groups to commit themselves to the Thirty Day Prayer Experiment. He goes on to say:

> Prayer makes us sensitive to God's will and may lead us to others who need a small group. Even people who are fully convinced that it's a great idea to start a group need to submit themselves through prayer to God's purpose and leading. Try this prayer: 'Lord, I believe that You are leading me to start a group. If this desire in me is from You, increase it and make my next step clear.'

> The prayer experiment will also help you find the people who are being led to join a prayer group. God has a plan and purpose for every one of us; therefore it is essential to pray for guidance to determine who should be invited into the fellowship of koinonia. Try this prayer: 'Lord, lead me to those people or those people to me whom You want to be included.'

> As you pray make a list of the names that come to mind. Also stay open to unexpected encounters, where people of whom you had not thought whilst praying are suddenly and sometimes surprisingly revealed to you in your daily routines. God has mysterious ways of bringing people together.

> **Approaching individuals**. Go to these people one at a time. If only one comes to mind, remember you can start your group with just two people. In time and with prayer it will grow.

> Whenever you approach someone, pray for God's leading in what you say. A good way to break the ice can be something like this: 'I have been needing in my own life an opportunity to deal with (you fill in your own honest content) and the part that God plays in it. I want to start a small group where people can share their concerns and joys, and I was wondering if you would be interested.'

> If they say, 'That's not for me at this time,' don't be discouraged. Only God can lead people to say 'yes', so go on to the next person on your list with confidence and approach him or her in the same prayerful manner.[5]

COMMENCING A CLUSTER OF SMALL GROUPS

Begin by establishing one core group using the suggestions given. Then, following some of the ideas mentioned earlier, seek to involve this group in helping others appreciate the potential of small groups, as they share the benefits being experienced. This group will provide potential leaders or co-leaders for the cells to be formed.

Enlist and train potential leaders. In the first parish in which we formed small groups, training began before we caught the vision of the possibilities of small groups! I never cease to be amazed at the way God works out his purposes frequently without our being aware of it at the time. Often it is only in retrospect we see the plan. We gathered together the people referred to the church from a Billy Graham Crusade, to establish them in their new-found faith and prepare them for membership. Others joined with them and over 70 people packed into our lounge room each week for these sessions! The evening included informal fellowship, praise, group prayer, an illustrated lecture and discussion. After two years the number dwindled to 25. We sought to discern what God was saying to us through this decline in interest. Through a series of events while absent from the church, I caught the vision of the potential of small groups. This was shared with the remaining 25 and we decided to make the group a training ground for potential leaders (and co-leaders). We struggled to learn something about how small groups function, develop some leadership skills and evolve a plan to introduce our vision to the congregations.

These leaders received a preparation for their tasks which few small group leaders experience. Crash programmes do not allow for adequate teaching in doctrine, introduction to the Bible and church history, which these leaders experienced for nearly two years, together with the significant group experience.

This enables the potential leaders to learn how to lead through involvement in an actual group. Effective leadership is modelled for them and, as the group develops, opportunities are given to share the leadership.

Enlist potential members. Each potential leader could be encouraged to follow some of the suggestions already made for forming a group. We have commenced clusters of cells for youth and adults in a more structured manner to good effect. A list of prospects was compiled from the lists of those associated with our churches. The list was divided into geographical areas and a leader assigned to each section.

Most leaders received a list of up to 30 names but ended up with an average of 12 in their final group. The leaders visited each person on their list, drawing attention to the prior publicity in the church paper and special mailings, and sharing their own experience of being a group member. They gave further information and issued an invitation to attend a launching dinner and a 'sample' small group experience. A blanket invitation was also given to the whole church by mail and pulpit announcements to ensure that no one was overlooked.

At the launching dinner, the new programme was outlined and response forms issued, upon which people indicated their interest and the nights they were available. Further forms were available at the weekly church services for those not able to attend the dinner. These were then sorted into common times and geographical areas and leaders assigned. They then visited each person in their group and invited them to an inaugural meeting in the host homes.

When commencing youth cells in one parish, we began by making a comprehensive list. This comprised all young people in the existing youth groups and others from past and present Sunday school rolls. These we then divided into groups based upon age, locality and mutual interest. Most groups contained a balance of 'actives' and 'inactives'. By 'inactives' I mean young people who have little or no association with the church. Difficulty was later experienced in some groups where there was a greater number of 'inactives'. Fewer groups with a better balance would have made the task more effective. The two leaders appointed for each group visited the home of each young person assigned to them, which permitted a discussion with the parents about the new programme and established an important personal contact.

In setting up one small group programme in a Presbyterian parish where I was called in to act as consultant, we used the elders' districts as the basis for the groups. Each elder was trained as a group leader and visited those in his/her district to invite them to join a group, in most cases held in the elder's home. In two or three districts, where there was little response, the elders combined their groups and acted as co-leaders.

A long-term approach. Some innovators in the small group movement have taken a long-term approach when commencing clusters of small groups. Their method, in brief, was to lead a cell themselves until the group became established. (The time this took varied from group to group.) As experienced group facilitators, they modelled a good leadership style. The group learned about leadership and small group techniques by demonstration. These leaders recognised and developed potential leadership within their groups until they felt confident they could relinquish leadership. They then commenced another group, repeating the process. There is much to be said for this long-term approach.

HANDLING RESISTANCE TO CHANGE

Research shows that only approximately 2.6% of people act as change agents in a given situation. It can be expected that if the vision is shared effectively, another 14.4% will join the movement for change almost immediately, with 34% following sometime later. Another 34% will become involved after a considerable delay, but 16% will continue to resist any effort for change.

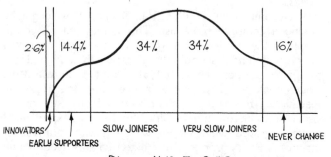

Diagram N°12 : The Bell Curve.

Ross Kingham gives some helpful suggestions to enable the initial movers to understand and handle aspects of resistance to the introduction of small groups in the local church.

> If there are a number of small group enthusiasts in a church you will find it a worthwhile exercise to perform a **role play** and become people who object to the introduction of small groups. You may find that your imaginary people just do not want to know about them. You may find they recall past failures to introduce new concepts or techniques. You may find that the participants reveal they feel threatened by change, or that they fear it means the same old workhorses will have to do the work, or be leaders, or organisers.

> You may find a reluctance in the person playing the minister to delegate authority or responsibility for church members' nurture or guidance. You may find people saying there is no room in the church programme for something new. You may find people saying they do not want little holy huddles dotted around the church, wallowing in subjectivity.

> Having verbalised many of the objections, how do you deal with them? Successful change in a church depends on the personal spiritual growth of the members and their sense of freedom to take part openly and honestly in the on-going process. At heart I believe we all want to be free, to grow. But to be actually given

the challenge, the opportunity can be a shattering experience.

Most of our fellow congregation members may appear fixed in their societal, their community, their home and their church roles. I would particularly plead for understanding for one of the people most fixed in a role—the clergyman. For many clergy the small group idea is a totally new one. These people need our love and understanding. They need to know that we are not criticising their ministry if we are enthusiastic about small groups.

Another factor which militates against inducing change through small groups is that our church buildings are not designed for coping with the pattern. Some pew backs are so high you cannot turn round to see the person behind you. If you try to alter the physical design of the church you are once again cutting across tradition or the fact that the basic floor plan of a church cannot be changed without ripping the whole thing apart.

There is temptation for the small group proponents to move out of the local church fellowship. This solves or avoids conflict, but it means that the small group cannot merge with the larger body of believers. Alternatively, even where there are a number of different types of small groups in a church, there will be some church members who will totally stand outside them, or even withdraw (hopefully temporarily) from the church. [6]

References

(1) Samuel S Shoemaker, *With the Holy Spirit and with Fire* (Harper and Row, NY, 1960).
(2) John L Casteel, *Spiritual Renewal through Small Groups* (Association Press, NY, 1957), p. 191.
(3) Sara K Little, *Learning Together in the Christian Fellowship* (John Knox Press, USA, 1956), p. 31.
(4) Lyman Coleman, *Growth by Groups* (Growth by Groups, USA).
(5) Paul Everett, *How Do I Start a Small Group?* (In-Touch, July 1987, Vol. 1, No. 2).
(6) Ross Kingham (extract from a chapter he contributed to *Building Small Groups in the Christian Community*, by the author).

Chapter 8
Sharing the Good News Together

It is the main task of the church to provide the conditions and circumstances in which God may awaken people or reawaken them. Church leaders must learn how to prepare people for conversion. We must lead our people into those places where the wind blows, where the Holy Spirit is working. It is this writer's conviction that the most propitious conditions for awakening prevail in koinonia groups centering on Bible study.[1]

The experience of the church through the years has been that there is no single way of undertaking evangelism. People have come to faith on their own, through another's witness, in a regular church service and many in very large gatherings. In his examination of the church's recovery of its sense of mission, Athol Gill says:

The evangelistic programmes which will probably command most respect will be those

which treat the hearers as persons and respect their integrity;

which are able to meet them at the point of their present understanding;

which encourage long-term in-depth involvement with them;

which take place primarily out in the world as an integral part of the total ongoing ministry of the Christian community;

which readily incorporate new Christians into that ministry and contribute to its spiritual development.[2]

Small groups are one method of evangelism which in an effective way gathers up most of the points made here by Dr Gill.

In my parishes we developed a strategy which was based on lay people sharing their faith in small groups. We first used this method in our local churches to reach the unchurched. Later we gathered teams of up to fifty people to conduct weekend evangelistic events, sometimes long distances from our parish. These teams comprised our own members and people from other churches. Preparatory training was given in how to share their faith story, particularly in a group situation, and in how to lead a group.

Usually this outreach was conducted over a weekend, commencing with a combined evening meeting of praise and witness, or a dinner. This was followed by small groups in homes during which lay people spoke of their faith. A low-key invitation to commitment was also given during these home groups. A number of the methods described later were used in these groups. Lay people witnessed in a variety of ways during the normal Sunday church services, which were sometimes followed by further home groups. Many were wonderfully converted to Christ during these weekends.

We also helped our people use a similar approach to reach their neighbours through one-off groups in their homes.

Many other churches in Australia have used these methods effectively.

In Cambridge, England, St Barnabas' Church followed a regular pattern of twice-yearly evangelistic missions based on the Home Groups. The main thrust of the missions would be events put on it and by the groups themselves, such as dialogue evangelism supper parties. Often an evangelistic team from outside would come to conduct the mission, but they would really be a resource to be used by the Home Groups. Initially of course, groups found this difficult, as they had no non-Christian friends to invite, but, by repeating these events regularly, people became aware of the opportunity and learnt to make friends as well as to invite them. Basing the missions on the Home Groups took a lot of the organisational hassle out of the process, and the dialogue evangelism approach increased the confidence of members to share their faith.

In this chapter we are concerned about short term or one-time groups whose main purpose is to develop relationships to win people to Christ. These are the bridging groups to the Christian church. In Chapter 3, 'Keys for Effective Small Groups', suggestions have been given for enabling an evangelism dimension to ongoing fellowship groups.

SOME ADVANTAGES OF USING SMALL GROUPS

Here are a few reasons why small groups provide such an effective and credible structure for evangelism:

They offer a bridge for shy people
Shy people may be painfully uncomfortable in crowds or large groups or they may be wary of church gatherings and church buildings.

They are personal
One person in a crowd may be very lonely and feel very insignificant. In a small group that person will respond to the group's care and concern, and to the group's recognition of his/her identity and worth.

A small group allows maximum participation
Each person has the opportunity to ask questions, to participate in the discussion and to share ideas and feelings.

They are flexible
The length, time and venue of the meeting can be varied and the programme need not be fixed in a definite pattern.

There is a minimum of organisation needed
Large amounts of time, energy and money are not required. Nor do we have to wait for church councils to move.

Evangelism is localised
A home is identified with the gospel in a neighbourhood.

They encourage spontaneity in evangelism
Two or three people with the sense of mission and a love for people can invite a few neighbours and friends into their home with the minimum of effort.

They are informal
A relaxed, natural atmosphere is possible.

Communication is easier
In the small group situation personal problems may be shared and solutions, both practical and theoretical, can be offered. We may be able to present the Christian message more easily and clearly. Difficulties can be discussed, problems clarified and knowledge shared. The small group

offers a very natural situation in which we can share our personal faith stories.

FRIENDSHIP/CONTACT GROUPS

Purpose
These groups, held in homes, are intended to reach irregular church attenders and the un-churched. They are concerned with creating a situation in which bridges of friendship can be built. Hopefully a foundation is laid upon which deeper communication can take place at a later stage. A non-threatening situation is provided, where the people invited determine the degree to which they wish  to be involved. The programme is essentially of a 'getting acquainted' nature. A climate is created in which the Holy Spirit can work to the extent he chooses.

Who to invite
Begin by inviting a couple of Christian friends to help you. Pray and plan together. Preparation of refreshments and other items for the evening can be shared.

Aim at having no more than twelve attend. Sometimes these will share a common interest. Be optimistic in considering who to invite. Often the most unlikely people will accept. Your list of invitees will include people from your broad network of relationships, including neighbours.

How to invite
Generally, the best invitation is a personal one. However, there is some advantage in sending a hand-written (or printed) invitation and following this up with a telephone call or home visit, as this gives opportunity for the invitation to be discussed prior to the personal contact.

Be sure to state clearly the purpose of the meeting. To simply call it 'a social evening to get to know each other' is possibly the best way to describe it.

Indicate the times for commencement and conclusion.

Preparation
Name-tags for each person, prepared beforehand, are helpful for group fellowship and assist the leadership. The lettering should be large enough to be read at a distance.

Have cheap note pads and pencils available for the 'Get-acquainted' game. Ashtrays should be readily available without people having to ask for them. Seating should be arranged to enable each member to see the rest of the group. Light background music could be playing as the guests arrive. But do not use 'religious' music.

Programme
Introduce people as they come, give them name-tags and allow plenty of time for informal conversations.

Use one of the get-acquainted exercises in the Appendix. 'Interviews' is a non-threatening game. The questions can be varied to suit those who attend. Do not use questions which probe (e.g. 'What is your aim in life?'). Keep them general at this stage. The 'Guess Who Fishbowl' is helpful for those who know each other well. Again, watch the questions you choose.

As the main purpose of the evening is to develop friendships, the programme should not be too heavily structured. Have some well chosen questions in mind to address to the whole group after the above game. These should seek information rather than opinions or feelings. Some questions will arise naturally out of the initial sharing.

The refreshments should be buffet style to encourage more mixing.

Finish on time.

Some hints
Listen carefully to people. Show a real interest in them.

Be alert to expressions of need—whatever they may be (e.g. physical, emotional, spiritual, etc.). Follow up on these.

Don't be easily shocked by what some may say.

Avoid controversial subjects.

Be natural.

Do not be surprised if people want to talk about spiritual matters.

Be sensitive to the desire or otherwise of the whole group to pursue these matters.

Pray about the meeting beforehand and ask others to support you.

Your own close communion with God will be your best preparation.

EVANGELISTIC GROUPS

These groups could be part of a structured local church evangelism programme or spontaneous group.

Purpose

Unlike Friendship/Contact Groups, these have a specific aim to present the Christian Good News, with a call to faith in Christ. When people are invited to such groups, it should

be made clear that the group will seek to explore seriously the meaning of the Christian faith for today. These are generally one-off groups, sometimes providing the option for further get-togethers for those who indicate interest in pursuing further the matters raised.

Preparation

Most of the suggestions for invitations and preparation for a Contact Group will apply.

Be prepared with some suitable booklets for those who wish to make commitments or think more about what was said.

PROGRAMME IDEAS FOR EVANGELISM GROUPS

In ongoing fellowship groups with a focus upon Bible Study, the Holy Spirit in his own time and way will address the uncommitted present and call them to faith through the study of the Scriptures. The programme ideas suggested here are mainly to reach those people who may not be prepared to commit themselves to a continuing group. The Bible will still play an important role in each of these programmes but to varying degrees.

Precede most of the following options with a **get-acquainted game** such as 'Interviews' found in Appendix A.

Have a party!

Rebecca Manley Pippert, author of *Out of the Saltshaker and Into the World*, writes:

> A wonderful way of evangelism is to have parties. I believe that a spiritual ministry is infinitely easier when there is already an atmosphere of openness, love and trust.

Here are some ideas:

A barbecue party to which each person brings and pools their 'eats'. This could be followed by an informal sharing by all on:

The first time I tried my hand at cooking . . .

My grandma's or mother's special meal . . .

If I didn't have to pay the bill, the place I would like to eat and the meal I would order are . . .

What I like most about barbecues is . . .

The one thing that really burns me up in life is . . .

To climax the time, tell with enthusiasm a suitable Bible story such as the 'barbecue' on Mt Carmel of Elijah and the prophets of Baal (1 Kings 18:17–40) with a simple evangelistic application.

A skills party. Each brings something he/she has made such as craftwork, cake, etc. and talks briefly about it. Others may have musical skills they use for the entertainment of the group. Some may choose to talk about their work, garden, sport, etc. with some item to show relevant to that.

This could be followed by a talk on God's creative genius, illustrated by slides, posters or items from the creation (flowers, leaves, etc.). A brief witness by the speaker concerning the ways God has recreated his or her own life, or has brought new life and hope into difficult situations, could help focus on God's forgiving and renewing love in Christ.

Other suggestions which could be used as the major segment in a 'party' are:

A concise presentation of the gospel followed by dialogue. Use a sensitive speaker who can give a simple, brief talk and follow with discussion. We have frequently used visuals to illustrate the presentation. These have been either diagrams, cartoons, pictures and summaries of main points, using flip chart, posters, overhead projector, video, film clips or slides. Audio cassettes of suitable speakers could be considered for some isolated situations.

Questions to help facilitate the dialogue could be:

What did you think of the message?
Did it make sense?
Is it your experience?
Would you like it to be?

A Christian film or video on a subject of interest to the group which can lead to discussion. The questions suggested above could be used here also. Be sure to carefully select a well-presented film or video and preview it with a couple of discerning friends well beforehand. Some will not be suitable for the purpose of this group.

A specialist speaker on a topic of general interest to participants. A talk on a theme of general interest giving a Christian perspective by a specialist who is a practising Christian. Issues to consider are: Understanding and Helping our Teenagers; Family or Marriage Enrichment; Coping with Crisis; Growing Old Gracefully; and others. Follow with question time and discussion.

A discussion of a selected book. Give a copy of the same book to each person a few weeks prior to the meeting. Ask them to read it and be prepared to discuss their reaction to the book.

Faith-story telling. Invite one or two sensitive people who have a vital up-to-date Christian experience and can express themselves reasonably well. These can be invited to share the story of their experience of God's grace at work in their lives. (This witnessing needs to be specific and have an air of reality about it.) The meeting is then thrown open for the group to respond. (The questions already suggested could be useful here.)

Alternatively, the leader could interview the witnesses using questions such as the following:

For how long have you had a meaningful faith?
How did you find this faith?
What helped you make this discovery?
What prevented you from taking this step earlier?
How is it working out in specific situations in your life now?

The heart of Christianity

Using the same pairs as for the 'Get-acquainted' session, have each pair discuss for approximately 5 minutes: 'What do you consider to be important things about Christianity?' Each pair lists only *four* points between them. All points are restricted to one or two words, to help in the following collation.

The findings of the group are recorded on a chart by the leader taking one point at a time from each pair.

A number is then placed in front of each point to facilitate the feed-back from the next stage.

Taking 3 to 5 minutes each pair considers the list on the chart and selects *four* of the points they now think to be at the heart of Christianity. Reports from the pairs are recorded by placing a tick next to each of the numbers listed.

Opportunity is then given for any to share why some of these points are important for them personally (particularly those with a cluster of ticks). This segment is introduced by the leader pointing out that of the many things we have been taught, we tend to retain those things which have been supported from our own experience. Therefore it would be reasonable to assume that the items listed have to varying degrees been experienced by members of the group. Facilitate the sharing then by asking: 'Would anyone care to share some personal incident in which one of these has been part of his/her own experience?' or 'What experience has proved one of these points to be real for you?' or 'Why has one of these points become important for you?'

The leader may sensitively ask questions to draw a person out, to clarify or help a person express him/herself.

We usually have one or two mature Christians present, who have been trained in telling their story, to help facilitate the group. However, they are taught to withhold their contributions until others present have had opportunity to respond.

Levels of warmth

The group can share in a random fashion on the basis of these questions:

How did you heat your home when you were young?

Can you recall any good experienced around the place where the heat was centred?

Which person was the centre of warmth in your home?

Can you recall some warm experiences you had of God when young?

What does God mean to you now?

(See Appendix for full outline of this method, together with some alternatives.)

General questions

What inspires you most about the creation?

Who is Jesus Christ to you?

When did God become more than a name to you?

What do Scripture promises, such as the following, mean in your own personal experience? (Optional)

'The steadfast love of the Lord never ceases, his mercies never come to an end; they are new every morning; great is your faithfulness.' (Lamentations 3:21–23)

'I am with you always.' (Matthew 28:20)

'Nothing can separate us from the love of God . . .' (Romans 8:38,39)

SOME OPTIONS FOR CONCLUDING MOST OF THESE PROGRAMMES

The final step is for the leader to seek a response of faith, using one of these options:

A brief impromptu talk based on some of the main items raised during the session.

A short talk explaining the way to respond in faith to Christ, using some visual aids.

A suitable booklet explaining how to become a follower of Jesus Christ is given to all present. The leader then asks all to follow in their own copy as the main points are covered. (Each of these options is followed by opportunities for commitment through silent individual prayer. This is then followed by an open response, completion of a card, or the recording of names in a disciples' book. In some circumstances, none of these options will be appropriate, but an invitation is given for enquirers to talk to the leader after the meeting.)

If there has been no apparent interest during the meeting by those who are uncommitted, close with a brief prayer of thanks for the evidence of God's mercy and love in the things shared. (Often during the following informal refreshment-time we have found a seeker who, whilst too shy to do so in the group, will speak to the leader afterwards.)

Modern versions of the New Testament and a few well chosen books/booklets could also be available for any to take.

Be available to people immediately after the group or at other times outside the group.

Take a long-term view. Follow-up people who showed interest—and those who did not appear to!

References

(1) Robert A Raines, *New Life in the Church* (Harper and Row, New York, 1961).

(2) John Mallison, *Youth Outreach and Evangelism* (The Joint Board of Christian Education of Australia and New Zealand, 1975).

Chapter 9
Caring for New Christians Together

The references to the 'disciples' as a corporate body are much more frequent in the Gospels than are references to individual disciples. Most of the references to individuals refer to failures on their part; while the references to the group as a whole more often speak of their joy, understanding or achievement. 'There is simply no substitute for getting with people, and it is ridiculous to imagine that anything less, short of a miracle, can develop strong Christians.'[1]

Accepting by faith God's gift of forgiveness and new life in Jesus Christ is the first step we take in beginning to live as a Christian. Growing to become the person God wants us to be is a long-term goal, requiring all the help available to us through the Holy Spirit working within us and through other Christians.

Like new-born human babies, those who are 'born again' spiritually need special care to help them become established. Most new Christians are very unsure of themselves and can easily become uncertain, get discouraged and fall away.

BONDING WITH A MATURE CHRISTIAN

Christian fellowships which take seriously their care of new Christians assign sensitive, mature persons as undershepherds or helpers, to take a special interest in the new disciples. They do this by making them feel wanted; helping them through their traumas; personally introducing them to people who share their exhilaration and recognise the significance of their decision to follow Christ; and by praying for them and discipling them.

Norm was a carpenter who had a pastor's heart. He took seriously his assignments to care for others, especially young people and new Christians. We assigned him to follow-up a builder and his wife who were converted. He frequently shared meals with them in his home, brought them to church where he sat with them, introduced them to others and made them feel comfortable and wanted. To help this couple develop their devotional life, he met with them for breakfast once a week, during which time they read the Scriptures and prayed together.

In addition to this one-to-one care, new Christians should be linked to a nurture group, as soon as possible after they have decided to follow Christ.

WHAT IS A NURTURE GROUP?

Nurture groups are short-term groups, usually lasting six to eight weeks, which provide support to help new disciples of Christ begin their life together in a caring fellowship of Christian love. The group consists of some experienced Christians as well as the beginners.

A home is usually the best venue because of the intimacy and warmth it provides. Where the 'undershepherd' or 'helper' system is in place, the new Christian is invited and accompanied by this person to the group.

THE PURPOSE OF A NURTURE GROUP

In a nurture group new Christians are helped to take some first steps and are given some very basic 'food' and support. Relationships with their new-found Lord and other members of their new 'family' are carefully developed in an atmosphere of care and concern.

Although the Bible will play a very important part in the group, the aim is not simply to do Bible study. The group will primarily try to care for and encourage new Christians, making them feel wanted and accepted. It will be a place for new Christians to get to know others, share experiences and ask questions.

There is sometimes a tendency for mature and well taught Christians to underestimate the importance of the 'Getting-acquainted' parts of the programme. But these are especially important for those with little or no church background.

A nurture group is also like a bridge helping new Christians into the wider fellowship of a local church. The group is a smaller version of the larger church. It is important that new disciples are not pressured to join other groups or organisations within the church at this stage; they need to become established first.

THE COMPOSITION OF THE GROUP

There is an increasing emphasis in Christian education upon inter-generational work—a mixed age group with all working together. This is a healthy trend away from the division into youth and adults and the splitting up of the family, which has happened in most church programmes. Some churches may therefore choose to run their nurture groups on an all-age basis.

However, for the small and more intimate group such as a nurture group, there can be value in dividing people into peer groups, particularly where there are extremes of culture and background amongst the members. It would be best for people with a similar background to struggle together with the problems of witness and lifestyle.

PLAN IN ADVANCE

When a local church is planning an evangelistic outreach programme the structure for the nurture groups should be set up at the same time as the outreach is being planned, to ensure immediate follow-up. Churches frequently neglect making these plans in advance, resulting in a time delay in which valuable support is not available when the new disciple is often in greatest need of it.

The local church which has evangelism as part of its ongoing programme will need to be alert to the continuing need to provide nurture group experiences to support new Christians.

THE OBJECTIVES OF A NURTURE GROUP

You should be able to identify the following objectives in a nurture course, some of them in each session:

To provide opportunities for group members to get to know one another

The aim is to establish deepening relationships without forcing the pace. Sometimes the sessions will include talking in pairs and sometimes there will be opportunity to talk with the whole group.

To ensure that spiritual foundations have been properly laid

Those still troubled by failure and sin need to accept Christ's forgiveness; those still unsure need to be assured of the presence of the Holy Spirit. All need to be given help in being open to daily receive all the grace and strength God has to offer and to learn to maintain a relationship with Jesus Christ.

To encourage regular Bible study

By the time the group finishes, new disciples should know how to handle their Bibles and have studied a few significant passages for beginners in the faith. Learning to pick out the main points in Bible passages and to see how the Bible applies to daily living will be key experiences for new Christians.

To develop confidence in beginning to pray aloud

The new Christians should hear others pray and, starting with silent prayer and simple word and sentence prayers, build up enough confidence to begin to pray aloud themselves.

To enable group members to begin to share their faith

New Christians are often the most effective witnesses—both to non-Christians and older Christians. The group should encourage everyone to begin to talk to others about Christ and to share with the group any difficulties they have had.

LEADING THE GROUP

Remember how important it is that new disciples have a good experience of a caring, concerned Christian community, where they will feel accepted and significant.

Do everything you can to make the group meetings **times for experiencing true Christian love**.

If possible, **have some spare copies of the Bible** in an easy-to-read, modern translation (preferably the Good News Bible or the New International Version). It will help if everyone has the same translation.

Begin and end on time. Don't let the session drag on.

Make the meeting interesting and lively. Keep the pace going and avoid long talks.

Use visual aids whenever possible. They are a tremendous help in understanding and retaining the message. Simple sketches, phrases and words are all that are needed. You could use felt pens with sheets of newsprint (attached to a piece of hardboard with snap clips), chalk and chalkboard, and an overhead projector if one is available.

Keep things simple. Avoid using clichés or technical Christian words, which may mean little or nothing to a newcomer to the faith. A useful exercise is to write down short and simply worded definitions of words and phrases such as 'conversion', 'grace', 'commitment', 'discipleship', 'Christian experience', and 'Christian lifestyle'.

Don't swamp people with too much information; it will only confuse or discourage them and they won't retain it.

Be sensitive to the needs of individuals—that means being ready to listen!

Think carefully before using hymns or choruses in the meetings. Most non-churchgoers will find the practice a little strange to begin with. If you do sing, choose your songs carefully and try to include some well-known, traditional ones, or those with familiar tunes, as well as modern, informal choruses. You may find that some members do not know any, so do not introduce more than one new one in any meeting.

Be aware that many newcomers will know little about the Christian faith and how to live with it. Most will not know how to read the Bible or how to pray. Concentrate on telling them **how**, not stressing that they **ought**. Many will have difficulty finding passages in the Bible. This is where it will be helpful if everyone is using the same version and preferably the same edition. You can then give the page number with the passage reference. Do everything possible to avoid embarrassment, and give people plenty of time.

Be unshockable! Those with no church background may have no idea what is and is not 'acceptable' in Christian circles. Be ready to step into awkward situations to prevent embarrassment.

Encourage questions. The new Christians will be trying to understand and absorb many new ideas. They will need opportunity and time to sort out these new thoughts. Asking questions and talking about how their faith affects their life will be invaluable, so be patient with them.

Emphasise that the Christian life is a growing experience. Remember that understanding and commitment are both things that grow.

Demonstrate by personal example how to share experiences with others in the group. Allow plenty of time for members to share their own new experiences—don't fill every silence with your own words! This will help new Christians gain confidence in expressing their faith.

Encourage shy members to participate, but don't force them. Help them to know that it is all right to have a problem and to talk about it.

Be careful not to put pressure on people to conform to _your_ ideas of Christian lifestyle. This could inhibit openness and sharing, or even stop people coming. Give new Christians time to grow as the Word of God speaks to them.

Serve a drink and maybe some light refreshments at the end of each session. This gives a relaxed atmosphere for further informal fellowship and you may find that the most open conversations happen at this stage of the proceedings. Ask your hosts to be responsible for this.

Arrange some opportunities for informal social get-togethers with no structured programme. Spouses and families can be invited.

A PROGRAMME TO FOLLOW

A six-session course for nurture groups called 'Caring for New Christians' is now widely available in different languages. This was first put together by a small number of others and myself for use in a Billy Graham Crusade held in Sydney. It was further developed by Eddie Gibbs, myself and others for use in Mission England and has since been revised.

The course takes up the themes of Beginning, Being Sure, Growing, Being Obedient, Being Established and Continuing.

Each session includes group building exercises, simple Bible studies, prayer and times for informal fellowship.

To give some idea of the session design (you may want to design your own course), the first follows this plan:

Get acquainted (using the Interviews game found in Appendix A).
Sharing—an opportunity for all to talk about their commitment and clarify what they have done. The questions forming the basis for this sharing are:

Can you think of one word to describe how you felt when you decided to follow Christ?
What had helped you take this step?
What differences has it made?

A talk to help the new Christians understand what they have done.
This will outline in a simple manner the steps involved in committing their life to Jesus Christ. (See end of this chapter.)
Prayer in silence with suggestions given by the leader.
Refreshments.

COMBINED GET-TOGETHERS TO COMMENCE AND CONCLUDE

There is often value in holding a combined meeting of all those who have become Christians, or are wanting to find out more about being a Christian. The 'helpers' or 'under-shepherds' are also invited. An informal evening is best, with time to get to know one another and for sharing and worship. Some of the mature Christians as well as the newcomers could be asked to briefly share their faith-stories. An interview may be more appropriate with some. Do not make an initial meeting like this too long. Make it a bright, warm time of celebration. Refreshments or a light meal would make a good ending to the occasion.

This combined meeting may be used to launch the home-based nurture groups or to conclude them, or both.

WORKING WITH CLUSTERS OF GROUPS TOGETHER

There may be occasions when leaders, who have completed the training programme, do not feel confident to lead the whole nurture course. In this case, the groups could meet together on church premises. The minister and/or some experienced lay people could lead the meetings, with most work and sharing being done in small groups led by the trained leaders. If you do this, be sure you have individual seating, so that you can split up easily into groups.

QUESTIONS NEW CHRISTIANS ASK

New Christians will have many questions after they begin to think through the implications of their commitment, and especially when they begin to share their new-found faith with others. The group, and those assigned to help them personally, can assist in answering these questions. In the revised edition of *Caring for New Christians*, key questions raised by new Christians (suggested by Paul E Little in his book *How to Give Away Your Faith*, IVP) have been listed and brief answers given. The questions are:

How has Christ secured my forgiveness?
How does Christ live in me by his Spirit?
How does God speak to me through the Bible?
How does God invite me to speak to him?
How does Christ want to have the central place in my life?
How does Christ want me to share his love and the Good
   News about him?

How will the church help me to grow in my Christian life?

Group leaders and the assigned helpers need to be familiar with the questions and appropriate answers. If any of them fail to emerge and you think that they are particularly important for some individuals to grasp, look for an opportunity to raise the questions yourself.

A TALK FOR BEGINNERS

Here is an outline of a brief talk I have always given in the first session of a nurture group. It takes no longer than 15 minutes if it is carefully prepared and visuals are used. Although overhead projector acetates, prepared in advance, are probably the best way to present the material, plain paper and a felt pen are quite adequate in a small group.

1. God loves us and made us for a close relationship with himself

God created us 'to be like himself' (Genesis 1:27) which gives us both status and responsibilities in the world God created. One way in which we are 'like God' is in having moral and spiritual capacities—we are far more than mere animals.

God created us capable of knowing him.

But God did not create puppets. He made us capable of choosing between good and evil.

This circle could be taken to represent how God made us— his potential for humankind.

Diagram Nº13

2. We have not become what God intended

The original intimate relationship with God (Genesis 3:8) has been broken right from the beginning of the human race.

Now we choose naturally not to live God's way. 'Everyone has sinned, everyone falls short of the beauty of God's plan' (Romans 3:23, J B Phillips).

Diagram Nº14

This warped circle could represent the distortion of God's potential for humankind by the impact of sin from within and from outside. This allows the 'world' to 'squeeze' us 'into its own mould' (Romans 12:2, J B Phillips).

3. God did for us through Jesus Christ what we could never do for ourselves

Because God loves us he made it possible for us to have our close relationship with him restored.
'Christ is the visible likeness of the invisible God' (Colossians 1:15).

Through Jesus Christ, God dealt with the problem of sin which prevented us from being 'like himself' and spoilt our relationship with him.
'God has shown us how much he loves us—it was while we were still sinners that Christ died for us!' (Romans 5:8).

When we accept what Christ has done, our relationship with God is restored. From this relationship we now have the power to become what God intended us to be.
'The secret is simply this: Christ *in you*! Yes, Christ *in you* bringing with him the hope of all the glorious things to come' (Colossians 1:27, J B Phillips).

4. We need to receive what God offers in Christ

We must desire to have our broken relationship with God restored, to be sorry for our attitude of rebellion and by faith accept Christ and what he has done.

Diagram №15

We often refer to this step as making our 'commitment' to Christ. We trust Christ to save us from sin and commit ourselves to his kingly rule over our lives. We are then 'born again'—made alive in Christ (John 3:16).
Christ becomes the focal point around which our life begins to revolve.
'Christ, the hidden centre of our lives' (Colossians 3:4, J B Phillips).

5. Disciples of Christ have a new power within them

The Holy Spirit of God gives us new spiritual resources which help us to overcome those influences of evil which have spoilt our life.

The Holy Spirit gives us a new perspective on life and deepens our relationship with God.
We do not have to try to make a success of our new Christian life on our own. It is a partnership, with God as the senior partner.
'I have the strength to face all conditions by the power that Christ gives me' (Philippians 4:13).

Diagram №16

6. Our relationship with God needs to be maintained

For any relationship to grow one needs to spend time with the other person. In our relationship with God this is achieved by *prayer, and by knowing and understanding the Bible. It also grows through fellowship*—all that the community of God's people experience and share together in worship, celebration of the sacraments, mission and service.
And we grow by learning to *obey* God—following his leading and intention for each aspect of our life.

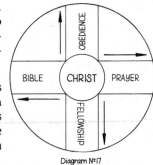

Diagram №17

Another way of expressing this could be to take the model of a simple wheel. If the hub is Christ and we are the rim, we keep in contact with him through the spokes.

We could also express this by seeing each of the ways we maintain our relationship with God likened to those things which are essential for a new-born baby to grow and mature.

PRAYER
Air (a hymn writer calls prayer 'the Christian's vital breath').

BIBLE
Food.

FELLOWSHIP
A family where care, support, sharing and love are experienced.

OBEDIENCE
Exercise to help us develop and keep fit and healthy.

Reference

(1) Robert E Coleman, *The Master Plan of Evangelism* (Revell, 1964).

Chapter 10
Learning Together

Try to learn what is pleasing to God.

(Ephesians 5:10)

When a group studies the Christian faith and its relevance to life, the Holy Spirit can work renewal in mind and life. Study has always been seen as an integral part of Christian growth and fellowship. In calling people to follow him, Jesus said, 'Take my yoke upon you . . . learn from me.' He was known as a rabbi or teacher. Jesus challenged people to seek the truth and find their freedom in that enlightenment (John 8:31,32). To become a follower of Jesus Christ is to commit oneself to a passionate search for truth. The word 'disciple' means 'learner'.

Christ's great commission to his followers included: '. . . teaching them to observe all that I have commanded you . . .' (Matthew 28:20) The New Testament church was committed to serious study: '. . . they devoted themselves to the apostles' teaching.' (Acts 2:42) Paul exhorted Timothy:

'. . . what you have heard from me . . . entrust to faithful men who will be able to teach others also.' (2 Timothy 2:2)

In his letter to the disciples in Rome, Paul said, '. . . be transformed by the renewal of your mind'. (Romans 12:2) There is a direct relationship between the renewing of the mind and the transformation of the life. A disciplined study of the Christian faith and its relevance to the whole of life lies at the heart of vital Christian witness. Many small groups stagnate because their focus has been purely upon emotional response; they have viewed Christian experience as essentially feelings. High moments of joy, praise and a variety of feelings result from the Holy Spirit being at work in the individual and the small group, but it is a fatal mistake to avoid serious intellectual pursuit. Indeed it is neglecting a God-given faculty which God obviously would not have given his creatures if it could not be a means through which we can draw closer to him.

In all our study we need to avoid the other extreme of becoming too intellectual. A group can suffer as much from people batting ideas back and forth without digesting or assimilating them. It is easy to hide behind a mask in discussion and never let the truth being discussed seep down into one's life. Enlightenment of the mind should be linked with genuine piety. 'Be renewed in the spirit of your minds and put on the new nature, created after the likeness of God . . .' (Ephesians 4:23,24)

Commitment to Christ and his cause is inevitably linked with our study in small groups. In all Christian education, development of knowledge and understanding should lead people to a new or deeper commitment to Christ. A personal response to Christ should have the central place— a commitment involving acceptance by faith of the free, yet costly, grace God offers to us in Jesus Christ, and a surrender of our whole being to his Lordship. 'Conversion' experiences can be expected to take place in small groups where the Word of God is encountered with open minds.

As the group studies with a genuine desire to discover the relevance of the gospel in our contemporary world, it will become aware of specific claims of Christ in particular situations. Every study should have an element of call to commitment to specific thought, feeling and action, accepting the risk and the danger which may be involved in the latter.

able experience. I cannot imagine the disciples being bored with Christ's teaching! God is the God of the unexpected. He is always surprising us! Learning of him and his will for us, under the guidance and inspiration of the Spirit, can be serendipity—experiences of unpredictable, happy surprises.

The learning methods dealt with in this chapter and the relational, inductive Bible study methods introduced elsewhere in this book will help captivate interest, include laughter (as well as possibly some tears), result in learning which will not be soon forgotten and facilitate changed lives.

God gave us the capacity to smile and a sense of humour. Let us use these beautiful gifts and enjoy our learning together as we explore the best news ever to break upon this world!

EFFECTIVE LEARNING

In many small groups the traditional pattern of the church's teaching ministry has been followed, where learners have expected to be told by their leader the facts and what to think about them. However, learners are much more likely to adopt an idea they have discovered themselves than one that has been told them.

It is sometimes said that people remember 10% of what they hear, 30–50% of what they see, 70% of what they say, and 90% of what they do. While this is an over-simplification

HAVE FUN!

Contrary to many people's past experiences, learning can be an enjoyable experience even when struggling with weighty spiritual matters. The Christian gospel is 'good news'. The essence of that gospel is 'joy and peace in believing' (Romans 15:13). Christian education should be a pleasur-

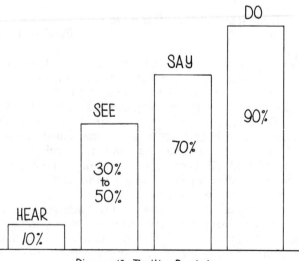

Diagram 18 : The Way People Learn

and disregards some other important factors involved in remembering or learning (which is not the same thing), it does draw attention to the importance of participation in learning. People learn more by experiencing things for themselves than by being told about them.

'The vast majority of people learn through the whole of their personalities, their senses, their relationships. The greater the sense of participation and involvement in a situation, the more the whole of one's faculties are exercised in that situation, the deeper the lesson being taught in the situation becomes embedded into life.' (1)

It takes longer to get facts across using discovery learning than it does by lecture, but discovery will be more effective. No one approach is always right and the lecture still has a place. However, people must be helped to develop skills in seeking out information for themselves, reflecting on their experiences, interpreting their findings and applying them to their everyday lives.

Learning is not restricted to formal teaching situations. On the contrary, the greater part of learning probably occurs informally, through experience in all kinds of life situations.

Learning from experience takes place both consciously and unconsciously. A child learns many skills without consciously being aware of the process taking place. However, here we are essentially concerned with the development possible when we take time out to think about and analyse our experiences.

We could learn far more from our rich storehouse of experience. This learning will be made most efficient when we reflect consciously and deliberately on what really happened in our present and past experiences. This will need to be climaxed with resolutions for future action, based on the insights gained.

When used in Scripture, the word 'know' means more than to know about someone or something. It means to have a personal experience of that person or thing. It involves knowing both intellectually and experientially. Christ's method of training the Twelve was that of action followed by reflection. He combined both teaching them theory and involving them in doing, and he alternated this with practice. Many of their experiences were followed by times for reflection together. They learnt from experience, but deeper learning took place as Jesus helped them consciously to reflect on their experiences and try to discover what new insights there were for them in what took place. This is known as **learning by praxis**.

In our daily lives we do not generally have time to reflect upon experiences in the structured manner set out below, although learning will be present to some degree. However, in the structured situation in a small group, it will aid learning to study and follow this pattern.

To learn from experience, people need time firstly to look at what happened. They need to recognise specific aspects of the experience.

Who was involved and in what ways?
What were the circumstances?
What surrounded it in time?
What were the facts?

The process of recognising the facts of the experience needs to be followed by an analysis of it.

Why did it happen that way?
How did the people involved behave?
What was helpful and what was a hindrance?
What was the outcome of the experience?
How did the people involved feel about it?

Appropriate resources are then introduced into the process to deepen and broaden the learning. Christian groups will explore relevant Bible passages, using some of the various methods introduced in this book to discover the relevance of the Christian gospel to situations. A variety of other resources can also be involved at this stage.

The learning climaxes with a time of seeking to discover the relevance for the learners personally. This involves generalising, drawing together all that has been learnt and applying it to their life situations.

Here are some questions to help facilitate this:

What have I learnt which will help me when next I find myself in a similar situation?
What should I be prepared to do when next I face a similar event?
What specifically would be involved in applying this?
Am I really willing to work at applying these new insights to my own life situation?
Am I prepared to take the risk and make the effort to

forsake my old patterns of behaviour and deliberately put new ones into practice?

The principal thesis of this kind of learning is that learning is only learning when it results in some new behaviour. That thesis is consistent with the gospel of Christ. Christianity was never meant to be purely intellectual. It is meant to result in changed lives. (Matthew 7:24–27; James 1:22–25)

In *Learning Through Encounter*, Robert Arthur Dow[2] lists eight factors which are basically required to make this kind of learning happen in a small group situation.

1. Maximum participation by the learner who is a respected member of the group, not because of his/her knowledge, but because of the resources of his/her own experience which he/she brings to the group.
2. The individuality of each person is respected.
3. It applies the theories of human development, taking into account the expectations of the person at their particular stage of development.
4. It requires an understanding of the small group process—how to interact, the roles people play, decision-making and development of group cohesion.
5. Shared leadership is encouraged. The teacher is an acknowledged learner, too. Other members can then display leadership in areas where they can provide solutions to group problems.
6. Flexibility and spontaneity are keys to learning, wherever they may lead.
7. Experiential learning is 'personal goal' oriented. It depends on the learner's response.
8. It always deals with living issues. Relevance is its main aim.

LEADERSHIP OF LEARNERS

In the learner-centred approaches to learning, the role of the leader/teacher is quite different from that of the traditional didactic up-front teacher-centred approach.

Leader-centred learning is characterised by:
Emphasis upon facts;
What to learn;
Teaching by telling.

In contrast, with learner-centred learning there is:
Emphasis on individual discovery;
How to learn;
Learning by doing.

In leader-centred learning, the role of the leader is that of

Instructor-Initiator:
Selects topics and resources;
Verbal source of information;
Explainer;
Stimulator;
Critic of ideas and skills;
Motivator of all that happens;
Sees groups as a whole rather than as individuals;
Is usually the assigned leader.
This kind of leadership results in passive small groups.

In the learner-centred situation, the role of the leader is that of

Enabler-Facilitator:
Topics and resources chosen by group to meet common needs;
Selects suitable learning method;
Involved with individuals;
Leader is a learner-participant;
A guide through the learning experience;
Provider of part of the resources for learning;
Available as a consultant;
Generally elected or 'emergent' leader.
This kind of leadership leads to active small groups. It should be pointed out, however, that the Instructor/Initiator role and the Enabler/Facilitator role are not mutually opposed or contrasting. A sensitive leader will perform both roles at certain times, the emphasis, hopefully, more on the latter.

LEARNERS ARE PEOPLE

Know your group members
It is important to have more than a superficial understanding of who our group members really are. We should seek to know what people are thinking—the kinds of pressures they experience in their homes and their work situations, the books they are reading. We only gain this kind of knowledge as we observe, talk with and take time to listen to them. There are no short cuts to getting to know people at this level. It takes sensitivity and a genuine interest in people, and time.

Knowing your group also involves having some understanding of the general characteristics of an age group. This is particularly important in leading the group in study.

Younger teenagers learn in a different way from older teens and adults. Study methods, topics and resources will be different for these age groups. We know people play different roles in groups. A good leader will seek to understand these roles and how to help people who hinder the group. A wise leader will also try to have some grasp of people's emotional or psychological needs and how they can be met through the group experience. This may seem a formidable amount of skills but a good leader will always be seeking to improve his/her effectiveness.

Recognise their limitations

Many people will come to a group with restricted knowledge of the Christian faith and limited experience. A leader must be sensitive to this, if people are not going to be made to feel embarrassed. Some will not know their way around the Bible, many will not know in which order the books occur. So they will have sparse knowledge of its content. Others will have only a superficial Christian experience and may never have prayed in a group before. Group members often have reading problems. Others have problems in written expression and spelling. An alert leader will avoid the deep embarrassment which can occur when such people are asked to read or write in front of the group.

Build self-esteem

'The feeling of self-esteem is important since it is the point of reference of all one's behaviour. The value people place on themselves is determined by the extent to which they feel themselves to be accepted, participating members of a group.'[3]

Many experiences in life help to destroy our self-image. Christ came to set us free from the shackles a sinful world has put upon us. He came to develop the real person God intended us to be. If leaders are to help others actualise this, then they themselves must have come to grips with who they are, have accepted the forgiveness and renewal Christ offers and be daily opening their lives to the power and love of the Holy Spirit. Leaders must be able to accept themselves, because God, in Christ, accepts them. Effective leaders will know their limitations and be aware of their 'gifts', potential and strengths. They will humbly but confidently seek to develop these and make them available to others. A leader will then be in a position to help others in a similar search.

Self-esteem influences all our behaviour. It is important to accept each individual as a person of worth, even when one does not agree with their ideas. 'Persons are more important than information.' What happens to the individual learner is the important thing.

Help people to change

The Christian gospel is the good news of the possibility of change. (John 3:3, 2 Corinthians 5:17). Life can begin again. In the Christian small group this complete about-face in thinking, goals and direction can take place through the Holy Spirit working through the leaders and each member. This complete turn around is one form of change. With some it may be a quickening of pace in moving towards our goal through new insights and motivation to see more clearly the way in which we have been going.

Change will fall into different categories—knowing, thinking, feeling (attitude) and doing (behaviour). Another way to see it is in terms of relationships—to God, to others, to ourselves, to our environment. All worthy change is the work of the Holy Spirit. Our techniques, study methods, understanding of people and appropriate leadership may all help but the spiritual growth is essentially God's work. We sow the seed, others tend the garden, but God is the one who gives the harvest. A wise Christian small group leader will be sensitively praying and expecting growth in faith and lifestyle in the group.

PREPARING THE STUDY

Prepare in advance

Hasty preparation does not produce the best results. However, when hurried preparation is forced upon us we can trust God to make up for our lack of adequate time. It is hoped that knowing more about how to prepare an effective study will make you want to spend the time needed to prepare adequately.

Involve others

The distinctly New Testament metaphor of the church is that of a body with all members functioning. Mutual ministry, the priesthood of all believers and the development of the gifts of all members of the body is prominent in the New Testament (Romans 12, 1 Corinthians 12 and Ephesians 4). Leaders should be player-coaches and not solo performers.

A Christian small group provides an ideal situation to discern, affirm, develop and use the variety of spiritual gifts of the members for mutual upbuilding. Therefore, when tasks are delegated, it is not primarily to decrease the load of the leader, but essentially to develop the individual ministry of each member.

Group members can be involved in the preparation of any study. It may be prepared by a number of people but presented by one. More than one member can present different facets of the study.

The majority will need help in fulfilling assignments. Each needs to understand what is expected of them and to know that assistance is readily available if and when they need it.

Some will fail. Help in reflection on their failure can lead to new learning and growth. Affirmation and encouragement will readily be available from a secure and sensitive leader.

Have a specific aim

A vague aim usually results in vague study. You cannot accomplish a goal if you do not know what it is. Many groups will follow prepared study materials which have clear aims for each lesson, but they will not necessarily adopt the aim as stated. Other groups will prepare their own studies based on the expressed needs of the group. Begin by writing down your specific session aim. An aim seeks to state what you want to happen and/or what you want the group to learn. Be concise and specific. Your aim will fit into one or more of three basic educational goals: Knowledge—thinking; Attitude—feeling; Behaviour—doing.

Follow a plan

It will help to have an ordered study session. The outline will depend upon the resources and method which are chosen. If you are using prepared study material, a plan will be suggested. However, always be flexible with all prepared material and adapt both the material and the session outline to your particular group.

In the section of this chapter dealing with experience-centred learning, an outline of an inductive method was given.

Two patterns found helpful are:

1. **Establish the 'life need'**. Discover the relevance of the Christian gospel to that need. Seek a life response in terms of behaviour, attitude and belief. Plan specific action and begin working on it.

2. **Study a passage of Scripture**. Discover the 'life-need' dealt with by it. Seek a response.

USE TEACHING AIDS

Teaching aids help implement learning. They introduce another level of sensory perception into the learning experience. They help hold attention and add interest. They visualise abstract concepts and increase retention of knowledge.

Audio and Video aids are numerous. Recordings of music or talks are available from Christian bookshops and libraries. Secular records provide rich resource material. Record your own copy of speeches and discussions from special radio or television programmes or meetings. News broadcasts contain up-to-date material for discussion.

Visual aids which can be used include: pictures, maps, charts, drawings and posters. A Snoopy wall poster shows Snoopy embracing Charlie Brown. The caption reads: 'Dogs accept people for what they are.' There is a good discussion starter!

Printed aids, such as books and pamphlets, make good resources to draw upon as group studies. Certain comic strips like 'Peanuts', 'Fred Bassett', 'Dear Abbey', 'Hagar' and many others have some insightful comments on life. News of people and the world, and editorials in daily newspapers can be helpful aids to the group.

Projected aids include overhead projector transparencies which are easy to make yourself. Some pre-printed sets are available commercially. A segment of a movie or a single slide can be shown for discussion to illuminate a point.

WHAT TO STUDY

Deciding what to study is a major decision for every study group. The needs and interests of the group should guide us here. The first consideration should be: 'What are the members interested in studying?' Too often we find well-meaning leaders informing their group of the study programme to be undertaken.

When the group concerns have been identified, a number of alternative resources could be proposed.

There ought to be some comprehensive plan or overall design that seeks to give a balance to the study. Interests ought to be balanced by needs of the group.

When considering resources, it needs to be remembered that most leaders are busy and need handbooks and other resource material that will require the least amount of preparation. If leaders are unaccustomed to leading or expressing themselves about spiritual truths, then resources for leaders are crucial.

While much of the resource material available is helpful, all too often it can be either too lengthy, too intellectual, or not sufficiently related to everyday living. Therefore, all resource material should be carefully scrutinised and, if possible, a period of experimental use allowed, with due regard to the spiritual and intellectual development of the participants.

I asked some group leaders to list what they considered **the basic requirements of a successful study**. Here are some of the suggestions made:

A study needs to answer a human problem and point to a better way of living.

It needs to be kept simple.

It needs to clearly set out the aim, especially for the guidance of the leader.

It must give opportunity for group discussion and provide questions that promote discussion.

The questions for discussion need to help the group relate the principles outlined in the study with their own needs and circumstances.

It should be based on the Bible. One comment was, 'We don't want another sermon with someone's ideas. We want to know what the Bible says.'

It must have an outlet in the actual everyday life of the group.

There is little value in studying about Noah, if this is not connected in some way to everyday living.

A study plan needs to be long enough to give approximately three-quarters of an hour to an hour for study, but not too long so that it has to be skipped through hurriedly, thus missing various important points.

The study needs to deal with a topic which grips the imagination of the group and holds their interest.

When the Christian church, in the power of the Spirit, has evangelised and faithfully cared for new Christians, teaching has played a vital role.

In small groups, people are re-discovering the renewal of mind and life as they confront the Scriptures with openness and a will to please God. They are using methods which not only result in more effective learning, but facilitate many pleasurable experiences and surprises as they grow in Christ and reach out in witness and service to others.

References

(1) Douglas S Hubery, *Teaching the Christian Faith Today* (Joint Board of Graded Lessons of Australia and New Zealand, 1965).
(2) Robert A Dow, *Learning Through Encounter* (Judson Press, 1971). Used by permission of Judson Press.
(3) O A Oeser, *Teacher, Pupil and Task* (Tavistock Publications, 1955), p. 34.

Chapter 11
Studying the Bible Together

Let not thy Word, O Lord, become a judgement upon us, that we hear it and do it not, that we know it and love it not, that we believe it and obey it not; O thou, who with the Father and the Holy Spirit livest and reignest, world without end. Amen. — Attributed to Thomas à Kempis

Many reasons have been given why the Bible should receive serious attention. William Barclay, in his book *Introducing the Bible*, sets forth a number of convincing reasons. He commences by drawing attention to the first chapter of the Westminster Confession of Faith, where it states that the books of the Bible '. . . are given by inspiration of God, to be the rule of faith and life'. It continues, '. . . the whole counsel of God, concerning all things necessary for His own glory, man's salvation, faith and life, is either expressly set down in Scripture, or by good and necessary consequence may be deduced from Scripture;

unto which nothing at any time is to be added, whether by new revelations of the Spirit, or traditions of men'. That is a tremendous position given to the Bible in the Christian community. It means that '*the Church accepts this ancient book as having final and binding authority*'.[1]

Barclay then goes on to explore why the Bible is so special. He claims we get close to the reason for its uniqueness by reflecting on its effectiveness, and he quotes a few examples of lives which have been dramatically transformed by reading it. Barclay says *the Bible is still relevant and powerful because it is about people, and about personal relationships*. This means it is always relevant because people essentially do not change from one generation to another.

The last and supreme reason he gives as to why the Bible is unique and for ever indispensable, is that: '*The Bible is the one place where we find Jesus Christ*. The Bible is literally the only source book for the life and the words and the teaching of Jesus. Take the Bible away, and we would be left with fugitive memories, and subjective opinions. And this is inextricably linked with the last point we made. It is only in and through Jesus Christ that our relationship with our fellow human beings is the relationship of love, and that our relationship with God is possible at all. In it alone we are confronted with the portrait of the one person in heaven in whom these relationships become what they ought to be.'[2]

AVOIDING COMMON PITFALLS

The purely intellectual approach
A danger which should be avoided in small group Bible study is that of taking a purely intellectual approach. The danger here is to merely view the passage as containing a set of doctrines or propositions, and not see it as mediating God's Word that addresses our feelings and behaviour as well as our minds.

Associated with this pitfall is the problem of not seeing the passage related to the life of the community for whom it was originally written, and also related to our experience and life in the twentieth century. God's Word is concerned with living. Scripture never fulfils its prime purpose if it is studied in an abstract, intellectual fashion that is little more than a philosophical discussion of correct doctrine. Bible study must be speaking to the pains and joys we experience as human beings and as Christians, and on living out Christ's gospel in our age.

The nature and mission of the Bible is transformational. Our responsibility is not merely to believe it, we are to live it. Our concern in studying the Bible is with its 'experiential impact'. 'Unfortunately, most of us have been trained to think of and to read Scripture in terms of "truth to be understood" rather than "reality to live". One problem most small groups in the church will face is tied directly to this. How can the study of the Bible be meaningful in our group? For this many of us will have to re-learn our approach to Scripture.'[3]

Professor Ross Snyder, previously of Chicago Theological Seminary, has made a very significant contribution to this whole area of helping people discover the experiential relevance of the Bible. His 'Depth and Encounter' Bible study method has brought a new dynamic in many groups to which I have introduced it. I consider it to be one of the most effective and thorough of all the many Bible study methods I have used. It can lead to new levels of communication and sensitivity in interpersonal relationships within small groups. I have seen many receive a compelling word of God through this study method and come alive spiritually or move out into new experiences of freedom and spiritual power. The method with some minor additions is found in Chapter 12, page 104.

Professor Snyder writes:

The truth of the Bible needs to get into the places where people are living. When we find an important passage we should stay with it long enough to really grasp it — its core message, its feeling about life, what it can do to our own daily experiences. Too often we never stop to study precisely any particular verse, never dig and sweat intellectually or existentially; seldom become involved personally in the message of a particular passage of Scripture and, therefore, never really possess any verse. In group discussion we tend to make pious comments, knowing full well no one intends to take them seriously.

By approaching the Bible existentially we mean the involvement of the individual in the message of a particular passage of Scripture. You ask 'What does this passage of Scripture say to me, for my life, right now?' Instead of asking, 'Why is there suffering?' you ask, 'How do I react to suffering?' It's important to understand this point if Bible study is to be more than a mental exercise.[4]

Shared ignorance
The opposite extreme to the purely intellectual approach to Bible study is the danger of simply sharing ignorance. If Bible study is merely subjective we fail to move beyond the feelings, attitudes and opinions of the group. While the subjective dimension is necessary, effective Bible study also demands that we come to grips with the findings of reliable scholars and teachers and understand the Bible passage in  its historical and theological setting. We can overcome the

dual dangers of an imbalanced subjectivity and sharing of ignorance in a number of ways, such as:

(i) using a resource person to provide necessary historical, linguistic and theological background information (e.g. your minister, a Bible teacher or a well-read lay person);

(ii) providing printed resources for the group to use (e.g. commentaries, Bible dictionaries, guided Bible studies with explanatory notes);

(iii) having one or more members of the group research beforehand possible areas requiring specialist feed-in, discover the necessary information, and introduce it to the group at the appropriate time;

(iv) recording during the meeting matters requiring specialist information and at the end of the session inviting members to research the various areas and share their findings at the next meeting.

By using a variety of these means, learning can be stimulated. In the main, use group research to discover needed information. Occasionally, a specialist can be used to discuss problem areas and so reinforce or clarify the discoveries the group has made.

A person does not have to be a scholar to read and study the Bible with understanding. But anyone who desires to take the Bible seriously will also need to take advantage of what others have learned. The findings of scholars can open the treasures of the Bible to those of us who do not have the technical training and commitment to do our own hard research. Do not fall into the trap of thinking that the findings of scholars are not important. Seek to use the fruits of scholarship without being burdened with the jargon and the methods of technical scholarship.

Ideally all group leaders should do some serious systematic study of the Bible to better equip them to lead the study of the Bible effectively. Courses for the laity in Bible background, an overview of the Bible and hermeneutics (how to interpret the Bible) are readily available through lay training centres, Bible colleges and theological colleges. There are also numerous correspondence courses. However, ask the advice of your pastor or a mature Christian leader, as not all will suit your background and some are lacking in balance, depth and reliable scholarship. Every leader needs the kit listed later in this chapter and where it is not possible to undertake the above study, the study of these books will help.

There are a number of well prepared courses which a local church could conduct. Leaders and as many members of the small groups as are able should be encouraged to be involved. The learning will lift the level of Bible study in the groups.

The Kerygma Bible Study in Depth course takes a thematic approach, tracing through the great Biblical themes of Salvation, God's Faithfulness, Kingdom of God, Righteousness, Wisdom, Worship, Hope, etc. It is designed to be used in small groups with a skilled leader. There is built into it a relational dimension to prevent it being purely academic. The resources are readily available in North America and Australia (Joint Board of Christian Education, 2nd floor, 10 Queen Street, Melbourne, Vic. 3000).

The Bethel Bible Study Series, prepared by the Adult Christian Education (Madison, Wisconsin, USA), is also available in Australia (Adult Christian Education Foundation, 67 Lawford Street, Chullora, NSW, 2196) and other countries. It takes a narrative approach, giving an overview of each of the books of the Bible. Leaders of the course are required to undertake special training.

The new 'Mastering the Basics' course produced by Serendipity USA (available in Australia, Serendipity Christian Resources, GPO Box 1944, Adelaide, S. Aust., 5001) is designed for use in small groups with leaders who are prepared to do some serious preparation. It covers a book of the Bible in 6–14 weeks and provides in-depth scholarly resources whilst retaining a relational dimension.

Superficial treatment

Superficial treatment of the passage is another potential problem. This danger is particularly acute if the group does not realise the importance of serious Bible study, is uncommitted to their task and to one another, or fails to use a commentary or other specialist help. The problem can also arise if you try to cover too much material in one session. It is usually best to limit the group to a passage with a reasonably self-contained unit of thought.
The natural paragraph divisions in the RSV are generally a useful, quick guide. However, the leader will need to exercise his/her own discretion. Reference to one or two

commentaries will also give guidance regarding the optimum number of verses to cover in one session.

There is a great deal to be gained in occasionally staying with only one verse to dig deeply into its meaning and explore what it is saying to each person's situation. Snyder's 'Depth and Encounter' method is helpful here.

Failure to get an overview

Small groups have not always had a good model of Biblical studies. Generally Bible study has been too piecemeal.

There is a need for a good overview of the Bible, to study it as a complete unit rather than in the fragmented way it has been studied. This is a large undertaking and obviously a verse by verse study cannot be undertaken within the group. The speed with which the study moves will vary from book to book but it is important to avoid getting bogged down or, on the other hand, not captur-

ing the main message of a particular book. Generally the group members contract to read a certain number of chapters, or a whole book, in between meetings. Some will want to do their own reading of commentaries on the weekly segments.

Innovative ways have been developed to help people get a broad panorama of the Bible. Some of these are not suitable for use in small groups and are studied individually or in larger gatherings. However others, such as 'Mastering the Basics' and 'Kerygma', are specifically designed for a small group setting. (See earlier reference to these resources.)

Neglecting the immediate context

One further common pitfall is failure to study the passage in its immediate context. Also if the standpoint of God's full revelation in Jesus Christ is not considered, 'sub-Christian' interpretation can result. A number of parts of the Old Testament, for example, do not align with the teachings of Christ (e.g. the 'eye for an eye and a tooth for a tooth' law). Whilst such passages must be seen in their original historical setting, we must look beyond them to God's fuller revelation of himself and his will which we find in the New Testament. Also difficult or ambiguous passages in the New Testament must be interpreted in the light of what is clearly shown elsewhere in the Bible as God's will as revealed through Christ in his earthly life or through his Spirit.

Not lead to action

Bible study in small groups has received just criticism because it has not always resulted in action.

> Do not merely listen to the word, and so *deceive* yourselves. Do what it says. Anyone who *listens to the word but does not do* what it says is like a man who looks at his face in a mirror and, after looking at himself, goes away and immediately forgets what he looks like. But the man who *looks intently* into the perfect law that gives freedom, and *continues to do this*, not forgetting what he has heard, but *doing it*—he will be blessed in what he does. [Italics are the author's.] (James 1:22–25, NIV.)

In Bible study, we should seek to sense, and then go and do, God's will. It carries with it a commitment to do God's will as he leads. We need the 'freedom to be responsible'. Freedom is found in obedience. The purpose of the Bible is to transform human lives and situations.

Group members need encouragement to seek the relevance of the Scriptures for specific situations in each of their lives and also for it to become a reality for them. When a person says, 'This is what I believe. I must act now in obedience to God's Word to me,' the group can provide motivational support by praying in the group and covenanting to uphold the person in prayer between group meetings. A pastoral call in person or by telephone, offering help and assuring them of continuing support, can further facilitate their actions.

Accountability is being rediscovered by many as a further motivation for action. Opportunities for reporting progress, or otherwise, can have positive effects provided unreal guilt is not generated due to a legalistic stance by the group. While accountability implies legitimate expectations of those wanting to take their discipleship seriously, it must always be within the context of grace.

STEPS TO EFFECTIVE IN-DEPTH BIBLE STUDY

These steps can be used for small group or personal Bible study. When used in a small group, members individually work on steps 1 to 6 prior to the meeting and then share their findings together. The group can then take the roles set out in steps 7 and 8.

A leader of a group will also find this helpful in preparing his/her role as a resource person.

1. **Personal preparation** (Get right with God.)
Be open to what the Holy Spirit has to reveal. Be ready to obey.

2. **Research** (What does the passage actually say?)
Make patient enquiry into the text.
Read and re-read in a variety of versions.
Gather information on people, places and situations mentioned.
Note references to time and sequence.
Seek out the meaning of the main words and phrases.
Ask questions of the passage, beginning with 'How . . . ?' 'Why . . . ?' and 'What . . . ?'
Re-write the passage in your own words—as you would say it.
Keep it simple and brief.

3. **Interpretation** (What does it mean?)
What was the original intention of this passage? What gave rise to it being written?
Compare it with other passages of Scripture.
Look up cross references. Let Scripture interpret Scripture.
Refer to a commentary (only after you have done all this work).

4. **Application** (What could it mean for me?)
Think of the ways in which you would be different if you took this seriously.
If you put this into practice, to what persons and situations would you have a different approach? In what ways?
Rev. Dr Terry Fullam uses a simple acrostic 'SPACESTEP' to help in applying Scripture to our lives:

S – Is there a **sin** to confess?
P – Is there a **promise** to receive?
A – Is there an **attitude** to cultivate or avoid?
C – Is there a **command** to obey?
E – Is there an **example** to follow or avoid?
S – Is there **something** for which to give thanks?
T – Is there a **truth** to believe?
E – Is there an **error** to reject?
P – Learn to **pray** the passage.
  [Used with permission.]

5. **Action planning** (What will I plan to do?)
From Step 4, select one or two things which you could begin working on immediately. Think of the steps you will need to take. Make a plan of action.

6. **Timing** (When will I begin?)
Set some realistic deadlines for some of the main steps in your plan.

7. **Support** (With whom will I share my intent?)
List the names of one or two Christian friends with whom you will share your plans and seek their support, especially in prayer. (Your small group may be the ones you choose to support you in this.)

8. **Accountability** (When will I report progress?)
Set a time with your friend/s in Step 7 for talking over your progress, or otherwise, in working through your plan.

AN INTEGRATED PARISH PLAN FOR BIBLE STUDY

In many churches around the world, the Bible study in small groups has been integrated into the total life of the congregation.

Many years ago I observed this model in the East Harlem Protestant parish in New York and adapted it for my own parishes. The original model, as I remember it, followed the plan set down here.

A well-presented booklet prepared by the parish set out their own lectionary for the year, following a theme for each week and incorporating original artwork related to these themes. Every member received a copy and was encouraged to follow these readings in their own devotions.

The staff met early in the week, during which time one or two of the staff presented an exegesis of the passages from their lectionary, which would be the focus of the preaching for the following Sunday. The staff discussed the passages and added further thoughts to those given.

All the small groups studied the relevant passages. Notes were made of the highlights of the discussion and sharing. These insights were then fed into a further staff meeting later in the week and, together with the staff's work, were woven into the preaching on the following Sunday.

In one of my parishes I introduced Scripture Union 'Daily Bread Reading Notes', with about half the congregation committed to read them. The groups used the small group study guide in the notes each week and, on the following Sunday, the staff and I preached on the passages studied, incorporating insights gleaned from the work of the small groups. Each time a new book of the Bible or a special theme was commenced, I would have a small, special segment in the Sunday services to introduce this.

In many Uniting Church parishes in Australia, the 'With Love to the World' notes, based on the International Lectionary, are now used widely. Much of the preaching is based on this lectionary and some parishes have their groups also study these passages.

A variety of other resources including 'Mastering the Basics', mentioned previously, also lend themselves to this integrated approach.

A BASIC RESOURCE KIT

It should go without saying that any study group leader must be both committed to and prepared for his/her role. Part of the practical outworking of such commitment and preparation is the building up of a small resource library. Such a library may be the responsibility of the group leader, the group itself, or the wider church; but in any event, the library should be available to all members of the group. Its regular presence in the group for quick reference will help prevent the sharing of ignorance of difficult Biblical matters.

These are some of the basic resources:

Bibles

It goes without saying that your main resource is a Bible. These fall into two broad categories: standard Bibles in a variety of translations and study Bibles.

There are a variety of study Bibles in both the Revised Standard Version and the New International Version. These have centre references, notes and an abridged concordance. The Jerusalem Bible with notes should not be overlooked.

One or two modern translations will also be useful, for example Today's English Version, the Living Bible, and do not bypass J B Phillips' translation—it has a lot to commend it. The Eight Translation New Testament contains these and other translations on two adjacent pages, for easy comparison.

The new 'Serendipity Small Group Study Bible' has 'warm up' and study questions next to every passage throughout the Bible. The three progressive sets of questions linked to each passage can provide the main part of the programme for a group meeting. Many groups now make this the base resource for all group members. It also stimulates thinking about the text when used in conjunction with other study resources.

Commentaries

Acquire a good one-volume commentary of the whole Bible. In addition you should, if possible, have individual commentaries on any book of the Bible you are studying. There are a number of paperback commentaries available, such as 'The Bible Speaks Today' series (general editor John Stott), Torch, William Barclay and Tyndale series. However, as the single commentaries are of varying standard, even within a series, seek the advice of your pastor or a teacher of Biblical studies before making any specific purchase of these or the one-volume commentary on the whole Bible.

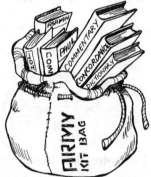

Ensure that the commentaries you choose include both the theological and historical dimension, together with a general introductory section to the book concerned. There are quite a number of commentaries available, reflecting differing theological standpoints. It will be up to the leader to select what he considers to be suitable. Some popular commentaries in addition to those mentioned in the previous paragraph are: The *Jerome Biblical Commentary*,

The *New Bible Commentary* (IVP), The *Interpreter's One Volume Commentary on the Bible* (Abingdon), The *One Volume Bible Commentary* by William Neil, and the new *Peake's Commentary on the Bible* (Nelson), edited by H H Rowley and Matthew Black (contributors include F F Bruce).

Bible dictionaries

Bible dictionaries give a background to the different customs, place names, characters and theological words that appear in Scripture, arranged in alphabetical order. They are ideal for quick, ready reference. Popular one-volume dictionaries are: *Harper's Bible Dictionary* (Harper & Row); The *New Bible Dictionary* (IVP); The *Hastings Dictionary of the Bible* (T & T Clark); *Interpreter's One Volume Dictionary of the Bible* (Abingdon); and *Dictionary of the New Testament* (Colin Brown, Editor—Zondervan).

Concordances

These help locate specific verses or names in the Bible. There are a number of small abridged concordances on the market, but pay the extra for one of the following: *Nelson's Complete Concordance of the Revised Standard Version*; *Cruden's Complete Concordance of the Bible* (Authorised Version); *Morrison's Analytical Concordance of the New Testament* (RSV), Westminster Press; *NIV Complete Concordance* (Hodder & Stoughton); *N.A.S.B. Handy Concordance*.

Bible background books

Choose from this selection: *The Bible With Understanding*, G Dicker (Joint Board of Christian Education, Melbourne); *Introduction to the Bible*, John H Hayes (Westminster); *How to Read the Old Testament*, E Carpentier (SCM Press); *How to Read the New Testament*, E Carpentier (SCM Press); *New Testament Foundations—A Guide for Christian Students* (2 vols.), Ralph Martin (Eerdmans); *A Theology of the New Testament*, G E Ladd (Eerdmans); *The Lion Handbook of the Bible* (Lion Publishing); *How to Read the Bible for All Its Worth*, Fee & Stuart (Zondervan/S.U.); *Understanding the Bible*, John Stott (S.U.); *User's Guide to the Bible*, Wright (Lion).

Other resources

There are other resources to include in your kit. A **concise dictionary** of the English language will help words come alive; a **Bible atlas** and a **theological word book** such as *A Theological Word Book of the Bible* by Alan Richardson (SCM).

BIBLE STUDY AND THE HOLY SPIRIT

We began this chapter by referring to the Westminster Confession. After declaring that the Bible contains all that is necessary for salvation, the Confession goes on: 'Yet notwithstanding, our full persuasion and assurance of the infallible truth and divine authority thereof, is from the inward work of the Holy Spirit, bearing witness by and with the word in our hearts.' It further states: 'We acknowledge the inward illumination of the Spirit of God to be necessary for the

saving understanding of such things as are revealed in the word.' We need the Spirit to enable us to fully understand the meaning of the Word of God. Through the Holy Spirit God gives us the grace to be willing and able to put into action his revealed intention for us. In other words, study of God's Word and prayer must go hand in hand.

Barclay wisely exhorts us:

> We do well to approach the Bible with George Adam Smith's great prayer on our lips:
>
>> 'Almighty and most merciful God, who has given the Bible to be the revelation of thy great love to man, and of thy power and will to save him; grant that our study of it may not be made in vain by any callousness or carelessness of our hearts but that by it we may be confirmed in penitence, lifted to hope, made strong for service, and filled with the true knowledge of thee and of thy son Jesus Christ: this we ask for thy love's sake. Amen.'

References

(1) William F Barclay, *Introducing the Bible* (The Bible Reading Fellowship, 1972).
(2) Ibid.
(3) Taken from *A New Face for the Church* by Lawrence O Richards, p. 178. Copyright © 1970 by Zondervan Publishing House. Used by permission.
(4) Ross Snyder, from a pamphlet describing his 'Depth and Encounter Bible Study Method'.
(5) Ibid.

Chapter 12

Creative Ways to Study the Bible Together

In this chapter you will be introduced to Bible study methods—some old and well proven; some new, from overseas or written locally, and offering great promise. Where we have been aware of the source, it has been acknowledged and where possible permission gained to reproduce it. However, many of these methods have come to us in a roneoed form with no acknowledgement. We regret we have not been able to trace and recognise their origin.

In most groups it is advisable to start with a method suitable to a newly formed group; for example, the 'Swedish Symbol' or 'Silent Sharing Method'. After one or two sessions the group can move to a deeper method of Bible study.

Most of these methods require a degree of honest sharing. If groups are content to operate behind their 'masks', this lack of openness will result in a superficial application to life. Honesty will not come automatically and often there are barriers of in-built resistance and years of lack of openness

to be overcome. Sensitivity and patience will be needed. Where the leader is secure enough to model this openness, the group will find it easier to open up with each other and struggle together to put into practice God's intentions for their lives, revealed through the Scriptures.

Do not over-use any one method. Vary your method as this helps to hold interest and broadens the learning experience.

For variation and greater depth, combine some appropriate aspects of different methods.

Finally, be open to the Holy Spirit! Bible study can be a vital and lively asset for the Holy Spirit, changing people for the better in a way that will honour God and influence others with whom they live and work.

INDEX—BIBLE STUDY METHODS

Below is a list of the methods included in this chapter, to help you quickly locate them:

1. DEPTH AND ENCOUNTER BIBLE STUDY

This method was developed by Prof. Ross Snyder, while at Chicago Theological Seminary and is used with permission. It is for those who are serious about growing in their discipleship.

A focus is made on only one verse. Each stays with it long enough to really grasp its core message and what this can do to his/her journey through life. Too often we never stop to study precisely any particular verse, never sweat over it intellectually or actually become involved in the message. This method seeks to lift the group out of abstract debate and get each person struggling with the meaning and the application of the Scriptures to his/her life situation.

It involves active listening to each other's work on the passage without superimposing our own thoughts. The aim in the initial stages is to help each develop his/her own thoughts by at least one or two persons in the group stating what was communicated to them. The person being received is then given opportunity to add to or correct what the others understood from what he/she said.

Only after all have shared their individual work, and been encouraged to do further thinking, does the group get into general discussion.

The method also avoids the common problem in relational Bible study of sharing of ignorance. A specialist is brought to the group to give some sound exegesis of the passage *after* the group has struggled with the passage.

The value of this method of Bible study lies in the distinctive way we carry on the discussion. Note that the method of sharing is different from the usual methods of group discussion where everyone jumps right in with his/her ideas. With this approach we are meeting one another where each of us lives. Our purpose is to help each one of us become clearer in our grasp of Christian truth. We are after development, not debate.

If members of the group plunge in immediately with, 'This is the way I translated it, . . .,' the more vocal people will tend to dominate, the depths of each person may never be revealed, and the members of the group may not learn the difficult art of **creatively listening to another person**. Furthermore, we are not being trained in our own translating and contemplation of the Bible.

Here are the steps of this 'Depth and Encounter' method:

1. **Individual work:**
   Silent prayer:
   'Lord, help me to grasp the meaning of this passage and enable me to express it clearly and then take it seriously.'
   Write out your own translation:
   Pray as you think and write.
   Try to use different words to those in the various translations as far as possible.
   Endeavour to put in your own words each of the main words before you write out your translation.
   Write it as *you* would say it. Imagine you are writing a letter to a friend.
   Make it clear; keep it simple.
   Ask yourself: (Do some serious thinking)
   'What would happen if I took this seriously?'
   'Would I see certain persons and situations differently?'
   'Would I do anything differently?'
   'What would I care for?'
   (Write down one or two ideas that come to mind. You may not necessarily find an answer to each question.)

To help in responding to the above questions refer to Diagram 19 on page 105.

2. **Work Group** (divide into groups of 4 to 6)
   N.B. These are not discussion groups. These are essentially opportunities to share. There will be more listening than speaking. All will work hard at concentrating with loving sensitivity on what others are saying.
   Each person in turn is given opportunity to share:
   All give their own translation and thoughts with explanations if needed.

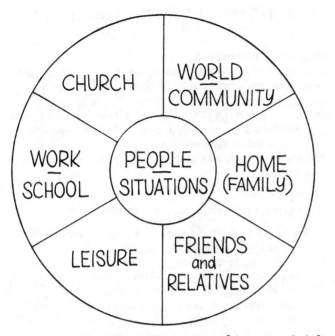

Diagram 19: For Helping Application of Learning to Life

One or two persons in the group may state what has been communicated to them. The person being received is then given the opportunity to add to or correct what others understand from what he or she has said.

The group helps each person develop his or her thinking and does not criticise or pass judgement. Questions to help another test his/her thinking may be: 'How would you apply that to this situation?' or 'What would you say to this idea?' The aim is to help the person grow or develop an idea **but still keep it his or hers. We are after development not debate**.

3. **General discussion:**
After each person in the group has been so received, a general discussion on whatever has been awakened in the group is profitable.

4. **Bring into the group specialist resources:**
After your group has had a few sessions on a portion of the Bible, bring in a specialist in the Bible. Have this person explain the meanings of the key Greek or Hebrew words in the passages, and help the group grasp,

somewhat dramatically, what this chapter meant to the people who first heard it.

Then ask the specialist to share what excitement this passage aroused in him or her (not give advice to other people on what they should do).

It is important to be clear how this differs from inviting a Bible expert to come in to lecture and then, after this person has told the group what to think, having the group discuss what the expert has said. In this approach the lecturer is expected to be open about how the passage addresses him personally.

In the absence of a special Bible teacher, consult a few commentaries. Dig the material out for yourself. *Caution!* Don't go to the reference until you have come at the Bible directly with your own life, and your group has behind them three or four solid sessions.

5. **Further reflection and steps to action and growth:**
It is useful to follow the previous steps with further opportunity for each person to reflect in silence on their own work, in the light of the specialist feed-in, and make possible additions or amendments. This can also include a time for developing a simple plan to implement the challenges to action. Each individual makes a list of specific proposed actions in order of priority, with a noted deadline after each for commencing to do something about it. One or more of these can be shared with the group and prayed over. Groups which are serious about supporting each other in their growth will expect reports of progress or otherwise to future meetings.

Kinds of passages to study by this method
The suggestions given below indicate the *type* of passages which lend themselves well to this method of Bible study. On the whole, narrative passages are not so fruitful for translation. Only one verse, or one unit of verses which can be kept in mind at once, should be used. Never take a whole chapter; too many points would be glossed over.

In many instances, the passages given here would be broken up into smaller units for study. They deal with frequent problems and the offer of life which Christ makes.

Romans 8:1–19;
12:1–2
Philippians 1:27–30;

Ephesians 3:16–19
Hebrews 12:1–17
James 1:1–4,12,19–27

2:1–13, 4:4–13
2 Timothy 2:1–5,
14, 15
Matthew 5:3–16

1 John 1; 2:9–11
1 Peter 2:1–10;
3:13–17; 2:9–10
John 15:9–21, 26–27

2. EIGHT QUESTIONS

This method may be used individually or in small groups. Each person or group is given a sheet of paper, with their eight questions printed so that there are enough spaces left for writing in the answers. When all have finished, the summing-up can be a comparison of all the answers of the individuals or small groups. If time is short, the two most important questions are: 'What is the central meaning?' and 'What act of obedience follows?'

Preparation required:
(a) A copy of the questions for every person or each group. If working with one group, the questions may be placed on a chalk/blackboard, chart paper or overhead projector and blank sheets of paper issued.
(b) A chalkboard or substitute will be needed for summarising.

The eight questions:
1. What are the scenes?
2. What are the difficult words (either because we do not understand them or they have been used so often they have lost their full meaning)?
3. What is the relation of this passage to the whole context in which it occurs?
4. Why is it in the Bible at all?
5. What is the central meaning? (Ask what the passage says about God and his attitude to us, about our attitude to him and about our attitude to each other.)
6. Can you illustrate this central truth from the life of the church today or in the past?
7. What is the meaning of this passage for our own group today?
8. What act of obedience follows from this, for the Christian community and for each of us individually?

Passages suitable for this method:
The Parable of the Great Supper—Luke 14:15–24
The Raising of Lazarus—John 11:38–44
Jesus and the Accusing Pharisees—Matthew 15:1–20

3. HEAD—HEART—AND HAND

Preparation required:
The group as a whole is divided into small groups so that all may have the opportunity to share. Each group needs a competent leader.
(a) Provide paper and pencils and a Bible for each person.
(b) Materials for reporting and recording findings from the group will be needed.
Enthusiasm to see this method through to its conclusion is also needed.

Group work:
Each group works together through these steps:

1. **Head:** Here the facts about the passage are discovered, such as the meaning of the words; build-up of the story; context: for what, to whom, by whom it was written—what kind of people were they—what were their needs, etc. This may be done by the leader verse by verse, or by the group using one of the other methods. (Where a cluster of groups are working together in the same setting, a skilled person may present this method in a plenary session.)

2. **Heart:** The passage is read silently and each individual tries to find the heart of the passage (central meaning) for himself or herself that day. (The 'Silent Sharing' method may be used.)

3. **Hand:** This phase deals with **action**. The leader accepts reports from each member, summing up at the end to give an overall picture of what has been discovered. For a few minutes these findings are discussed to find which is the most important one for the group (although individuals may make their choices as well).

Action often falls into three sections:
Some obvious group action for the group, church or community.
If there is a feeling that the group needs to know more, further study may be planned. (Make sure that this does not become an escape route.)

Individuals decide for themselves on the things which need to be changed in their lives.

Plenary: Where a number of groups are involved, opportunity should be given for reporting on any significant aspects of the experience, particularly the action planning segment.

Example of a passage suitable for this method:
A changed life in a New Society—Colossians 3:1–17.

4. HUMAN NEED AND CHRISTIAN ACTION

This method will help groups to become more aware of the suffering of fellow humans and to explore the application of the gospel in practical ways of caring.

Step 1: The leader or member of the group presents an **actual situation of human need**. This may be in the form of suffering through a crisis, a neighbour's difficulties, a problem at work, a situation in the church, or in the town/suburb. It is flexible but needs to be specific.

Step 2: The problem having been set before them, small groups of four or five **discuss the situation** with what Christian insight they have. To quote William Barclay, 'One needs to get inside the skin of another person to see what they see and experience what they feel.' This is what the members are asked to do: to study each person (not only the apparently 'wronged' person or the one suffering misfortune, but each one) in order to see the situation from every angle. After half an hour, the leader (or member leading) records the reports on a chart but makes no comment on them.

Step 3: The groups are now **given a Bible passage** which has been selected beforehand by the one leading, and chosen because of its relevance to the topic. Only now is the Bible used. Another half hour at least is needed for this. Now deal with these questions:

(i) Having looked at the passage, is there anything there which prompts us to change the thoughts we had earlier? Are there any guidelines which may help decide what action to take either as: (a) individuals, (b) the group, (c) the church community?

(ii) From what we have learnt in the Bible passage and the situation presented to us, what should we include in our prayers of: (a) confession, (b) thanksgiving, (c) petition?

Step 4: Reassemble in the large group and **share findings**. Only now can the one leading the group make any contribution.

Step 5: Determine what action is to be taken. What is God calling us to do? What will be involved? Who will take the initiative? When will we begin?

Step 6: Close with a time of **group prayer** using the points which have come from Step 3. The leader concludes this prayer segment.

5. HUMAN TRANSFORMATION METHOD

This Bible study is an adaptation of the procedure outlined by Dr Walter Wink in his book *The Bible in Human Transformation*. This method requires the leader to have some background in theology and biblical exegesis.

Preparation required:
Before the study group meets, the leader prepares a thorough exegesis of the passage, used as his/her basis for a carefully thought out series of questions, to guide the group into a greater awareness of the historical and theological background and meaning of the passage.

Step 1—Analysis
By means of the leader's prepared questions, the group analyse the account, working together on their own exegesis of it. The leader may need to provide some specific technical information, or guide the group when they seem bogged down or headed in the wrong direction. Questions may be asked also concerning the recording of the incident, for example: Does it appear in any other Gospel? Do the accounts differ? Why? What is the meaning of certain words, traditions, etc.

Step 2—Picturing the message
The aim is now to enter more deeply into the story. By means of historical imagination, and using the critical analysis of Step 1 as a check on sheer speculation, the passage is thought through again and members are asked to seek to relive the passage. In this step, questions (for example, concerning what the early church understood about the nature of God and his relationship with man, or who Jesus is etc.), may be raised as a direct result of information from this section. If questions from this step are factual, then the danger of premature self-reflection (which

fails to allow the unexpected and 'offensive' elements in the text to confront the group) may be avoided.

Step 3—Putting yourself in the picture

In this step the leader uses questions to help the members closely identify with the characters in the Gospel story. The members are helped to use these ancient characters as mirrors of their own lives which involves imagination, serious thinking and honesty. The leader will need to set the pace by modelling this openness, application and involvement but will need to avoid manipulating people into going further than they are prepared to go in being open.

Transformation can take place during this phase. The members may hear the voice of God and feel the power of the Holy Spirit, in a way similar to those who experienced a transforming encounter with Christ in the original story.

Questions based on the story of Mark 3:1–6 could go like this:

What is your 'withered' or 'crippled' hand? In other words, what aspects of yourself do you identify in this character? (Allow a short pause for people to reflect and gather their thoughts.)

What is the 'Pharisee' in you?

Is there a 'sabbath' day in your life? Is there a special part of your life that you keep for yourself? Is there a part that you refuse entry to the work of the Spirit of God?

Why then does your 'Pharisee' not want your 'crippled hand' healed, or want God to work in your life?

How does Jesus fit into the picture?

How can Jesus relate to our 'Pharisees', 'sabbaths' and 'withered hands'?

(The session in our example ends in prayer, with the members reaching out to God for their various needs, and at the same time supporting one another in prayer. The conversational prayer method could be effectively used here.)

Step 4—Creative expression

In this concluding segment each member is asked to creatively express some aspect(s) of the passage studied. This may be done using poetry, crayons, paints, or clay, in the members' free time between sessions and brought to share with the group at the next meeting.

6. THE MEDITATIVE USE OF SCRIPTURE

(Based on a session led by Rev. Gordon Cosby of the Church of the Savior, Washington, D.C.)

The meditative use of Scripture is one of the most significant ways in which the Christian is addressed by God. It is an art which needs to be developed. It is not study, nor is it merely reading—it is letting Christ address us.

This method requires sufficient time to do it unhurriedly. Some or all of the work could be done prior to the group meeting or a longer period allowed for the group meeting.

The method is **ideal for retreats** where time is not a constraint. Sometimes I have allowed two hours for this in such a setting.

The whole purpose of this experience is to help us hear our destiny and to fulfil it. However, it is easy to develop devotional life apart from mission. The question which is ever before us in true meditation is, 'What is God's call on my life now?' That call will have certain characteristics:

There is a feeling of ultimateness, a feeling of being dealt with by God.

There will be a feeling of impossibility—a tendency to brush off as seeming ridiculous. On the other hand, do not miss it because it seems so simple.

There will be persistency—it will keep coming to you if you are continuing to be a growing person.

Change will take place within us as the Holy Spirit takes hold of this event. Growth takes place with this type of day by day encounter with the living Christ. What transforms life, making it spiritually vital and dynamic, is the cumulative power of the Word of God.

The whole of the individual work should be undertaken in complete silence. Silence may be a problem for some because they may be afraid of a dark disturbance, or that Christ may make real demands upon them which go beyond their present level of availability to him. These possibilities should be mentioned beforehand and encouragement given to trust God's love for us. Some may need further support, such as working in silence alongside the leader with the option to break silence if necessary.

Individual work (in silence). Up to an hour or more should be allowed.

(1) Preparing
Open the Bible at random. Select your own passage. Ask

for the guidance of the Holy Spirit as you read. Let him select the passage which you need most at the moment. Some will find it more helpful to begin in the Gospels and read on until a passage captures your attention.

Select a brief passage. Sometimes it will only be a phrase because we want to encounter it at depth. A long passage will not permit this in the time we have available.

Pray. Ask that you may be personally addressed by God through this Scripture. Pray for the guidance of Scripture. Ask for courage to meditate upon it, for this is a dangerous business ('it is a terrible thing to fall into the hands of the living God'—it may mean being told to go to Nineveh!!) It will be tragic if we are disobedient and costly if we obey. Pray, 'Lord, I want you to get hold of me.'

Use the passage 'not as a model for morality but as a mirror for our identity' (Sanders).

(2) Picturing
Try to picture the original event—get into the event by bringing the past to bear upon it. Use your intellect and your imagination. It will help to write notes as you proceed.

(3) Pondering
Get into conversation with Christ. He is there within you and beside you. He is in you and you in him. Christ is talking to you now; listen, talk it over with him. Ask him questions about yourself, such as 'What are the implications of this passage for my life?' Write notes on your inner stirrings. The Scripture provides the approach for you to get in touch with the Christ who is alive and ever present with his people.

(4) Dialogue Prayer
Hold a conversation with God. Express innermost feelings, not feelings you think you ought to feel. Do not pretend. Write out your prayer. Record what you say to God, in response to his word to you through the passage you have meditated upon. Write what you imagine God to be saying in reply. When we are in a close relationship with a person, we can closely predict what their expected response might be. God has revealed his character to us in the Scriptures. We know sufficient about him to have some ideas concerning the replies we could expect from him. Let it flow back and forth until you feel the dialogue has finished. Keep what you say brief and precise. What you feel God is saying must be consistent with his nature and intentions revealed in Scripture, supremely through the Lord Jesus Christ.

Sharing
This can be done in small groups or in a plenary session. Not every member will be asked to share. Usually it is best to ask only those who received a compelling word from God—something they feel is a strong call to action. The dialogue prayer is not shared.

7. PRAYING THE SCRIPTURES

An ancient form of seeking to hear God speak to us through the Scriptures is attributed to Saint Benedict (c. 480–c. 543). The basic form has been adapted for use by small groups as set out below. Groups which have used this method over a period of time have found it extraordinarily rewarding. This guide is supplied by Tony Neylan.

Method
At the outset the leader describes the sequence below so that all are familiar with what to expect.

1. One person **reads aloud the Scripture text slowly and prayerfully** pausing at the end of each sentence. All can follow in their Bibles or just listen.

This is followed by a period of silence during which all ask themselves, 'Has a particular word or phrase captured me?' That word or phrase is allowed to unhurriedly echo silently within.

The person who read the text now prayerfully speaks aloud the word or phrase which stood out for him/her. Allow a brief silence as the others drink in that word. Other members of the group say their word or phrase, pausing after each person speaks.

2. A second member of the group reads the text slowly and prayerfully.

Then there is a second period of silence. Each rests in the scene and stays with a particular word or phrase.

The second reader now speaks the word or phrase (the same word as previously, or a new word) which he or she found significant. Other members of the group say their word or phrase, pausing after each person speaks.

3. Let the group put away their texts and listen to a third slow and prayerful reading.

This is followed by a third period of silence.

The third reader speaks the word or phrase and follows it with a mini-prayer, making use of the word or the words in the phrase.

4. Remain for a little while in a prayerful silence. Then one person speaks of his or her experience of listening to and praying the above text. Was there something which spoke to them in a particular way? Did the text connect with some aspect of their life? Perhaps there was some sense of a silent and peaceful spirit which cannot be put into words.

Continue around the group. One person speaks at a time, without comment from others and without discussion.

8. RELEVANCE TO CURRENT EVENTS

This Bible study is a good tonic for a group which is becoming too introspective and is having difficulty seeing further than themselves! The leader selects an appropriate Bible passage which is discussed in small groups. (The Head–Heart–and Hand method would be appropriate here.)

Each group is then given a recent newspaper and they are asked to discover in the paper any news item upon which the passage throws light. These questions may be asked:

1. Why is the passage relevant to the news item?
2. Is there something I personally could do about it? Should I be more informed? Would it be costly to my own integrity? Is there a similar situation close at hand?
3. What is the group feeling about the news item(s)? Is there any action for the group to take?

Findings should be shared in a plenary session and, if possible, any suggested course of action should be recorded for the group to see each subsequent week, and plans made to set it in motion.

A fitting close would be to link arms, or join hands, in a circle, symbolising that all members are part of that decision and each has the support of the other. Each may share in prayer of commitment—either in several words or simply one word, 'yes'.

9. ROLE PLAYING THE BIBLE

(Adapted from Robert C Leslie's book, *Sharing Groups in the Church*, Abingdon Press, Nashville, 1971, pages 31–44.)

The Bible is a document of timeless experiences, about which everyone knows something in their own life. By talking about their personal experiences, each individual speaks as an expert about the life that they know best.

1. Introduction
Read the Scripture reference out loud using different voices for different characters where applicable as well as a narrator for continuity, and using modern translations freely.

Thus, even before the study begins, a number of the group members are involved actively in the procedure.

2. In Small Groups
Discuss the associations stirred up in your mind by the passage of Scripture. You are an expert on what associations come to your mind. Share these associations in as personal a way as you can with the study group. (If the group is more than twelve, divide into groups of about six.)

The leader can help set a contemporary note by sharing an association of present-day life and encourage personal associations by group members to the story.

Discuss the following question: 'What do you think this story is really about in terms of relationships between people?'

As the small groups struggle with this question, they begin to sense the contemporary relevance of the Bible. Only at this point is biblical interpretation introduced. There obviously is a place for informed understanding about biblical research. The point is, however, that the Bible often gives examples of life experiences that are typical of any age so that specific contexts are less important than the central message.

Discuss your reaction to . . . Here the leader introduces an aspect of the story which might have been overlooked and, in so doing, may raise a major theological question. This can lead easily into the next issue.

3. Plenary
Discuss together in the large group with the leader what it means to . . . (Here **the main theme of the story** can be discussed).

Robert Leslie gives **two examples** of the method:

The first based upon the story of Joseph and his brothers in Genesis 37:2–8,12,28 illustrates the first steps well. He then chooses Genesis 45:4 ('God sent me before you to preserve life'). He follows this up by asking the large group to discuss 'What it means to live a life directed by God'.

The second focuses upon the story of Zacchaeus in Luke 19:1–9. He begins by asking, 'Have you ever been "up a tree" like Zacchaeus?' Then, 'When have you felt cut off?' The plenary discussion follows naturally: 'When you felt cut off, what helped?'

This discussion leads easily into a consideration of how Jesus went about reaching Zacchaeus and of the meaning of an invitation to have a meal at home.

He then suggests an additional item of discussion:
In the same group of six, discuss the meaning of Luke 19:9 ('And Jesus said to him, "Today salvation has come to this house, since he also is a son of Abraham"').

After the small groups have talked together about the meaning of 'salvation, the leader can interpret salvation as a new kind of relatedness, a relationship that includes both the person-to-person (i.e. Zacchaeus restored to his Jewish community from which he had been alienated) and the person-to-God (wrong relationships made right) dimensions.'

10. SILENT SHARING METHOD

This method is very simple and may be used with youth and adults. It is also a good means of introducing beginners to Bible study.

Preparation required:
Every person needs a Bible.
Choose the passage carefully, according to the needs of the group.
Have a chalkboard or chartpaper on which findings can be recorded.

Method of approach:
Give instructions to the group before indicating the passage they are to read.
Tell the group that, on their own, they are to look for **one verse** which:
  either **'means most to me** in this particular passage',
  or **'sheds new light** on the Christian life',
  or **'is God's message for me** at this moment'.
Inform them that this step is **done individually and in silence**.
Indicate that they will be asked to share their answers when they have finished reading.
Now give the Bible reference to be studied.
Leader should read also and should be prepared to share first, giving the reasons why the verse was chosen.
Others in the group share also. Significant answers may be recorded on a chalkboard or chartpaper.
If some share the same verse, they may have different reasons for choosing it.

General discussion follows.
Conclude with each person praying in silence or audibly for the matters the person to their left shared.

Some suggested Scripture passages:

Romans 12:9–21	Ephesians 4:1–16
Psalm 139:1–10	1 Corinthians 13:1–13
John 15:1–14	Colossians 3:12–17

11. SWEDISH SYMBOL SHARING METHOD

This is also a very effective method for a group not used to Bible study.

Preparation required:
Find a suitable passage. This method is most suited to the teachings of Jesus (particularly parables) and sections of the Epistles.
Ensure Bibles are available for each person.
Make copies of the worksheet. (You have permission to photocopy it for your group.)
If copying facilities are not available draw the symbols, together with each explanation on a chart or the like. Provide sheets of paper for each to draw their own worksheet. They can just draw the symbols (or use numbers) and refer to the chart for the explanations.
Have commentaries, a Bible dictionary and a concordance available for any questions which may arise.
The leader should study the text carefully in advance in order to be better prepared to answer any questions personally.
Have an aid available on which to record the possible summary at the end.

1. Read the passage
The passage chosen is read either aloud by the leader, using expression, or by the group as a whole so that they are all involved right from the beginning.

2. Individual work
Individual study of the text follows for ten minutes with the aid of the symbols below. An explanation of each symbol may be needed.

The relevant verse numbers are written next to the appropriate symbols and a brief note made of the ways in which the symbol relates to the verses chosen.

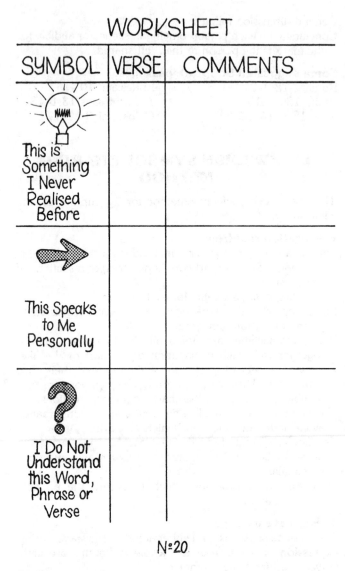

WORKSHEET

SYMBOL	VERSE	COMMENTS
This is Something I Never Realised Before		
This Speaks to Me Personally		
I Do Not Understand this Word, Phrase or Verse		

N°20

3. Group work
The group comes together for all to share their work on one symbol before proceeding to the next. The leader usually shares first.

Notes can be made on a chalkboard or substitute of some of the main findings, particularly under the candle and question mark symbols.

General discussion follows.

In anticipation of some questions not being able to be answered satisfactorily, have commentaries etc. on hand for reference.

Questions still unanswered are noted and answers sought from a specialist prior to the next meeting.

Any person can share what they plan to do, and when, concerning the 'arrows' they noted. The leader should share first.

Prayer should follow for those who shared. Do this in a similar way to that suggested at the conclusion of the Silent Sharing Method.

Some suggested Scripture passages:

Matthew 20:1–16; Luke 7:36–50; Ephesians 2:13–20.

Extension
This method can be extended by adding two more symbols:

I don't really understand this but I want to say yes. There is something about it which seems great!

I have questions or doubts about this, but it moves me. (The word for this symbol is Interrobang. It is a combination of question and exclamation marks.)

This is not new, but it comes through to me now with greater emphasis and meaning.

12. CREATIVE EXPRESSION

Most of the Bible studies in this book have been limited to verbal or written expression. For the more adventurous, creative expression of what each interprets the Bible to be saying can be a very 'freeing' and enriching experience.

We need also to remember that some people have difficulty in reading and expressing themselves verbally. The exploration of other ways of interpretation is an encouragement to them as they feel their contribution is accepted, and they in turn feel themselves accepted as a worthwhile member of the group.

Another advantage of creative expression is that one has to think more deeply about a passage to express it in this way. This work may be done as 'homework' between meetings to allow for more thought, concentration and time.

However, some extremely good work can be done quite quickly. Some people are stimulated by being able to express themselves in a free, non-critical atmosphere.

Here are some ideas (let the Holy Spirit kindle your imagination!)

1. Make a montage or mural
Take a word, 'salvation', for example, and express its meaning by a montage (pictures and words cut from magazines and pasted on paper), or mural. This allows for a diversity of 'sub-headings' which together give a better picture of the totality of the word. Where this is done between meetings, members may like to discuss one another's contribution before beginning the study for the day, which may be on that topic or it may be an expression of what has been previously discussed.

Create a collage using scrap material—cloth, paper, foil, ribbons, laces, herbs, seeds, etc. The collage can be abstract and symbolic (expressing feelings, concepts) or realistic (depicting incidents) in style.

Created by a group on a large scale and combined with montage, painting or weaving, this can be used to decorate a room to create an atmosphere of worship, or express joy, etc.

2. Writing a poem, prose, short story, prayer or song
Alternatives need to be given if possible so that at least one method is always on any one member's level of achievement.

3. Drama
Try some spontaneous 'acting out' of a story; perhaps you could give it a modern setting or take one facet of an incident reported in the Bible. For example, if the group is discussing the healing of the blind man, take it in turns blindfolding one's partner and leading them around the house. Discuss how it felt to be blind and what it felt like to see again.

4. Painting or drawing
Take a theme like 'I am the light of the world' (John 8:12) and illustrate, using paints, soft crayons, felt pens or charcoal.

5. Write a brief play or a musical drama
This may be done as a group effort or by two people working on it together.

6. Other ideas
These include making a mobile, clay modelling, abstract modelling from bits and pieces, and writing or finding a song that expresses the theme of a passage.

If working systematically through a book of the Bible, Creative Expression, together with a variety of other Bible study methods, will give a freshness of approach and a new vitality to the group. It is important to remember that we do not have to be artists to paint. What is wanted is the expression of each person's thoughts. To expect masterpieces destroys the whole purpose of freedom of expression.

Encouragement needs to be given to members to 'try'. Most will hesitate, especially the first few times, but it will not be long before many talents will be appearing which may have been either dormant or undiscovered.

Chapter 13
Praying Together

Intercession is the most promising way to meet our neighbours, and corporate prayer, offered in the Name of Christ, the purest form of fellowship.[1]

In small groups people are exploring the meaning and purpose of prayer. They are rediscovering the power released through prayer. God's promises are being taken seriously. Barren stereotyped procedures—which have straitjacketed much of our small group prayer—are being discarded, and new and exciting skills in communicating with God are being developed. The power of the Holy Spirit, in his role as the divine enabler in prayer, is being experienced anew.

I keep receiving reports from many countries around the world of new Small Group prayer movements amongst both Protestants and Catholics, some existing within the established church structures, others not. Sometimes it may be just two or three concerned people meeting spontaneously.

Many prayer cells meet across denominational barriers. There are many Catholic parishes across my own State where over fifty intercessory prayer cells meet weekly—some pray for me regularly.

The experience of the church is that there is no real progress in true Christianity without prayer. Periods of spiritual power in the church have been preceded by and sustained by great prayer. No limit can be put to its power. I find that many people really want to pray but do not know how. Most are very limited in their prayer experience. For many, the extent of their learning in prayer has been listening to public prayers, or the reciting by rote of prayers they learnt in their childhood. Often people meeting in small groups for Bible study, sharing and prayer are aware that their prayer time is ingrown and lifeless.

In Small Groups we have an ideal situation to provide help for people in personal and corporate prayer.

I have set out in the next two chapters a variety of methods to enable group prayer to become more dynamic.

WHY PRAY WITH OTHERS

There are many reasons why we should pray with others. The three I suggest are: Jesus prayed with others; the early church practised it; we experience untold advantages in praying together.

Christ taught us to pray individually in isolation and he did so himself. But that was only one aspect of his prayer life. Even when he withdrew to a quiet place, this was not necessarily for solitary prayer. As he was praying alone the disciples were with him (Luke 9:18). Peter, James and John were with him on the high mountain (Luke 9:28) and accompanied him into the Garden of Gethsemane. To record his prayer in Mark 14:33, they must have overheard it. The Lord also prayed habitually with the apostles. If we are to be his disciples, to 'learn' from him, we must pray alone and we must pray with others.

From the very beginning the apostolic church was a community at prayer. It was upon a company at prayer that the Holy Spirit was poured out on the Day of Pentecost (Acts 1:14). The first converts 'joined with the other believers in regular attendance at the apostles' teaching sessions and at the breaking of bread services and in prayer'. In the crisis of persecution, the assembled church spontaneously resorted to prayer (Acts 4:23–31). When Peter was imprisoned and threatened with execution, 'many were gathered for a prayer meeting' in the house of Mary, mother of John Mark (Acts 12:12). Barnabas and Paul were dedicated for their special task following a time of prayer and fasting by a small group of five church leaders in Antioch (Acts 13:1–3).

We experience advantages in praying together because Jesus said that the mind and will of God can come to us more clearly when we pray with others (even though he insisted that we find solitude and be alone with God).

If two of you agree on earth about anything they ask, it will be done for them by my Father in Heaven. For where two or three are gathered in my name, there am I in the midst of them. (Matthew 18:19–20).

When we pray alone, it is difficult to sift our selfish desires from our real needs and our own will from God's intentions. So when we pray with others as a group, we have the advantage of testing our assessment of God's will against the group's insights.

From that same passage in Matthew, we deduce the greatest advantage of praying together—the promised presence of Christ in the midst of that fellowship. All through the ages when Christians have assembled for prayer with a common purpose and a deep sense of unity, they have been aware of the unseen Presence and have encountered the living Lord.

There is also a deeper joy in praying together, an added vitality, a plus difficult to define. It is rather like the difference between eating your meal alone and sharing in a party feast. Eating together is not the same as eating in solitude; the something more is the company, the fellowship. So it is with prayer.[2]

THE PERFECT PATTERN FOR PRAYER

In answer to his disciples' request, Jesus gave to them and to us what has become known as the Lord's Prayer. The pattern it sets out is very simple, but very comprehensive. It is at one and the same time a prayer to use by itself and a pattern for all prayer. Many small groups are finding an enriching experience as they study this prayer in depth.

Some using a resource such as *The Plain Man Looks at The Lord's Prayer* by William Barclay, have taken a section at a time to expand their understanding of prayer. Others have benefited from paraphrasing the prayer individually or as a group. The pattern which the prayer follows has been studied by some groups, which then follow this outline for private and group prayer experiences over a period to give direction to their own prayer. Maxie Dunnam's *Workbook of Living Prayer* (Upper Room, Nashville), suggests two seven-day segments working through the Lord's Prayer, and then using the pattern as a base for further growth.

William Barclay says, 'The pattern of the Lord's Prayer must be the pattern of all prayer, for it begins by giving God His proper place, and it goes on to take life's past, present and future to God, the Father, Son and Holy Spirit.'

Helmut Thielicke in *The Prayer that Spans the World* likens the Lord's Prayer to the rainbow colours of the spectrum. He says, 'The whole light of life is captured in this rainbow of seven petitions'. He gives another refreshing interpretation of this greatest of Christian prayer resources. Numerous other books are on the market to assist the group in plumbing the depth of this immortal prayer.

THE FORMS OF PRAYER

The study of the Lord's Prayer will open up the order in which Christians have found it helpful to pray. It may help to deal with them here and make some comments which are applicable to prayer in small groups.

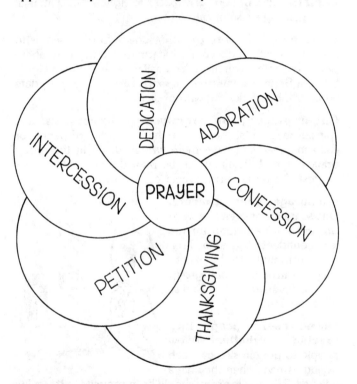

Adoration is the rarest of all prayers. In this we do not even say thank you, we simply adore. We think of the greatness of God—how incredible that he should bother to hear us at all! Dwell on the person of God, his love and his holiness.

It often helps to view a scene from a mountain look-out. Stand on a cliff overlooking the sea, or concentrate upon a flower. A picture of these can be used as an aid.

An appropriate passage of Scripture from the Psalms, such as 111 and 121, Isaiah chapters 6 and 40, or others describing Christ, his nature and purpose such as Philippians 2:5–11 and Colossians 1:15–23 can be meditated upon, collectively or individually, leading to adoration.

It is unnatural for this prayer to be prayed in isolation from other forms. But it is a good discipline for spiritual uplift, even in a group, to use it sometimes.

Confession in group prayer is best undertaken in silence. Do not hurry this. Allow a time to recall past failures. Encourage the group to be specific. Bidding prayers can help: 'Think of a relationship with another that you may not have taken the initiative to heal,' or 'Think of words you may have spoken which have not been suitable for the occasion,' or 'What action spoilt your witness last week/ yesterday?' Assure them of forgiveness as they have asked for forgiveness in the name of Jesus; quote a promise such as John 1:9. Encourage the group to accept by faith, apart from feelings, what God offers to them by his grace. In silence, or audibly, let them then praise him in general terms.

In our prayer workshops we have found it helpful to have participants write the sins they confess on a piece of paper. Then, as an act of faith, they draw a cross over what they have written and tear the slip into small pieces. A paper cup is passed around each group to receive the pieces. As it is passed around the person passing it says to the next person: 'As you have confessed your sins to God, in the name of Jesus you are forgiven.' On occasions, we have completed the time of confession and assurance of forgiveness by placing the contents of the paper cups in a large metal container and sending one person outside to burn them. The person has returned saying, 'The records of our sin are completely consumed in the fire of God's love in Christ. Praise be to God!' The groups reply, 'Praise be to God! His grace is sufficient for all our sins! Blessed be His Holy name!'

The general confession (Psalm 51), particularly in a modern translation, is a useful form of group confession. To paraphrase 1 John 1:9 individually can help confirm the reality of God's love and forgiveness.

Thanksgiving is the natural step to follow an experience of the certainty of forgiveness, through God's grace in Jesus. Again help people to be specific. Bidding prayers can further help as people recall particular experiences of God's goodness. For example: 'Reflect on persons, situations, experiences you can be genuinely grateful for at home this week,' or 'Can you recall a time when you have been specially loved or had the opportunity to show love since we last met?' or 'Can you remember the gratitude you felt as you lay down to rest after a hard day's work?' Health, friends, books, fun, work, life's challenges (and a thousand others!) are all topics for thanksgiving.

Thanksgiving should also include expectations of future fulfilment as an affirmation of our faith in God's ability to answer our prayers.

It will also go beyond ourselves to thanking God for the blessings others have received in the group and beyond the group to our friends and widening out to world situations.

Petition is the next step. W E Sangster says 'Keep petition in a minor place. Nothing more reveals the juvenility of our prayers if we pray with persistence and passion only when we want something for ourselves.'[3]

Again we should be specific. It is helpful to have each member write out a prayer of petition as a response to a meaningful Bible study segment. These can then be prayed silently or audibly around the group in turn. Each can be followed by members putting their hand on the persons next to them and praying, 'Lord, grant . . . 's prayer.' Some find it helpful to keep a confidential spiritual diary, in which they record prayer responses to significant learning experiences.

Intercession, or praying for others, is selfless prayer. In it we exercise one of the most sacred aspects of the ministry to which we are all called. This is our 'priestly' role. We become 'bridge-builders' between people in their need and God, the source of undeserved favour. A concerned person listens for expressed needs rather than inventing their own assessment of another's needs. Again prayers need to be specific. Avoid allowing the gathering of information about others for prayer to degenerate into gossip.

In a number of groups we have found it helpful to keep a group prayer journal. In a notebook we wrote on one page the date and items for prayer, keeping the opposite page open to record future answers to these prayers. This not only prompts specific regular intercession, but engenders specific thanksgiving as answers to prayer are noted from one meeting to another.

In our networks of cells, a weekly list of parish and community needs was provided by our prayer convenor for distribution to each group. A copy was supplied to each group member, with space provided to add additional points. These were then added to in the various groups.

Dedication is an aspect which follows naturally after intercession. This is the 'Lord here am I, send me' response to human need or 'with eyes wide open to your mercy I present myself to you, Lord, as the least I can do. Use me as you will'. Sincere dedication can be an awesome thing (Acts 4:29–31).

SOME KEYS FOR PRAYER CELLS

Limit the size of your group. Six to eight is sufficient if all have a strong sense of call to pray.

Teach people how to pray. Include a 'Lord, teach us to pray' segment. Endeavour to learn something new about prayer each time you meet. You will not need to spend long. Study a Scripture passage, an extract from an appropriate book or a hymn dealing with prayer.

Gather prayer points from your group for praise and special needs. List these on a chart, on slips of paper for each member and have them written down in the group prayer journal. They should be prayed along with prayer requests from the parish prayer convenor.

Encourage short prayers.
One sentence or even one word prayers will be helpful for the less confident, and as a discipline in thought to the experienced. Introduce your group to Conversational Prayer (Chapter 15).

Do not coerce people into praying verbally. Allow people to pray in silence, each saying 'Amen' when they have finished. The whole group should be introduced to the value of times of silence for meditation, waiting, time to think, reflecting and responding to God personally.

Introduce variety into meetings. Group experiences should not be dull and uninteresting. Vary the meeting format. Introduce new prayer methods. Use a guest speaker, a recording or use visual aids in the 'how to pray' segment of your meeting. Arrange for an occasional combined meeting with another group.

Keep a balance in prayer. Do not over-emphasise intercession to the neglect of adoration (reading or singing a psalm could help), confession (usually in silence) or thanksgiving (spend much time here).

Pray positive prayers. Negativity indicates doubt and lack of faith. Positive prayers believe 'mountains' can be moved by a God who 'specialises in things thought impossible'. And it only requires a small seed of faith for that to happen!

Make your groups Christ-centred. Focus on the Living Word, the Risen Victorious Christ, ever present when his people gather. Worship, affirm and love him. In each meeting explore some relevant aspect, no matter how briefly, of the written Word.

Be punctual. Start and finish on time.

Allocate your meeting time. A simple plan is to spend one-third of the time in learning about prayer, one-third for sharing and for introducing and receiving prayer requests, and one-third for prayer.

Pastor each other. Spend time getting to know each other and repeat this for new members. Care for each other in prayerful and practical ways. Follow up on absent members.

Seek to develop a vital group. Spend time getting to know each other and encourage honest, open sharing. Pray and work at becoming a fellowship of love where people feel accepted and significant.

Put legs under your prayers. Make yourselves available to be part of the answer to your prayers. True intercessory prayer should lead to corporate and personal action in meeting the spiritual and practical needs of others.

Organise some informal groups just to make contact with others, possibly those being prayed for, to develop friendships. Building relationships with non-Christians is an important aspect of pre-evangelism. (See Contact Groups, Chapter 2, page 16 and Chapter 8, page 75.)

Develop Prayer Triplets. They can be sub-groups of a prayer cell or quite independent. (See Chapter 1, page 9, and Chapter 2, page 18.)

THE PLACE OF THE BIBLE IN PRAYER

The Bible has an important role to play in personal and corporate prayer. One person has said it comes alive as the Word of God when read and responded to in the context of prayer. The Bible should be the heart of the corporate life of the group.

A small group which hopes to grow in its prayer life must have a good grasp of biblical teaching to make a firm base for their prayers. The purpose, potential and possibilities of the Christian's prayers are arrived at by studying God's revealed Word on the matter. The many books on the subject only supplement this data.

The greatest contribution the Bible makes to prayer is that it reveals to us the true nature of the Divine Person to whom we offer our prayers. Even groups which have prayer as their main aim seldom, if ever, maintain real vitality without regular and frequent reference to and meditation upon the Bible.

The Bible is a treasure house of written prayers from the stories of some of the greatest persons in prayer the world shall ever know. Jesus, the patriarchs, the prophets, the psalmists and the apostles all have left us an eternal heritage of prayers prayed in real life situations. Here is a sample of some of these prayer resources the Bible provides:

Prayer for preservation and protection—Numbers 10:35–36

Prayer for a sick child—2 Samuel 12

Prayer for understanding of affliction—Samuel 21:1–12

Prayer in national danger—2 Chronicles 14:11

Prayer as intercession—Job 42:7–10

Prayer for preservation here and hereafter—Psalm 16

Prayer for confession and a broken heart—Psalm 51

Prayer for peace—Isaiah 26

Prayer for the oppressed—Lamentations 5

Prayer as taught by Christ—Matthew 6:1–13

Prayer habits of Christ—Mark 1:35

The intercessory prayer of Jesus—John 17

THE ROLE OF THE HOLY SPIRIT
IN PRAYER

The Holy Spirit is God at work in us in the here and now. He is our life. Prayer comes alive not because we have correct understanding of the theology of prayer, nor because we have developed some special techniques or because of our regular disciplined application to its pursuit, but essentially because God is in it. The Holy Spirit is the key to vital prayer life, individually or corporately.

And in the same way—by our faith—the Holy Spirit helps us with our daily problems and in our praying. For we don't even know what we should pray for nor how to pray as we should; but the Holy Spirit prays for us with such feeling that it cannot be expressed in words. And the Father who knows all hearts knows, of course, what the Spirit is saying as he pleads for us in harmony with God's own will. (Romans 8:26–27)

There can be no activity of prayer with any significance if the Holy Spirit is not at its heart.

References

(1) Dietrich Bonhoeffer, *The Cost of Discipleship* (SCM Press).
(2) Stephen Winward, *Teach Yourself to Pray* (Hodder & Stoughton), p. 86.

Chapter 14
Creative Ways to Pray Together

Pray in your own way! There are twelve gates into the holy city and a thousand different doors to prayer. When we pray we are entering a vast expanse of truth which leaves room for much experiment and many approaches.[1]

To communicate with our Heavenly Father who loves us so deeply should be a wonderful experience. God has given humankind the gift of creativity and imagination and this rich endowment should be used to make prayer a lively, varied, satisfying activity.

These methods and ideas are given as suggestions which should be adapted to each situation. Not everyone will find each item helpful. Therefore they will need to be used with discretion.

SPOKEN PRAYERS

Conversational prayer offers a creative dimension to group prayer experiences, so Chapter 15 deals entirely with this method.

Enabling spontaneous prayer
Spontaneous spoken prayer may be a frightening experience especially for newcomers to group prayer. Some people like to have time to 'think out' their prayer if praying in a group with others, while others may be so afraid of their own voice that they never have the courage to speak. As an aid to spontaneous praying, a leader may encourage members by asking the group for a few suggestions of people or topics to include in the prayer, and then formulate these into prayer. Alternatively, the leader may open and

close in prayer and ask the group members to mention their topic or person for prayer. The leader should try to keep the prayer simple in order to encourage others to understand that praying aloud is something anyone can do. We need to remember also that spontaneous praying is a basis for an adult relationship with God and not all people have attained this maturity.

Chain prayer

Chain prayer involves each person praying in order around the group. Its main drawback is that people can feel forced to pray, resulting in embarrassment. However this can be avoided by stressing the validity of silent prayer. Those who wish to pray in silence can simply touch the next person when they have completed their silent prayer, or if they do not wish to pray. Chain prayer can be used for each segment of prayer, going around the circle once or twice for the period of Adoration, then around the chain again for Thanksgiving and so on. Confession is generally in silence with each indicating when they have concluded. It is often used for one segment only with a different procedure for the other aspects.

One word bombardments

These are helpful in encouraging those who are new to group prayer. Each spends a brief period in silent reflection and follows this with a prayer focused into one word or a brief phrase. For example, in Adoration, time may be spent in meditation upon an attribute of God or the promise of Christ's presence in the group. The group responds as each feels moved, with 'Jesus', 'Father', 'Our Lord', 'You are here', 'We adore you', etc. This is especially helpful for Adoration and Thanksgiving. When used for Intercession the person's name only is used, or the specific situation mentioned.

I have sometimes photocopied a hymn for all to sing, which deals with the nature of God. As it is sung each person underlines words relating to God. After the hymn, in a spirit of prayer, each says one of these words with feeling, one at a time.

Litany response

In this a prepared prayer is used with a copy for each member to follow. The leader reads brief portions which are followed with prepared responses for the whole group to read. These are readily available in older or modern forms. Copies of the Book of Common Prayer or other equivalents could be borrowed, or photocopies of certain sections made. A number of hymns, old and modern, lend themselves to this use, e.g. 'Jesus, with Thy Church Abide' and 'Saviour, when in dust to Thee'. The chorus of others can be used as the response, or the last line or two of appropriate verses adapted. Some groups write their own litany as the follow-up from a study, which is then used to conclude the group meeting.

Bidding prayers

The leader needs a book of prayers prepared for this purpose or a list is compiled, either by the leader beforehand, or by the group during the meeting. The leader then bids, or invites the group, 'Let us remember God's goodness to us', or 'Let us pray for our government', which is followed by silent or vocal response by the members. The leader may pray a brief prayer on the subject before moving on to the next point. The leadership can be shared with any number of members, each taking a different aspect.

Open-eyed prayer

We have been taught to close our eyes in prayer to help our concentration. It has become a rigid ritual unfortunately, 'All eyes closed . . . '. Occasionally try keeping your eyes open and focusing on a symbol, or worship centre or picture of the creation, and respond in prayer. This works especially well when the group is able to meet in a bushland, open country or garden setting or overlooking the sea.

Often when we discuss persons and situations for intercession in order to prepare a list of requests to follow, the time quickly slips away and someone in a surprised voice says, 'Oh! We have run out of time and will not have time for intercession!' It does well to affirm where God was during the conversation! He heard every word. A brief prayer acknowledging God's presence during the 'open-eyed' conversation and committing to him all that was mentioned can then be prayed without the group feeling their concerned conversation was not heard by God.

WRITTEN PRAYER

Group prayer is an art which many find difficult to launch into. Older folk particularly, who have not prayed openly, find it a traumatic experience. Beginners in corporate prayer often benefit from writing out a prayer and then reading it when the group prays. A natural way to do this is in response to a Bible study period. Participants write their own prayers, which they then read in the group. However, people should still be given the opportunity to not participate.

Some wise leaders have suggested to a person who is experiencing this difficulty that they prepare a prayer at home, which they may be asked to read to open the group or in the collective prayer sessions.

Paraphrasing

Paraphrasing traditional prayers or hymns is a useful exercise. A prayer either from the Bible, a book of prayers or a hymn-prayer, is rewritten by each individual. It is kept simple by using everyday words. A dictionary for each participant will help in putting technical words in a way each would say them. With long prayers or hymns, assign segments around the group. This work can also be done as a home assignment. The paraphrases are then read in group prayers.

Rewriting the 23rd Psalm

Psalm 23 would be the best known of all psalms, but it is written in terms with which we are not very familiar in our nuclear age. Shepherd and sheep had a close relationship and that association had far more meaning when the psalm was written. Try rewriting the psalm in the way you would say it in the colloquial language of your culture, using comparisons with which people are familiar. In *God is for Real, Man*, by Carl Burke (Fontana, 1967), the paraphrase of the 23rd Psalm says that the Lord is like a 'probation officer', a term that had special relevance for kids from the streets. Perhaps terms such as 'navigator', 'companion', etc. might be used. The idea is for the participants to choose a word that is their model of God. Having done that, move through the psalm, changing the ideas to whatever is relevant, keeping in mind the picture of God that was chosen. Then allow the psalm to be a prayer of affirmation and confidence in God.

Personalise the Lord's Prayer

While recognising that the Lord's Prayer is given to us in the plural so that it embraces all peoples, a fresh approach may be taken when we pause to personalise it. Take all words written in the plural and substitute 'My Father', and 'me' throughout, and replace old-fashioned words such as 'art', 'hallowed', etc. with words current in the vocabulary of today. After having discussed the changes in each group, then each quietly prays the prayer by themselves.

Dialogue prayer

This is a way of truly holding a conversation with God. Feelings are expressed without pretence. Each person writes out a prayer in the form of a dialogue with God, recording what he/she says to God together with what is imagined God is saying in reply.

When we are in a close relationship with a person we can almost predict what their expected response might be. God has revealed his character to us in the Scriptures. We know sufficient about him to have some ideas concerning the replies we could expect from him.

The conversation flows back and forth, until the person feels the dialogue has finished. Each segment of the dialogue is kept brief and precise. What each person imagines God to be saying must be consistent with his nature and intentions revealed in Scripture and supremely through the Lord Jesus Christ. Therefore dialogue prayer is generally best used with other than beginners.

THE USE OF SILENCE

Silence plays an important part in private and corporate prayer. People need encouragement and help in spending more time in silent meditation and contemplation. 'Be still and **know** that I am God' is a wise word for busy people in the twentieth century. **Planned silence** should be a regular part of all group prayer. Until the group develops an ability to use the silences, the time should be kept reasonably short. Suggestions may need to be fed in from time to time.

Some help should be given in using **unplanned silence**. When the group is praying verbally and a silence occurs, teach the group to continue to use the time in non-verbal prayer or listen for the voice of God speaking to them.

TOUCHING OR PHYSICAL CONTACT

Most of us know the power of touch—a friendly slap on the back; a hug; a warm handshake; the gentle, loving touch of our closest loved one; a child's arms thrown around us in a spontaneous welcome; a concerned friend's arms around our shoulder in a time of distress.

Jesus and his disciples touched people to heal and bless them. His followers have found the human touch in prayer to be important. Some will have reservations and others real problems in being touched by another, but it is often very supportive to hold a person's hand or put our hand on their shoulder as we pray for him or her. As in Jesus' ministry, somehow power is transmitted person to person by touch.

Laying on of hands

This is an ancient tradition practised by Jesus, the early church, and used frequently since, for setting apart persons for special ministries and for healing. In small groups it is commonly used when praying for one who has openly expressed a deep desire for special prayer for personal renewal, or for healing, or a fuller awareness of the Spirit, and to acknowledge special gifts or to confirm a person's call to a specific task. The  members of the group gather around the person and lay their hands on his head, shoulders or back.

Sometimes 'laying on of hands' by **proxy** has great meaning. A person in the group 'stands-in' for one who is not present, the others laying their hands on him. The 'proxy' person seeks to become one with the person for whom prayer is being offered.

Huddles

These can give a sense of concern for each member and deepen the sense of unity. All stand in a tight circle with shoulders touching. Arms can be placed on each other's shoulders or around waists, or hands can be held.

Cradling

This can be a supportive caring experience for someone who has shared deeply and seeks the group's care and concern in their problem. The person lies on his or her back on the floor. The group gathers around, then lifts the person to waist height and rocks him or her back and forth like a baby. Prayers may be spoken for the person while he or she is cradled. Usually a minimum of four persons on either side is needed. The process concludes by standing the person back on their feet.

BODY POSITION

Kneeling

This has traditionally been a common pose for prayer. It is an indication of humility and submission to our Sovereign God. For physical reasons not everyone will be able to kneel and when it is done for long periods some will find it more difficult than others. The pose can be varied by facing inward during most of the prayer period and changing to face outward during the period of intercession, as an indication of concern for others outside the immediate group. Most people will find it helpful to have a chair or table to rest against if the period is to be prolonged.

Lying prostrate

Lying face down on the floor is seldom done in prayer today, but it was a common pose in the Bible as an indication of complete submission to God. Young people have used this in recent times with benefit.

Reclining

Reclining is a relaxed position. A chapel in a retreat centre I visited had an inspiring art piece in the ceiling. The absence of any seating and a carpeted floor was a natural setting for this relaxed form of meditation and prayer.

Try this on a warm, clear night outdoors. Look up at the stars and the moon. The vastness of creation and the might of our Creator God becomes more real.

The wheel position

This is a more structured form of reclining for a small group to experience a restful unity. The group lie on the floor to form a wheel with heads facing inwards, each person being a spoke! Hands are raised and grasped and prayer made together with a deep sense of oneness.

Creative movement and dancing

These are used to amplify a prayer through body motion. The group stand at more than arm's length from each other with eyes closed. As the leader slowly recites the Lord's Prayer or another appropriate prayer or hymn, each expresses their thoughts by appropriate body movement.

Dancing has played an important part in the worship of God. The Old Testament tells of Miriam and the women with timbrels, dancing and singing praise to God (Exodus 15:20,21); 'David danced before the Lord' (2 Samuel 6:14); and the Psalms contain exhortations to 'Praise his name with dancing' (Psalm 149:3) and 'praise him with timbrel and dance' (Psalm 150:4). Not everyone will feel sufficiently uninhibited to participate in dance, so it will need to be used with sensitivity and as an optional prayer response.

Some groups play appropriate recorded hymns, songs or music to which each individual can make their own prayer response combined with dance.

FANTASISING

This is a creative use of our God-given gift of imagination in prayer. Taking a stationary, relaxed body position using creative movement, each person seeks to identify with the creation by playing a **fantasy role**. While background music is playing and eyes are closed, each imagines that he or she is a mountain stream, a cloud, a flower, a water-lily on a pond, a leaf or a tree. After a few minutes prayers are offered, stemming from the feelings experienced.

Fantasy trips

These are used regularly in therapy and can be put to good use by a sensitive leader in group prayer. We have found it particularly helpful in Confession or in Thanksgiving. Each sits or lies (if there is room) in a comfortable relaxed manner with eyes closed. Through centring their thoughts on their breathing, they seek to get in touch with themselves. Slow deep breathing helps the relaxation. After a brief period the leader asks each to imagine that they are lying relaxed on a carpet. It is a magic carpet which slowly lifts them up and gently conveys them through past events and experiences.

The leader reinforces this movement backward into the past, by asking: 'What were you doing before you came tonight? Was there anything for which you can be genuinely thankful? Where were you today? Who were you with? What did you do? What did you see? Can you recall something for which you can praise God?' Encourage them to begin by going back over the last few days. Then let them go back as far as they wish into their past till they recall a person, an event for which they can be truly thankful to God. The 'trip' needs to be completed with a bringing back to the present and a brief period of relaxation for de-roling.

When used for Confession, a segment for specific handing over of guilt and acceptance of forgiveness by faith must be followed by assurance of forgiveness, together with some reassuring acts within the group, each to the other. A brief period of sharing can conclude the experience, which will give opportunity to share any disturbing memories or feelings and inspiring or enriching recollections. The sharing could be introduced with: 'How do you feel after that experience?' Most leaders need training in this form of prayer.

PRAYER CONTRACTS

Too often group prayer is vague, especially when it comes to promises to pray for one another. The small group movement in Pittsburgh, USA, known as the Pittsburgh Experiment, initiated '30 Day Experiments' as one of its main emphases for individual and group prayer. One of their pamphlets explains:

> A thirty day experiment is simply this. We suggest that no matter what the problem or concern might be, if a person will only pray every day, as often as he thinks about it, or feels tension arise within himself, then God will help him to understand the situation and the other parties involved. We have seen this work in hundreds of situations. I have yet to see anyone who has been faithful and honest in daily prayer for thirty days, end up with their prayers unanswered.

The group can enter into a contract with a person to pray for any specific period: 7 days, 14 days or 30 days. It avoids the vague promises of support and encourages concentrated prayer for a specific period, at the end of which progress can be shared.

It often enriches this experience for the person who is the focus for this prayer, and at least one other who has contracted to pray, to keep journals for the period and then compare notes at the end. I frequently do this when counselling someone who is seeking guidance or trying to find their way through a difficult situation. Those apparently small messages from God in everyday life, so often passing unnoticed, are captured. Together, over an extended period, they often lead to clear insights.

PRAYER AIDS

Small cards

These could be approximately 130 mm by 80 mm (standard file cards are useful). They can be written on without needing a support and fit into the back of an average size Bible. Use them for each person to note the intercessory prayer requests for the day. Each may send their card around the group so that others may write a signed prayer request on it and return it to the owner as a reminder throughout the week to pray for the group. It has a variety of other uses.

Prayer record books

We found it useful to use a cheap school exercise book to record the requests for prayer in an intercessory prayer group. A separate page was kept for each meeting with the opposite page kept free for recording progress in answers to prayer at future meetings. From time to time, it was an inspiring experience of thanksgiving and praise to look back over the months and recall God's answers to our prayers.

Hymn book

A hymn book is a rich prayer resource for private and corporate prayer. For the non-conformist churches it is their prayer book. Many hymns are written in the form of a prayer. Use them for reciting together or silent meditation. Sing or read them as prayers. Let the leader slowly and prayerfully read a verse or so of a hymn of 'adoration' to commence the prayer time. In a time of 'confession' each may read in silence a hymn of 'repentance and forgiveness'. Sing together a hymn of thanksgiving. Paraphrase a hymn, putting it into your own words. The group members could each take a book and find a prayer that is meaningful for them. A hymn could be chosen for the group, and members asked to choose a verse as their special prayer for that day.

Books of prayers

There are many books of ancient and contemporary prayers which can be read or studied or paraphrased by the group.

Newspapers

These are useful in making intercession specific. Give each member a news page of a recent daily newspaper. Allow time for them to select a news item for prayer and underline the main points. Each gives a summary of the news item which is followed by group prayer. Or each can write a prayer in response to the news item they chose. These are then read in the group prayer time.

A variation would be to give each person a newspaper and ask them to choose an item that is of interest. (It may be a story, report, advertisement or cartoon.) Now ask, what is the relation between the article you have chosen and God?

Having established the connection, form a prayer around the theme. For example, with an advertisement designed to sell cars, the prayer may include thanks for all those involved in the production and design of cars, for those working on the repetitive production line; for migrant workers; for those injured in producing vehicles; a prayer for responsibility for those who drive; and intercession for those who have been injured in a car accident. These could be made more specific. We can pray for a realisation of our own responsibilities on social issues. It is not enough to pray that there will be no strikes—think about what causes are involved.

Symbols

These have played an important part in giving a common focus, stimulating reflection and facilitating a worship response to God. A cross, candle, loaf of bread, chalice, jug of water, open Bible, vacant chair, a simple drawing of a fish or dove, and other traditional symbols can be useful aids if they are varied.

The Creation

The world around us is rich with things to inspire our prayers. Ask each member of the group to bring some natural object with them to the next meeting. (This could be a flower, a leaf, a piece of bark, a piece of driftwood, a stone, etc.) Alternatively, if it is a day meeting (and depending on the locality) each person could go out and find an article. In any case, they are asked to conceal it so the others do not see what they have. Arrange the group in pairs, numbering A and B. Then ask A to close his/her eyes while B puts the 'found object' he/she has brought into A's hand. The article is felt by A, who may smell it or even taste it, while trying to guess what it is. When that has been done, A then gives to B what he/she has brought.

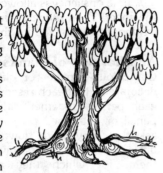

While each partner still holds the article which the other person has brought, ask each to try and imagine that piece of nature in its original state. Then ask: 'Does it remind you of God in any way?' Following a short period of silence, ask each to use their picture image as the basis for a personal prayer.

If the object brought to the group was a rock it may have reminded the person of the strength and stability of Christ's love—'He is my rock and fortress', etc. Members may like to share with one another their thoughts which led to the foundation of their prayer. The objects can then be placed together as a focus for worship.

Alternatively, posters of different parts of creation, a montage of cuttings from magazines of suitable pictures and words can be displayed and responded to.

If the group is meeting in a room looking out onto a garden or a wider view, get members to locate parts of the creation before them with which they identify. Some reactions might be: 'I would like to be more responsive to the Spirit, as those leaves are to the wind', or 'May my life become more beautiful like that flower', or 'Thank you for the silent growth that is taking place in your creation and in my life'.

THE BIBLE

The Bible will be our most useful aid to group prayer. Here we find many prayers of the patriarchs, prophets, psalmists, our Lord and the apostles. The Christian's understanding of prayer comes primarily from this book. Studies of the teaching and example of Jesus and the apostles will be an important aid to group prayer. The recorded prayers can be paraphrased, personalised or used as they are.

GENERAL

What are the words saying?
Keep alert for music, songs, an excerpt from a book, television or radio commercial, poem, etc. which may either form a prayer in itself or be an excellent opener for one. As an example of an 'opener' to prayer, play a record of 'My Favourite Things' from *Sound of Music*. Ask each person to list about ten of their favourite things and then move into a prayer of Thanksgiving. Or it may be a topical song chosen, leading to prayers of intercession.

God in everyday things
There are reminders of God all around us. Choose four objects and suggest they be the basis for prayer, or ask each person to contribute an object. One may choose a pair of glasses, a dictionary, map of the world or a coin, and the prayer could be 'Enlarge my vision, O Lord, to see meaning in the ordinary and the profound, and extend my vision to perceive the needs of others around me. Remind me there is a tangible way of helping those less fortunate than I am'.

Share a prayer
Ask each to choose as a partner the person sitting next to them. Explain that they will be given 30 seconds to think of someone, or some need in the world, for which they would like to pray. (This could be varied by asking them to think of a problem which they would not mind sharing with their partner, or to think of someone who means a lot to them.) Allow about 30 seconds for each to explain to their partner the prayer need.

Remind the group of Jesus' promise that where two or three are gathered in his name there he is in the midst (Matthew 18:20). Then say that in the silence of the next 30 seconds each will be asked to remember that promise and to pray for the need that their partner has just shared with them.

Appreciation of love
Using the chart No. 22, each person thinks carefully and tries to picture in their minds the names and places that immediately come to view. They describe the place briefly, be it home, town, church, bushland, etc. The same is done with the animals they remember. They then recall those who have loved them and those they have loved.

They use their lists as they pray quietly, thanking God for

THANKYOU GOD FOR YOUR LOVE AS I SEE IT EXPRESSED ALL AROUND ME			
A Place I have loved...	An animal who loved me...	People who have loved me...	People I Love...

Diagram № 22

the love they have experienced in the past, present and the future. (Prior to this last step, each group member might like to share one point from their list.)

A good introduction to this method would be to play the record 'Where is Love', from the musical *Oliver*. There are an abundance of relevant songs on this theme.

Expressing thanksgiving

Either provide for each member a copy of the following chart (No. 23) or a sheet of paper on which they can make their own copy by hand.

THANK YOU GOD FOR THE GOOD THINGS OF......(Date)			
Good Things I Did...	People I Enjoyed Being With...	Good Experiences (things that happened to me)	Good Reminders of you (God)...

Diagram № 23

A time of silence is allowed while each person completes the sheet. Then suggest that each rereads what they have written, thanking God for their recalled experiences.

Another way of thanksgiving

Cut coloured paper or gift wrapping in rectangles and decorate so that each resembles a parcel. Distribute one to each person (together with a pencil or felt-tipped pen) and ask that they write down a gift/s which God has given them, for which they are especially grateful, and which they do not mind the other group members seeing. Then using a board, ask each to come forward and place the gift parcel on it (with pin or masking tape). The leaders may ask if the gifts suggest a prayer.

The members may then move to a time of Thanksgiving, or one member may praise, using the names on the gifts.

Removing mountains

Ask the group to look up Matthew 17:20. Remind members that Jesus placed an emphasis on faith as the condition of appropriating God's love and power. Prepare several small cards (about 130 mm by 80 mm) and give one to each person. Explain that they are to write on the card the 'mountain' which they are facing at the moment (they can state it in very general terms if they wish). Point out that this will become known to the group later. Their name is not to be on the paper. When each has finished, the cards are collected, shuffled and distributed to the members.

Silently the person reads the other person's 'mountain' and prays for the mountain to be removed. Then each card is read aloud, the group pausing after the reading of each for quiet prayer.

Where the group has developed a fair degree of trust, names can be placed on the card and the card handed to the person on their left for prayer. The card is then kept by that person as a reminder for continuing prayer until the next meeting.

Reference
(1) Charlie Shedd, *How to Develop a Praying Church* (Word).

Chapter 15
Conversational Prayer

Roslyn Rinker, in *Communicating Love Through Prayer* and *Prayer—Conversing with God* (Zondervan), introduced an approach to group prayer which for many has lifted it out of its lifelessness and brought a new reality to group prayer. A deeper love and sensitivity for God and one another has been discovered.

Conversational prayer is this: Instead of each one present praying once and covering many subjects, each one prays as many times as they wish. Simple brief prayers are prayed, for only one subject at a time.

Conversational prayer expresses the real purpose of all true prayer—to put God at the centre of our attention, and forget ourselves and the impression we are making on others.

It is conversation directed to God who is with us and within us, as well as to each other. It contains three ingredients common to any meaningful communication which are:

1. **We become aware** of the other person—what they say, what they mean, how they feel.
2. **We pursue the same subject** by taking turns, listening, speaking, agreeing and giving thanks.
3. **We try to keep in tune** by not prematurely introducing a new subject, but by maintaining interest through participation in the current subject. [1]

Conversational prayer is a group of brothers and sisters in real conversation with their Father. It involves silences in which we listen for God's response in our spirits, and, like real conversation, it means listening to what others are saying to him.

It is speaking confidently, yet reverently, with a Person who really loves us and accepts us in Christ as we are. The conversation takes place in a group which is growing in love and concern for one another. This growth is not the fruit of their own effort, but the result of the action of the Holy Spirit.

Honesty, openness and simplicity with the One who really loves us and a group who accepts us is essential. But this will also be a growing experience. Part of that openness is saying 'I' when we mean 'I' and 'we' when we mean the whole group.

Each may pray as many times as they wish but each short prayer relates to the subject being pursued by the group at that time. There is no order for people to follow, each prays as moved by the Spirit.

Conversational prayer is an art which needs time and practice to develop. In our prayer workshops and in retreat situations I have found that even with people who have a real motivation to learn this prayer technique it has taken four half-hour workshops on successive days before most begin to gain some confidence in using it. Young people generally master the art more quickly than adults.

As Roslyn Rinker says: 'Conversational prayer is loving sensitivity'.

The five basic steps

There are five basic steps of conversational prayer which form an easily recalled framework. In summary they are as follows:

1. **Jesus is here**
   The power of worship.
   Realising God's presence.
   Accepting God's love.
   Matthew 18:19–20.

2. **Thank you, Lord**
   The power of thanksgiving.
   Speaking from our hearts.
   Freedom from fear.
   Philippians 4:4–7.

3. **Help me, Lord**
   The power of confession.
   Supporting and affirming one another.
   Receiving love.
   James 5:13–16.

4. **Help my brother and my sister**
   The power of intercession.
   Giving away our love.
   Receiving answers.
   Mark 11:22–25.

5. **Use me, Lord**
   The power of service.
   Declaration of availability to be involved with others in need.
   Isaiah 6:8.

Notice the progression in the steps.

1. We start with our Lord and worship.
2. Gratitude opens our hearts and our mouths.
3. We pray for ourselves and for those present.
4. We include those who are not present.
5. We are willing to be part of the answer to our prayer for others.

The purpose of these steps is to give a starting point and a workable plan to follow. They help bring direction and meaning to group prayer. To follow them requires attention and thus produces fresh interest.

The five steps in more detail

1. Jesus is here. This begins usually with a period of silent meditation possibly following some suggestions for creative imagination. The whole segment may be in silence but usually people will be motivated to verbalise their deep inner response to the presence of his Spirit. It helps for the leader to introduce this step by reciting Matthew 18:19,20.

The reading of a very brief meditation or playing a suitable recorded hymn or song which suggests the presence of Christ with the group can be helpful and bring variety. An appropriate symbol in the middle of the group can launch the group into meditation.

2. Thank you, Lord. This is closely linked with the first step. It is the natural response to the awareness of the Presence of a loving God so rich in grace. A period of reflection to begin this segment may help.

These first steps are a unit of worship in receiving love from God and responding in expressing our love and worship to him. The next three steps are a giving of love to others, both in the group and outside it. In 'step 3' there will be a beautiful experience in receiving love from one another as each person is supported and affirmed by other members of the group.

3. Help me, Lord. In this step confession and petition are the focus. This follows easily after the study of the Word of God. Wise and sensitive leadership will be needed here. Until the group develops deeper levels of trust and openness we have found it best to suggest personal confession in silence. Much will depend upon those in the group.

4. Help my brother and my sister. Here we enter into the power of intercession. It begins by responding to the individual prayers in 'step 3' and widens out to the families, friends and acquaintances of the group and to the community and world.

In explaining this step I find it clearer to divide it into two, making a distinction between the response to individual prayers within the group and the wider intercession. The first part takes place spontaneously immediately after each person has prayed their prayers of confession and petition. The second part takes place as a further separate step.

(a) Response during 'step 3'. Let Roslyn Rinker explain:

As soon as a person prays for themselves, another one or two should be applying a 'bandaid' of love upon that wounded spirit. Any revealing of the heart calls for immediate response on the part of those who heard the prayer. Let your prayer-response be brief, to the point, with thanksgiving and with love. And without preaching or suggesting. Prayer should involve neither of these. We pray for each other by name, back and forth sometimes, according to the discernment received through listening and loving. The response may be for example, 'That's just how I feel too, Lord', 'I have just the same problem, Lord, help us both', or, 'Help Jim to know we love him'.

(b) Intercession for other than group members.

Let it be creative and specific. After one person prays for a person or situation, one or two others in the group will support the prayer. In some cases the support prayers will be 'Yes, Lord'; 'that is our real concern too, Lord'; 'Lord, we share John's concern for his friend'.[2]

5. Use me, Lord. This is a natural progression for the sincerely concerned person. God does not do everything himself in answer to our prayers. He chooses to work through people. True intercessory prayer in the small group should lead to corporate and personal action in meeting the needs of others. A prayer group without a social conscience is a farce. Prayer and action make the finest combination for changing our world.

In this step we put legs under our prayers. We make ourselves available to be part of the answer, 'Lord, I'm available to bring your love and concern to Mrs Jones who lost her husband last week'; 'So am I, Lord—guide us as to how we can best minister to her'; 'Yes, Lord'.

After the prayer time, make definite plans to act upon the things the group felt moved to do during prayer.

The role of the leader

We have found it essential to have a sensitive leader to facilitate this prayer experience. The leader will be conversant with the process and able to sense when it is appropriate to move on to the next stage. The leader will also know how to handle people who are negative, critical or unwise in sharing their personal failures.

It takes time to learn

Some people, especially more mature folk, find it extremely difficult to adapt themselves to this new form of prayer. All should be made aware that this is a skill which needs time and patience to develop. A few never seem to master it. Most will find it hard to keep to one subject at a time or restrict their prayers to one or two sentences. Save embarrassment by acknowledging this from the outset. Encourage them to persevere.

References

(1) Roslyn Rinker, *Prayer—Conversing with God* (Zondervan).
(2) Ibid.

Chapter 16
'At Home' Groups

This is based on my experience with 'At Home' programmes held during a number of my parish ministries. In each instance many favourable comments were received from the participants. Such remarks usually concerned the pleasure of being invited to meet socially in the minister's home, and the opportunity to get to know other members of the congregation better. In one situation, two elderly church members, who had been attending the same church for forty years, confessed that the evening provided the first experience of conversing with each other beyond a merely formal short greeting after Sunday worship!

This intensive programme outlined here is very demanding of the pastor, his or her spouse and their family. It can easily be adapted to not need such a large involvement by them.

This programme has now been tried in other areas by some who have participated in my Small Groups Conferences where the concept was introduced. One minister reported:

We have found 'At Home' groups very effective in our area. Within a three-week period we were able to meet 180 folk in this way. Being a rural area, not all folk could travel easily to our home in the main town. Therefore, five meetings were held in our home, with three others being held in private homes in the outlying centres. These have been held to integrate newcomers to the parish as well as to assist us in getting to know the established congregation.

New folk have deeply appreciated the experience of acceptance and warmth that such an evening provides. They participate in one or two relationship games and talk informally over supper. By this means those who are either new to the area, or who have lived in the locality for some time but without feeling incorporated in a congregation, are helped to link up with others. Another interesting and unexpected by-product of these evenings has been the genuine uplift given to the 'older' members doing the welcoming. A number of these folk have stated later that they were thankful for what the evening had meant to them in terms of personal satisfaction and enjoyment, and knowing they had been able to minister to others.

Another minister reported:

> We followed your outline almost to the letter and found it to be most effective. Over a period of 12 nights we had 164 different people attend our home. Sub-committees were formed in each of the three centres in the parish to undertake the organization necessary. The church women supplied the supper for each evening.
>
> We followed your suggestion to use a set of slides. About 40 or 50 of general interest were shown. These had something to do with our personal experience, places we had visited and tasks we have undertaken. The best groups were between 15 and 18 people. These evenings were a tremendous strain on the whole family, but looking back, we feel it was well worthwhile. We now plan to hold further groups in the future.

Aims

An 'At Home' function has three aims:

1. To develop a deeper sense of community in a congregation/parish.
2. To enable the minister and his/her spouse to get to know as many of the congregation as they can in a short period of time at the commencement of a ministry.
3. To help the congregation to get to know the minister and his/her spouse.

When to hold 'At Homes'

'At Homes' provide an effective way to get to know a large number of people in a relatively short period. For that reason they are useful when a minister moves to a new parish to help them get to know their people quickly. However, I have used them later during my ministry in the same parish with equally good effect. In this case the programme took a varied form to that used in the original series.

It was my practice to use this type of group on a continuing basis to help orient newcomers. Names of new arrivals were recorded and when two or three couples were listed, they were invited to one of these types of group. A number of members of the congregation were also invited to help the newcomers integrate into the local church community.

Organisation

It is essential that ministers and their spouses do not get involved in the tedious details of setting it up. If the plan outlined here is followed, the minister will be heavily committed in the demanding visitation programme and his/her spouse will be busy hosting the meetings in addition to the normal daily schedule.

A small group of people with a good knowledge of the local church people should handle the organising. (These need not necessarily be church office-bearers; they could be a small group already in existence.) It can be explained that the minister and his/her spouse will be busy in the 'At Home' programme and wish to concentrate on getting to know people rather than getting involved with the organising.

Organising committee's duties

1. **Make master list**

   The group compile an up-to-date master list of people including all who have some connection with the church.

   Information can be drawn from the Sunday School Roll, Youth Group membership lists, Church Membership Roll, Women's and Men's Groups, etc.

   The list is graded into 'actives' and 'inactives'.

   The list is divided into areas and then into streets (in order of street number).

   Note: The minister does a crash-visitation programme. This method of listing enables systematic visitation.

2. **Make groupings**

   The list is divided into groups of 25. It has been found that 25–30 people need to be invited at one time to ensure an attendance of 12–15. This will vary from place to place.

   Each group should contain a proportion of 'actives'

and 'inactives' (say two-thirds 'inactives' and one-third 'actives').

These smaller groups are still kept in areas and in street order as far as possible.

It was found advisable to include some special groups, e.g. for young married couples and young people.

3. **Prepare group lists**

The group lists should be typed on loose-leaf sheets which fit into a small folder.

Have one page per group and three copies of each group list. (One copy is the minister's visitation list, one copy is kept near the minister's house or office telephone to record telephone replies, and one copy is filed.)

Layout of lists:

.... (Date of 'At Home')

NAME	ADDRESS	CODE "A" or "Ina"	OTHER INFO. Family Details, ways involved etc.

Diagram № 24: Layout of At Home List

4. **Enlist 'actives' to help**

The Organising Committee contact 'actives' in each of the groups to bring eats and help with the washing-up after the meeting.

5. **Prepare and post invitations**

The invitation should be printed, preferably in script, leaving a blank space for the name of the person/s invited and the date. They should be of a size which will fold easily into a standard envelope.

Suggested wording:

The Rev. John and Mrs Everyman invite you to be their guests at an informal social evening in their home on ....
commencing at .... p.m.
Supper (coffee/tea and dessert) will be served at .... pm.
To assist with catering arrangements, we would appreciate it if we could have a reply by ......
(one week in advance).
174 Pilgrims Way
Southaven 2999
Tel. 174–2999

Names and addresses should be typed on envelopes, which are then stamped.

Keep in batches with dates on front of each bundle.

Post invitations four to five weeks before date of each 'At Home'.

One person on the committee should be responsible for the regular mailing of the invitations.

Encourage replies by mail to prevent excessive telephone calls.

Notes:

If possible, use the minister's residence, even if it is not a very large house.

If this really is not feasible, and it will not be in some cases, use the homes of key members.

If people cannot come to an 'At Home' and reply to let you know, then plan an additional 'At Home' for them.

Launching

Discuss with the appropriate governing body of your church or parish the intention to hold an 'At Home' programme.

Photocopy or make a summary of these pages for all to know what is envisaged.

Seek to get their approval for this short-term activity to have priority over other activities as it will be extremely demanding.

Announce to the congregation that everyone will be invited at some time.

Work out dates for the 'At Homes' well in advance, and give them to the Organising Committee.

Visitation

Visit by lists, whether a reply has been received or not.
Call one week before the 'At Home'.

Make the call brief. Introduce yourself as the minister. Mention the invitation (you may find you will be picking up replies).

Express a hope that they might be able to share in this 'informal social evening'.

Call even if people have said they will not be coming to the 'At Home'.

If no one is home, leave your card with a note.

The evening

Have name tags prepared (in large print so that they can be read from across the room).

Be ready well in advance, introduce people as they come and allow informal conversation.

State aims of the evening.

Play the 'get-acquainted' game 'Interviews' (see Appendix A). The minister and spouse also participate.

Generally, a programme of slides is presented. This should last no longer than 30 minutes, be fast moving and could include slides relating to your own life, college training, marriage, children, some highlights of past ministries and slides of general interest. This could give insight into your own background and interests and build confidence as people learn of the experience which you are bringing to the new situation.

Serve refreshments (coffee/tea and dessert).

Say a brief 'family' prayer.

Finish on time.

After an overseas study trip I repeated this programme in order to report to the whole congregation and share insights which later became the foundation of a new direction in that church. I illustrated my report with slides and items I had collected.

Note: If people say they would like to come but cannot get a baby-sitter, perhaps it would be possible to have the Organising Committee make arrangements for this.

After the 'At Home'

Immediately after the meeting, make notes regarding attendance and any special things that have been learnt about those who attended and any follow-up to be undertaken.

These notes can be made on one of the lists of names supplied by the Organising Committee and later transferred to the pastoral care files.

Chapter 17
Young People Together

Rod Denton

Christianity began as a young people's movement . . . The original band was a young men's group. Most of the disciples were probably still in their twenties when they went out after Jesus . . . No one ever realised more than Jesus did that the adolescent years of life . . . are God's best chance with the soul.[1]

[The insights shared with you in this chapter have mainly come from Rod Denton's involvement with 350 young people in 40 small groups linked to Blackburn Baptist Church in Victoria, Australia. At the time of writing, Rod was minister for youth in this dynamic church. He felt guided by God to use small groups to build up the ministry with young people. It was a long and hard road, spanning a period of almost ten years. They began small, and slowly saw God bless the work as they sought to lay some firm foundations.

Many readers will be in entirely different situations to the one described here; where to form a few small groups (or even one!) for young people would be seen as evidence of great faithfulness by God. However, as the principles apply to most situations, I trust this chapter will enable all who work with young people to catch the vision and be encouraged to begin small as Jesus did, and then develop a solid base of deeply committed Christians which could be a launching pad for some of God's beautiful surprises!!]

The small group is vital to a growing youth ministry today. It may be possible to gather a large group of people and develop an attractive programme, but this of itself will not guarantee that anything is really happening in the lives of young people. Growth takes place best in the context of relationships, and small groups provide the best opportunity for relationships to be built.

George Bernard Shaw once commented, 'Youth is such a wonderful thing, it is a shame to waste it on the young'. Whilst there is some truth in this sentiment, it is also true today that young people are growing up in a world where they are subject to great stresses and pain. Consequently, developing spiritually mature young people is not an easy task in today's pressurised world.

FOUR KEYS

For this reason I have found it important, by way of foundation, to have a clear understanding of the following four key words if I am going to be able to develop an effective youth ministry:

Goal. What is it that I want to achieve?

Just before entering full time youth ministry the Lord impressed upon me Colossians 1:28 as my goal for ministry, 'to present everyone mature in Christ'. This has given me a sense of direction because I now ask how every activity will help further my goal before I proceed with it.

Strategy. How do I go about achieving this goal?

As I look at the life of Jesus, I see that he shared his life intimately with a small group of men in order to build them to maturity, to make them disciples. His main focus was with a few men rather than the masses, so that through those few men his ministry might impact the masses.

The strategy is one of discipleship, of raising up spiritual leaders who will have an impact on the lives of others. Discipleship is not primarily the sharing of a programme, or a manual, but the sharing of a life over a period of time. Primarily we need to be looking for better people rather than better programmes, as E M Bounds put it.

Structure. How do I organise our young people?

This is where small groups fit in. We may be able to impress people from a distance, but we can only make an impact on them up close. Leaders are set apart to shepherd and disciple small groups of young people, to develop relationships with them and be effective models for them. In the context of our overall ministry programme, I find the small group life to be the most vital part.

Programme. What activities will best serve to achieve our goal?

I find a common fault in youth ministry is that many leaders are programme oriented. They have programmes for programmes' sake and become event oriented rather than people oriented. It is important to remember that the programme must be a servant to the goal and every activity contribute toward this end. I keep reminding myself that, just because I am busy, it does not mean that I am achieving something.

It is important to define these four key words, because they provide a context for the formation of small groups. With this understood, we guard against small groups being an end in themselves, rather than a means to an end.

PURPOSE OF SMALL GROUPS

Although this subject has already been covered in this book, I want to comment on a few specifics in regard to young people.

Positive peer influence:
Peer pressure can be bad or good. Christian young people, at a vulnerable age, need all the support available to combat the negative peer pressure they face in the world. As young people have opportunity to pray for one another, encourage and affirm one another in regular small group meetings, an environment of positive support is created and they are learning how to live as members of the Kingdom of God.

Personal growth:
Small groups provide opportunity for young people to get involved and even fail without feeling a failure. Spiritual gifts can be identified and encouraged, accountability developed,

questions can be asked in a non-threatening environment and responsibilities allocated.

Family:

In an age where one in three young people come from broken families, whilst many others have inadequate communication with their parents, it is vital that they have a group where a leader, together with other members, can assist them in their social development and compensate to some degree that which may be lacking in their family life. For others, the small group is able to supplement an already existing healthy family life.

Mission:

Young people need challenges, but often lack the know-how and confidence to take initiatives whereby they may meet the needs of those around them and get involved in evangelistic or service missions. In small groups, under the guidance of a leader, they can plan and undertake projects that will minister to those in need and also create opportunities where they can include their non-Christian friends in group activities.

Identity:

The big cry on the lips of young people today is 'who am I?' The reason why the advertising industry is so successful is that it is able to create an identity in a generation that is confused and aimless. Young people more than ever need to be part of a group character-ised by relationships of trust and openness, where they can reveal the deep questions of their hearts and find answers from God's Word that help them establish their identities in a way that their Creator meant them to.

Sue was a shy insecure 12-year-old when she entered one of our Junior High groups. She had a poor relationship with her parents and her Christian faith was very weak. She was self-conscious and moody. During her three years in a Junior High small group, where her leader and small group members loved her and cared for her, she slowly but surely changed. By the time she was 15 she was much more stable in her personality and her faith had grown immensely. So much so that she led two of her friends to Christ and her family relationships have improved. Sue's small group and her group leader had created the necessary environment that provided healing and growth in maturity.

SMALL GROUP LEADERSHIP

Perhaps the most important groups in our youth ministry are the leadership groups. In each of our youth departments we have a leadership group that meets primarily as a small group and in the process of meeting also discusses its programme and any business matters.

One of the great tragedies of youth ministry has been the high turnover rate of youth leaders. Apparently the average length of ministry of a youth leader is around 18 months.

However, it has been our practice to ask youth leaders to make a three-year commitment when joining a ministry team, and this has been more than realised on average because our first ministry is to the youth leader. In other words, if there is a satisfactory input into the life of the youth leader, if they are being cared for, then each leader will be keen to give maximum ministry output over a number of years. Largely this input has occurred through the leaders' cell group and the leader of the department.

Our leaders' groups are structured so that leaders might develop strong bonds with one another. They share a common vision, they meet weekly to worship, study, pray, share and plan together. They have social outings and weekend retreats together and find that the effectiveness of their ministry in their youth departments is related to the unity that exists in their leadership teams.

In the normal course of meeting together leaders can share small group learning experiences with one another and receive instruction from time to time to better equip them for ministry. They also spend a night together at the beginning of each term to plan their small group pro-grammes and share ideas with each other. The principle of modelling is a vital key to learning and the department leader keeps this in mind as he takes the leaders through their small group meeting each week.

In addition, the leadership teams from all youth depart-ments come together for a time of celebration, sharing and learning three times a year and at the beginning of each ministry year they retreat for a weekend to pray and plan for the year ahead.

The department leader is responsible for bringing his

leadership team together and is looking for people who are growing in maturity and who are demonstrating the characteristics of:

Faithfulness: is this person reliable and trustworthy?

Loyalty: will this person work well in a team and be supportive of its leader?

Availability: will this person make ministry a high priority and determine to do one thing and do it well?

Teachableness: is this person humble and hungry to learn and grow?

Servant spirit: does this person really love young people and is that love a sacrificial love?

John is a young man with these character qualities. However, there is no doubt that the world would probably pass him over as a youth leader. He has a slight physical disability and consequently does not perform well at sport. He does not dress trendily, drives erratically and struggles with his self-image at times. But after two years as a leader he is now one of our most effective leaders. He is a reminder to me that whilst man looks on the outside, God looks on the heart and delights to take ordinary people through whom he might do extraordinary things. I do not know of a more important lesson I have learnt in my ministry than this.

The selection of leaders is one of the most critical points in our youth ministry and we dare not select people who have not already shown an ability to work well in their existing small groups. The words of Jesus where he said that a person should not be given greater responsibility until he has been faithful in the little things is so important. It seems that God does not promote people on potential alone and neither should we.

In summary, a good small group leader is one who has learnt to relate well with their God, their fellow leaders and the young people that have been entrusted to their care. Nothing much else really matters, whilst without these anything else is of little value.

FORMATION OF GROUPS

It is always our aim to try and place a young person in a small group as soon as possible for the reasons already mentioned.

If a person has been brought by a friend it is more than likely that they would join their friend's group. Possibly the group has already been praying for that person. On other occasions, the placement of a person would be made by the department leader in consultation with relevant leaders.

Leaders are encouraged to stay with their groups for three years which is the length of time a young person would normally stay in a youth department, i.e. Junior High, Senior High or 18 Plus. This provides the leader with a valuable opportunity to develop a friendship with the young people in their group and then through that friendship help them to grow as a disciple of Jesus Christ.

At the time of placing a young person in a group we find it helpful to take time to explain the purposes of a small group and where relevant, particularly amongst older young people, the responsibilities of a small group member. This creates a level of expectation and also an encouragement to participate in the group. It is true that a person usually gets out of a small group what they put into it. In other words, small groups are not an end in themselves but a vehicle through which effective life and growth can be generated.

As a group grows in size, it is always our intention to work to divide the group into two groups. This step must always be done sensitively and gradually and with advance notice.

A BALANCED GROUP LIFE

From experience we have found that most groups grow effectively when they keep a balance between the following four inputs:

Worship: our relationship with God.

Young people have an opportunity to be very creative in this area. Worship activities might include: listening to a record or cassette; singing with or without musical instruments; reading a psalm or passage of Scripture and affirming the characteristics of God that are mentioned; sentence prayers that focus on the person of God; being still before God and adoring Him in the quietness; and sharing a communion time together.

In some groups, all members are able to take a turn in leading a worship time, whilst in other groups the leader might need to have more involvement. In any situation, the example of the leader will be important, for it is not possible to take a group further than the experience of the leader.

Fellowship: our relationship with one another.
So much of the potential of a group's life depends on the quality of relationships that are formed in the group. It is important to remind group members that they are to live as servants to one another, that they do not primarily come to get something from one another but to give themselves to one another.

This is done in the group by using 'ice breakers' and getting acquainted exercises, by sharing prayer points and keeping a prayer diary, by creating prayer partners, by having group members share their life stories, by affirming one another's strengths and gifts, by following up absent or sick group members and by meeting one another's practical needs.

In addition to regular small group meetings, relationships are built as groups get together for social activities, meals, camping times and other recreational activities. In all of this, the goal of the group leader is to see group members grow to become his/her best friends.

Mission and Outreach: our relationship with others.
The group that fails to reach out beyond itself will grow fat and self-centred and begin to die. The group that exists for others will be full of life and see its members growing through practical ministry opportunities.

These can include reaching out to a wide range of people, e.g. those in hospitals, the elderly, disadvantaged children in the community and other countries, bringing non-Christian friends to a group barbecue or social, contacting fringe group members, supporting a missionary, becoming involved in social issues or taking a church service at another church.

It is often in these activities that gifts are discovered and young people are exposed to a wide range of real life issues that help them gain a better perspective on the world that their heavenly Father created and for which Jesus Christ died.

Nurture: our relationship with the Word of God.
As always, the Word of God is relevant to the needs of young people today. The challenge of leadership is to determine the needs of young people and develop a strategy whereby Bible study might speak to their needs and provide appropriate answers. Bible study must never be seen as an end in itself and so the practical application is always a vital part of the study.

Small group Bible studies can link in with the large departmental meetings where opportunity in the group is given to discuss and apply the large group teaching. On other occasions small groups might work through a Bible study book with questions and answers, listen to cassettes or watch videos, have a guest speaker, work through a passage of Scripture (using a creative Bible study method and resource books) and on other occasions develop basic discipleship skills.

Small group leaders need to be helped to develop skills in leading study in ways that are appropriate to the stage of development of their group. Inductive methods of Bible study, learning by doing, exploring relevance for life and supporting each other in putting it into practice are aspects of effective study which leaders need to understand and gain confidence in using. Very importantly they need to live out the truth that they teach, for young people need to see trust more than hear truth.

Although these four characteristics need to be held in balance in the life of a group if it is to grow, they do not need to be included in every group meeting. For example, some group meetings have been set aside for prayer and praise, whilst others have been totally used for deeper sharing and praying for one another.

Further, there may be different stages in the life of a group where it is important to place greater emphasis on one of these four characteristics. For example, when a group is first formed it is important to take time to develop relationships and so the fellowship dimension is of priority.

However, in general, if the group doesn't give attention to:

Worship: it will become dry.
Fellowship: it will become cold.
Mission and Outreach: it will become fat and self-centred.
Nurture: it will become sub-Christian.

A final key word is the word 'creativity', for our God is a creative God. It is my goal whenever leading a group to try to keep members guessing as to what happens next. Try to avoid predictability in leading a group.

THE PLACE OF SMALL GROUPS IN THE TOTAL PROGRAMME

Obviously, the small group meetings are only part of our total youth programme, but they are a very important part.

Each of our departments has regular weekly meetings, after church suppers, camps and other activities.

What we have found is that the older our young people grow, the more important the small group activity becomes and the less important are the range of large group activities. Consequently some in our Junior High groups may only meet each week for 30 minutes or so in their groups as part of the larger departmental meeting, whilst our 18 Plus groups meet weekly in a home and share in social activities together.

One of the advantages of small groups is that their members can work together to serve the whole department. All of our rosters are worked out on a small group basis, whether it be setting up the room for a department meeting, preparing refreshments after the meeting, preparing the programme for a department meeting or organising an after church supper. A the same time, it should be noted that we do not always conform to our basic small group structure when groups are required. Occasionally, in department meetings, we will break into ad hoc groups so that life and variety can be encouraged.

In all of this, the key word is balance: balance between small groups and departmental activities, balance between intimate relationships with small group members and opportunities to encourage new and caring relationships with all other youth group members.

OTHER COMMENTS

It has been important to ensure that female leaders disciple girls and male leaders disciple boys. This does not mean to say that groups cannot be mixed. It means that under these circumstances there needs to be a girl and a boy in leadership.

Youth small groups are encouraged to build bridges to other areas of the church. This can be done by visiting elderly people or having a small group exchange with an adult group.

Departments need to maintain adequate administrative procedures in order that all things are done decently and in order. Group leaders complete a weekly evaluation form and department leaders complete a monthly evaluation form, so that absentees may be cared for, prayer points circulated, new contacts noted and general trends observed.

Group leaders who spend key time in the homes of young people and have regular contact with parents gain the respect and trust of parents and, in the case of non-Christian parents, can build vital contacts.

Informal group times (e.g. social outings, meals, sporting activities, sleepovers, weekend retreats, youth rallies, etc.) are just as important in the leader's overall goals as are the regular formal small group meetings.

Training of new leaders is a vital part of any youth ministry. This is done by appointment of assistant leaders, leadership training courses and by providing various opportunities for growing Christians to get involved in ministry experiences.

We must continually gauge our effectiveness not so much by numbers, but rather by the growth that occurs in the lives of our young people. When young people start to grow in the likeness of Jesus, the results will be so noticeable and different to that which is happening in the world today that others will be naturally attracted to the life of the group.

Hang in there in your own great ministry with young people! Avoid the spectacular. Seek to dig firm foundations. Aim for quality growth with a few. Keep close to the Lord so you will be a living demonstration of the gospel. Pray about what you are doing, and pray for the people you lead. Then be prepared to be surprised!!

Reference

(1) J S Stewart, *The Life and Teaching of Jesus Christ* (The Saint Andrew Press).

Appendix A
Get-acquainted Games

These exercises are used to help people begin to develop relationships in the early part of their group experience. They provide a 'warming up' period which should create a congenial emotional climate. The intention is to help them feel comfortable, included and significant as they share some non-threatening information with each other. They also will provide one of the first important steps in group involvement, that of enabling the participants to hear their own voices and be listened to by the group. Sharing something of themselves in this manner should open the way for them to share at a deeper level later in the meeting.

These exercises are meant to be enjoyable, relaxed times—for that reason they are often referred to as 'games'. Leaders should seek to engender this fun dimension by their own relaxed attitude.

Interviews

A completely non-threatening game, of value when commencing a new group or for one-time small group meetings.

Setting: Small groups with even numbers of people. Upper limit of 12 people. Can be used with larger groups, but more time is required.

Time: Depends upon the number in the group; 4–6 minutes for the interviews in pairs. Usually takes a total of approximately 25 minutes for a group of 12.

Materials required: Small notepad and pencil for each person.

Procedure: Distribute pencils and writing pads for brief notes taken in the interviews. Briefly explain the method. Pair off the group, making sure that married couples or close friends are not put together. With the assistance of a number of suggested questions, one seeks to discover as much as possible about the other in 2 to 3 minutes. The process is reversed for a similar period.

Each person in turn then shares with the whole group what they have learned about the other.

Choose one of these methods for introducing the questions:

Put on a chart and place in a prominent position for all to
   see.
Dictate for the group to copy down individually (this is time-
   consuming).
Make a copy for each person with sufficient room left for the
   answers.

Questions for interviews: Sometimes all are asked to share four interesting things about themselves with their partner, however most people will need a set of questions to give direction and breadth to their interview.

Suggested questions:
Name?
Where do you live?
How long have you lived there?
Where were you born?
Occupation?
Married—family?
Interest—Hobbies? Sport? Clubs?
What is the nicest thing that happened to you in the last 12
   months?

These will need to be adjusted for use in groups for young people. Some possible inclusions could be:

Which school do you attend?
How many in your family?
What is your favourite television show?

(See Appendix B, 'Questions and Suggestions for Sharing', for more question ideas.)

Four Facts

This is for use with people who are well known to each other.

Setting: Small groups of 6 to 12 people. Because this is for people who know each other well, it is better to work with smaller sub-groups of 4–6.

Time: Depends upon the number; 15–20 minutes for 10–12 people.

Materials required: Small notepad and pencil for each person.

Procedure: Write down four facts about yourself:

My favourite game when I was a child was . . .
My hero when I was twelve years of age was . . .
My favourite kind of music right now is . . .
The place I would like to live if I could live anywhere in the
   world is . . .

Of the four answers, three should be true; one should be untrue.

When everyone has jotted down their four facts, get together in groups of four and let one person in each group start out by reading their facts. The others in the group try to guess which fact is untrue.

When all have guessed, the person should explain which answer was untrue and which were honest answers.

Repeat this procedure for each person in the group.

Guess Who Fishbowl

This game frequently helps people realise how little they really know about fellow group members or surprises them by demonstrating how misleading it is to 'typecast' or categorise people. It is useful for groups who know each other fairly well. It can be used at different stages in a group's life.

Setting: Groups of 6 or 8 sitting in movable chairs or on the floor.

Time: 30 minutes.

Materials required: A small sheet of paper and pencil for everyone, plus a bowl for each group of eight.

Procedure: The exercise is in two parts: Preliminary Exercise, with everyone working on their own; and Guessing Game, with everyone in groups of 6 or 8.

Preliminary Exercise (5 minutes)
Give everyone a sheet of paper and ask them to write down

four facts about themselves. (Do not let anyone see what you jot down.)

Your favourite radio or TV programme when you were a child.
Your hero when you were 12 years of age.
The place where you would like to spend a vacation.
One word that would best describe your life right now.

Fold your sheet of paper when you are finished.

Guessing Game (25 minutes)
Get together in groups of 6 or 8 and place your sheet of paper in the bowl for your group.

Let one person pick out one of the slips of paper and read the four facts or clues to the group. Then everyone tries to guess who it is. (The person who it is should play along by guessing someone else.) When everyone has tried to guess, let the person confess and explain their answers.

Repeat this procedure until you have removed all of the slips from the fishbowl.

If time allows, have a general discussion on what the game revealed.

Identity Card

The aim is to enable people in a large gathering to establish contact with a significant number of people not previously known to them, but also to break a large group into smaller groups in a non-threatening manner. (It can be used as well with smaller numbers.)

Time: 20 to 30 minutes (or less).

Materials: Small file cards or scrap card cut to size; pencils.

Procedure: Distribute cards and pencils, one of each per person.

Individual work: The leader selects a set of questions similar to those used in the 'Interviews' game.

These questions are presented as incomplete statements and read out by the leader. Each individual writes the statement plus their completion of it, e.g. 'My occupation is . . .'.

All of the statements are limited to the one side of the card.

Meeting others: All move around, meeting as many as possible during a 15-minute period, especially those who

they have not met before or who are not well known to them.

During these encounters, cards are exchanged, the statements read, hands shaken and a welcome given by each. Then each writes on the back of the other person's card a greeting or wish for the other and the writer's signed name. (For example, 'I hope this will be a growing experience, Bill S.'—'So nice to meet you. May God continue to enrich your life, Jill A.').

Cards are returned but the side with the greeting is not read at this stage.

Repeat this experience with as many as possible in the time available.

When the time expires, the pairs talking at that time sit together.

Only then are all the greetings, etc. on the reverse side of the card read by the owner.

Groups can then be formed by each pair finding two or three other pairs and sharing anything on their cards.

Humming Birds

The aim is to facilitate contact between all members of a large group in a related climate of fun and humour but also to break a large group into smaller groups in a non-threatening manner. (It can be used as well with smaller numbers.)

Time: Approximately 30 minutes.

Materials: A folded strip of paper concealing the title of a well-known song for each member of the group (one set of song title strips for each sub-group desired).

Procedure: The leader commences in a light-hearted manner stating that there is a great deal of talent and skill in the room which will be made evident through this exercise.

Each is given a piece of paper on which is written the title of a well-known song. Each looks at the title but does not share it with anyone else.

When the leader gives the word, each person will move around the room humming their tune until they find all the other members of the group with the same song.

Suggested songs: National Anthem, Three Blind Mice, Auld Lang Syne, Happy Birthday, Kum Bah Yah, For He's a Jolly Good Fellow, Mary had a Little Lamb, Jingle Bells, etc.

When the groups have been formed, each group sits in a

circle. Groups are instructed to discuss how they felt at the beginning and during the exercise.

Variations:
The leader can tell the participants how many others have the same song. This will accelerate the activity.

Instead of one song per strip, several songs can be listed. The first song is used to form pairs, the second song fours, and the third a group of any number for some later activity.

If time permits, the final group can then be assigned the task of coming up with a group name or a song title to express their feeling as a group.

Get-acquainted Merry-go-round

This works well where a large gathering has been subdivided into small groups; but it is also useful with a single group.

Time: 30–45 minutes.

Leader's note: The leader should complete the first three sentences, setting the pace for openness and honesty by his/her answers.

Procedure: The exercise is in two parts: Merry-go-round, with the outer circle in each group rotating every two minutes; and Synthesis, with each group of 6 or 8 re-arranged into one circle.

Merry-go-round (20–30 minutes)
Get together in groups of 6 or 8 and arrange the chairs or sit on the floor in a merry-go-round pattern, with 3 or 4 people in an inner circle and the same number in an outer circle. The inner circle should face the outer circle in each group so that everyone is facing a partner.

The leader will read the first part of a sentence and give you two minutes to finish the sentence and discuss your answer with the person you are facing. Then, the leader will call time and ask the people in the outer circle to rotate to the right.

When you are settled in front of your new partner, the leader will read out the next sentence and let you finish the sentence and discuss your answer with your partner for two more minutes. Then, the leader will call time and ask you to rotate again.

Continue this procedure until you have finished the sentences or run out of time.

My favourite time of the day is . . .
My favourite time of the year is . . .
My favourite place in the house is . . .
My favourite television show is . . .
If I could visit any place in the world on a vacation, I would like to visit . . .
If I had ten million dollars to use for the benefit of humankind, I would use the money to . . .
If I could smash one thing and one thing only, I would smash . . .
The greatest force in the history of the world is . . .
The greatest crime one person can commit against another is . . .
The greatest discovery I would like to make is . . .
The greatest value in my life at the moment is . . .
The thing that gives me the greatest satisfaction is . . .
The thing that I fear the most is . . .
The time I feel most alone is . . .
The time I feel most alive is . . .

Synthesis (10–15 minutes)
1. Stay in your same group of 6 or 8, but arrange your chairs or sit on the floor in one circle, facing each other.
2. Go around and let each person finish the first sentence below and explain their answer. Then, go around a second and third time, until you have finished the sentences or your time has run out.

   The person I learned most about in the last few minutes is . . .
   The answer that surprised me most was . . .
   The person in this group who seems most to feel about life the way I do is . . .

WARM-UP

The aim is to help a relatively new group get to know each other and provide an opportunity for some sharing of spiritual experience. It would generally not be used in the first meeting of a group which is to meet for a period.

Setting: A circle with each person in the group able to see the face of every other person.

Time: Approximately 60 minutes. A whole meeting could be given over to this exercise.

Materials required: None.

Procedure:

Step 1

What is your name?

Where did you live between the ages of 7 and 12 years?

What stands out most in your mind about the school you attended?

The leader proceeds to answer the first question then goes completely around the circle asking each person to answer the question. This is repeated for each question.

Step 2

How many brothers and sisters were in your family when you were between the ages 7–12 years?

During your childhood, how was your home heated? Can you remember anything humorous about it?

Leaders, in telling about how their homes were heated, should try to think of some incident that may be humorous or vivid concerning the heat in their homes. Perhaps being cold in the morning, or having to get up and fetch the wood or coal; perhaps the gas or oil running out or an extended electricity failure.

An Alternative:

Because some may have had memories of home or lived in an area where they did not need heating, consider these alternative questions:

Can you recall some experience in which you were very cold, e.g. while you were swimming, or in a situation in which you were without enough warm clothing or bed covering?

How did you get warm?

What feelings did you have besides being cold and then warm?

Step 3

During that time where did you feel the centre of human warmth was?

Was it a room? (e.g. the kitchen, parents' bedroom, dining room, etc.) Or it may not have been a room at all; it may have been a person around whom in retrospect you sensed an aura of safeness or warmth.

At this point the leader can explain that what we are actually doing is tracing the human experience of security. Our security is first known as a child in terms of physical warmth. As our horizon broadens outside of our immediate self, we sense our security in the warmth and acceptance of the people around us.

An Alternative:

Some people simply do not have any remembrance of a centre of human warmth in their home or in any person. The leader by mentioning this may put at ease people for whom this experience is not a reality. The leader should try to anticipate this beforehand and possibly change the above questions to read:

What location has good memories for you? Can you recall a place where you experienced acceptance, love and concern? Or somewhere where you had pleasant experiences so that you feel warm when you recall this place?

Which person has encouraged and cared for you most?

Step 4

When, if ever, in your life did God become more than 'a word'?

When did he become a living Being, alive in your own thinking and experience?

The group as a whole are asked these questions so that people can volunteer answers if they have any. This step can be optional, as it may be construed as threatening by someone who is afraid to reveal himself or herself.

We are not asking necessarily for an account of a conversion experience. This transition in one's thinking may have taken place while listening to a beautiful piece of music, watching a sunset, or in a conversation with a person who loved God. By this time the group may know each other well enough to volunteer answers right away. If not, the leader tells of their own experience.

After this last question has been asked, the group is in the midst of a discussion on the reality of God in human life. The leader may close this conversation by summarising the discussion and pointing out that, according to Christian belief, although everyone's experience of security and acceptance begins with physical warmth and graduates to human warmth, we are so made that our security will never be complete until we find it in God.

What this whole discussion does is to take people as a group of strangers, and within an hour's time get them talking personally with deep involvement about the deepest issues of human life. It can lead to people making commitments to Christ. The leader will need to be prepared for this possibility but should be sensitive and not try to coerce the group.

Appendix B
Questions and Suggestions for Sharing

Here are some further questions and suggestions to help facilitate sharing in small groups. All or some of these can be used in get-acquainted games and certain ones in connection with other relationship exercises.

Awareness of God (right relationship to God):
1. What impresses you most about Jesus Christ?
2. What event in the life of Christ means the most to you?
3. In what ways does the creation inspire you?
4. When did God become real to you?
5. Who helped you most in your understanding of God?
6. When you were a child, what impressed you most about God?
7. Of all the things you know about the nature or character of God, what means most to you personally?
8. When do you feel closest to God?
9. What one question above all others do you want God to answer?
10. If God is real to you, what gives you that certainty?
11. What do you most want God to do for you?
12. What does 'faith' mean to you personally?
13. When has God seemed furthest away from you?
14. What do you find hardest to believe about God?
15. 'God is love'—what does that mean to you personally?
16. Of all the teachings of Jesus Christ, what has come to be the most significant in your life?
17. How do you endeavour to show your gratitude to God?
18. Which word best describes God to you?
19. At what time in your life was God most real to you?
20. What is the most vivid experience of prayer you have had?
21. What certainty do you have that you matter to God?
22. In what way does your relationship to God make your way of facing life any different?

Self-awareness (right relationship to self):
1. Draw your own crest or coat-of-arms as you wish it were (which describes you) . . . and explain it to the group.
2. What would you do if you knew you could not fail?
3. What would you most like to do or be for the next five years, if there were no limitations (of family, money, education, health, etc.)?
4. Who is the most authentic person you have met? (Describe them).
5. What is your most satisfying accomplishment—ever? Before you were 6? Between the ages of 6 and 12? 12 and 18? 18 and 25? over 25?
6. Tell your three strongest points. Tell your three weakest points.
7. What is your happiest memory (at various ages)?
8. Describe the most significant event in your life.
9. Describe the characteristics of your 'ideal' woman or man.
10. What person besides your parents has been most influential in your life.
11. What present would you most like to receive?
12. List what your personal freedom depends upon.
13. Whose approval do you need the most?
14. In whose presence are you most uncomfortable? Why?
15. If you had what you really wanted in life, what would you have?
16. List your long-range goals. List your short-range goals.
17. Describe the most excitingly creative person you have known.
18. Write your own obituary.
19. List some creative ways to begin and to end a day.
20. What do you most daydream about?
21. What do you most trust in?
22. Who has most changed your life?
23. Where would you live if you could, and what would you do there?
24. Tell who you are, apart from your titles, honours, or your job description.
25. What is the best book (apart from the Bible) you have ever read?
26. What kind of social gathering or party do you like best?
27. Describe your favourite way of spending leisure time.
28. What feelings do you have trouble expressing or controlling?
29. What kinds of things make you irritated . . . furious?
30. What makes you feel depressed or 'blue'?
31. What makes you anxious, worried or afraid?
32. What gives you self-respect?

Inter-personal (right relationship to others):
1. Describe the person who has meant most in your life other than a parent or child. What is that person's outstanding characteristic?
2. Who was the first person you felt really understood you? What did they do? What were they like? What was their effect on you?
3. Are you the kind of person others confide in? Why?
4. What kind of person do you confide in?
5. What makes a person a good listener?
6. What kind of listener do you think you have been in this group?
7. How do you feel this group has listened to you, both corporately and separately?
8. What makes a 'good' marriage?

Responsibility to humankind (right relationship to the world):
1. What would you most like to do to be remembered in history?
2. What is your ideal for the future of society (both immediate and long-range)?
3. Describe your convictions about 'equality'.
4. How could you help to change an injustice of which you are aware?
5. What is the greatest current need in your community?
6. If you were willing, what could you do to change your church, your home, your neighbourhood, your school, or your job?
7. What disturbs you most about misuse of the physical resources in our world?
8. How do you personally react to the underfed and underprivileged in your country and in other areas of the world?
9. If you had limitless resources, how would you use them to benefit others?

General (for use in groups or individual reflection):
1. List the things that make or keep your life complicated.
2. List the things that you do to keep your life simple.
3. List the things that you could do to make your life more simple.

4. What do you find to be the worst pressures and strains in your work?
5. What do you find most boring and unenjoyable about your work?
6. What do you enjoy most in your work?
7. What shortcomings handicap you in your work?
8. What are your special qualifications for your work?
9. How do you feel your work is appreciated by others?
10. What are your ambitions and goals in your work?
11. How do you feel about the salary or reward you get for your work?
12. How do you feel about the choice of career you have made?
13. How do you feel about the people you work with?
14. How do you feel about the way you handle money?

Additional items for young people:
1. The three things that I do best at school are . . .
2. The longest trip I ever took was to . . .
3. I have these hobbies or things I like to do . . .
4. My pet is . . .
5. One of the best books I ever read was . . .
6. My favourite radio or television programme is . . .
7. If I could spend one day as I please, I would do these things . . .
8. The three things I want more than anything else are . . .
9. The three loveliest things I know are . . .
10. The thing I wonder about most is . . .
11. Three kinds of work I would like to do . . .
12. I think my best quality is . . .
13. Probably my worst fault is . . .
14. The three grown-ups I like best, next to my mother and father, are . . .
15. What I like best about church is . . .
16. The things I do not like about my church are . . .
17. The things that are different which I wish we would do at church are . . .
18. I think the Bible is . . .
19. One or two words which best describe God to me are . . .

Appendix C

An Order of Service for Communion in Small Groups

Notes:

The aim is the Upper Room atmosphere meeting around a table rather than the more formal atmosphere in a church.

It is intended that all members of the small group be involved in the leadership. The 'parts' should be given out well beforehand and practised prior to the celebration.

Hymns and Scripture songs should be included at appropriate places, each picking up the theme at that point.

The Scripture chapters given would be too long, so readers are expected to choose the section to be read. Each reader should follow on with how the reading ties into the life of the group.

The prayers following the readings may be replaced with extemporary prayers. Prayers for individual needs in the group and for others follow the John 15 reading.

Where a minister is not present, the words of consecration and institution can be omitted. It then becomes a fellowship meal, which is not, strictly speaking, a sacrament.

The Washing of the Feet can be done in a symbolic way.

We usually wash each other's hands which is more appropriate in many cultures.

The leader opens the service saying:

We remember how Jesus sent Peter and John, saying:
  'Go and make ready the Passover for us, that we may eat.
  With desire have I desired to eat this Passover with you
  before I suffer.'

SETTING THE TABLE

In the name of Jesus,
  we now set the table, that he may eat with us.
This bread and wine, and all the preparations we have made,
  we now offer to our Lord.
We, his disciples, having done as we were told,
  await his coming to take his place in our midst.

153

Let us pray:
Jesus, Lord,
the table is ready.
> We, your disciples, await your Presence.
Bread and wine cannot nourish our souls.
Our fellowship would soon break up,
> and each one of us would soon revert to type, unless you
> come and fill all things with your Presence.

In your Presence,
bread and wine are alive with the life that makes all things
> new.
Our fellowship becomes the body of Christ,
> and each one of us is lifted up to a new level.

INVOCATION

Come, Lord Jesus,
> take your rightful place as host at this your table.
Come, Lord Jesus,
> take your rightful place as Lord of your church.
Come, Lord Jesus,
> take your rightful place as King of our lives.
Come, Lord Jesus, come.

(Silence)
'Behold I stand at the door and knock,
if any man hear my voice and open the door
I will come in and sup with him, and he with me.'
Glory be to the living Christ who comes to us,
Glory be to the living Christ, mighty in the battle against
> the powers of darkness.
Glory be to the living Christ, who comes to save us.

Psalm 24 verse 7 can be sung here.

THE WASHING OF THE FEET

Reading from John 13.

I confess to God almighty, in the sight of the
whole company of heaven, and before you all, that
I have sinned exceedingly in thought, word and deed,
through my fault, my own fault, my own most grievous
fault, wherefore I pray God almighty to have mercy
upon me.
May the almighty and merciful Lord grant you pardon,
absolution, and remission of your sins, time for
amendment of life, and the comfort of his Holy
Spirit. AMEN.

O Jesus,
We thank you for your patience with us, your disciples.
We thank you that we can make a clean start once more.
We thank you for not holding our sins against us.

Here and now we pray for those with whom we have
quarrelled,
> those who have wronged us,
> those whom we have wronged.
We forgive them, even as you have forgiven us.

And if there are hidden tensions below the surface of our
> fellowship as we gather round your table,
> enable us to face them and set them right, for your own
> Name's sake we ask it. AMEN.

THE WAY

Reading from John 14.

Jesus,
> we will not be troubled or afraid as we face the
> future.
> We do not know what lies ahead,
> but we know you, and that is enough.
> So in quiet confidence we lay before you these
> things that concern us . . .

Jesus, the Way, the Truth and the Life,
You are the Way for us,
> even when we cannot see the next step ahead.
You are the Truth for us,
> even when the familiar landmarks of life disappear.
You are the Life for us,
> even when these mortal bodies crumble to dust.
Jesus, the Way, the Truth and the Life,
> armed with your peace,
> we face the future,
> sure that you will lead us safely home,
> in spite of our tendency to wander.
Jesus, the Way, the Truth and the Life,
> in you we put our trust,
> we will trust and not be afraid,
> because you live we shall live also,
> in time and in eternity. AMEN.

*The Creed, or some other affirmation of faith, may be said
here.*

154

THE LIVING VINE

Reading from John 15.

Lord we thank you for linking us together
  as branches in one great network . . . the living vine.
We thank you for our common concerns,
  and for the knowledge that you are working through us.
We thank you for the help we are able to give each other,
  and for the love of Christ at work in our midst.
We thank you for the wide outspread of this vine,
  the network of branches spreading out into every corner
  of the earth, spreading beyond earth, into heaven itself.

And now, linked together in the love of Christ,
sharing in the life of the vine,
united with the church on earth and in heaven we pray:

OUR FATHER . . .

THE INSTITUTION

*The words of Institution in 1 Corinthians 11:23–26 (or
Mark 14:22–23 may be used).*

In the name of Jesus we do this,
doing what he did, so that we may know him present in our
midst.
I now take bread and wine, as he did,
the fruit of God's good earth,
the products of the labour of our brothers and sisters.
They are your gifts, Lord,
and we offer them to you, so that you may use them.
As Jesus gave thanks that night,
so let us thank God now:
To you, O God, we lift up our hearts in thanksgiving,
For you have made us for yourself,
In you we live and move and have our being,
By your love in Jesus Christ you have rescued us,
By your spirit you renew us daily.
To you then we turn in joy and in love,
united here at your table with all your family,
those on earth and those in heaven,
and in that wonderful unity which you give us
we join in the eternal hymn:

  Holy, holy, holy, Lord God of Hosts,
  Heaven and earth are full of your glory,
  Glory be to you, O Lord most high.

Send down on us, and on these your gifts of bread and wine,
your Holy Spirit,
So that the bread we break and share may be for us
communion in the body of Christ,
and the cup we share may truly be for us
communion in the life-blood of Christ.
So may Christ live in us and we in him.
Here, once again we offer ourselves to you, body and soul,
to be your people, united in your love,
equipped by your Spirit to carry out the work of Christ.
And as your people we are joined together
through Jesus Christ our Lord.

THE DISTRIBUTION

Jesus took bread, broke it and gave it to them saying,
  'This is my body. It is broken for you.'

Bread is broken and passed round.

And he took the cup saying,
  'This cup is the new covenant. It is sealed in my
  blood. Drink from it all of you.'

*The cup is then passed round. When separate glasses are
used each pours out his/her neighbour's glass from a jug.*

The peace of the Lord Jesus Christ be upon you all.

THANKSGIVING

O God our Father
  We thank you for giving us these tangible tokens of
  your love.
  We thank you for giving us these visible signs of
  our forgiveness.
  We thank you for giving us this real pledge of our
  oneness,
    our oneness with you,
    and our oneness with each other.

With new courage we set out to face life,
  trusting in the inner reinforcement that Christ gives us.
With the new light you have given us,
  we tackle the problems which once seemed too great for
  us.
With the love of Christ in our hearts,
  we set out to serve the people we meet on life's journey.

We pray for those whom we shall meet:
  at home . . .
  at work . . .
  in our neighbourhood . . .
We think of those who suffer, especially any we know . . .
May the reality of the presence of Christ in our lives bring
  to each of these a blessing.

Father, into your hands we commit ourselves
  and all our loved ones wherever they may be,
  on earth or in heaven.

Glory be to God our Father who loves us.
Glory be to Christ, our living Lord and our Redeemer,
Glory be to the Holy Spirit, powerfully active in our hearts,
To Father, Son and Holy Spirit be praise and glory for ever.
AMEN.

[This order has been adapted from An Order of Service for a Small Communion published in *Worship Now*, The Saint Andrew Press, Edinburgh. We acknowledge with thanks permission to quote.]

Appendix D
Leaders' Meeting Check List

This is based on a check list used in the leaders' meeting of a network of adult groups in one of my parishes. Not all the items were dealt with in each meeting—however good leadership ensured the major items were covered.

1. **Praise**
   For what in our groups can we praise God?
   What have been some of our surprises?!
   (*This then led into a prayer time.*)

2. **Attendance**
   How many are there on each group roll?
   What was the average attendance in each group since last we met?
   (*These were then recorded in the master attendance book.*)
   Have irregular attenders been followed up by members or the leader?

3. **Group life**
   How does each group leader describe the quality of the life of their group?
   Are there any difficulties being experienced here?
   How can these best be handled?

4. **Pastoral care**
   Are there any group members requiring pastoral care in addition to that being received from the group?
   (Sickness, bereavement, financial problems, employment, marital or family difficulties, loss of interest, new or renewed commitment to Christ.)
   Who will undertake this special pastoral care?
   (*This led into a prayer time.*)

5. **Spiritual growth**
   What progress is being made in this area?
   Are there specific answers to prayer to report?

Are there specific problems being experienced by individuals or the group as a whole?

How can these be dealt with?

In what ways can we deepen the spiritual life of our groups?

Are the regular parish prayer notes being used in each group?

6. Learning together

How are the present studies being received?

Are there ways in which they can be improved?

Is the learning being applied to everyday life situations?

Have there been any requests for subjects to be covered in future studies?

Do we need to develop new skills in leading our groups in their learning together?

Have the study resources been ordered for future terms?

What stocks of the present study book are being held by each group?

(The curriculum for the year was decided upon at the evaluation and planning conference held towards the end of the previous year.)

7. Service

What action by the groups has arisen out of the study time?

What other service has been undertaken?

Are there aspects of the parish programme which could be handled by certain groups or the groups as a whole?

What are we doing to keep before the groups the needs of the community and the wider world?

8. Leadership

Who are emerging as possible new leaders?

In what ways are they being affirmed and encouraged to develop and use their gifts?

With what training events can they be linked?

Have they been invited to some of the present leaders' activities?

9. Growth

In what ways can we help our groups to grow?

What efforts are being made to enlist new members?

Are any groups approaching the point where they should consider dividing?

Who will we appoint as leaders and assistant leaders of the new groups?

Where and when will the new groups meet?

10. Finance

What is the state of the parish small group fund? *(Treasurer's report.)*

Have the group collections been properly recorded and paid into the central account?

What payments need approving?

11. Sharing of ideas

What new ideas or ways of doing anything raised in this check list have been found helpful?

In what ways can we improve what we are doing?

12. Special gatherings

(These included combined meetings to commence and end each term.)

How successful were these?

How can future meetings be improved?

    Special input (speaker, etc.)

    Programme

    Supper

    Getting people there

When and where is our next meeting to be held?

What planning do we still need to do regarding:

    Meeting place

    Programme

    Assignment of duties to each group—preparing location, promotion, aspects of programme, supper, welcoming group, etc.

13. General

Are there any changes to the time or location of any group?

Any other business?

14. Next meeting

When and where will the next meeting be held?

Who will have special responsibilities at that meeting?

    Training segment

    Leadership of prayer

    Special reports

    Other

Appendix E

Group Leader's Check List

This is based on a check list prepared for leaders in one of my parishes.

1. Group Members
Do I have my group roll book up-to-date?
(Members' names, addresses, telephone numbers, family members' names.)
Am I marking the roll each week?
Are there any who need following up?
Who will do this?
Am I praying for each member of the group?
Are we praying for each other as a group?

2. Programme
Have I made out a meeting plan with the timing for each item and who is responsible?
Have those responsible for different aspects been reminded?

Do they need any help?
Have all members received study materials, etc. needed before the meeting?
Have I found the answer to any questions, etc. raised last meeting?
Are there any notices to be given to the group? (Future combined events, parish activities, etc.)

3. Arrangements
Are there any matters to check with the host and hostess?
Are there any special arrangements to be made about transport, seating, baby-sitting, food, name tags?

4. Equipment and resources
Have I arranged for the visual aids needed? (Board and writing materials, masking tape, overhead projector and materials, etc.)

159

Is there any other equipment needed? (Audio or Video cassette players, record player, etc.)

Have I arranged for items for praise segments? (Hymn and song books, music book, musical instrument, musician.)

Are any other resources needed? (Spare Bibles, hand-outs, parish news sheets and prayer notes.)

Are there any materials needed for expression work?

5. Evaluation

Have I planned to get some informal feedback from the group as a whole or from individuals?

Am I recording this somewhere for future reference and for sharing with other leaders?

Do we need to do some more formal evaluation?

6. Leaders' meeting and overseer

Are there items I need to raise with the meeting as a whole or with the overseer?

Index

161

JOHN MALLISON

John Mallison was ordained a Methodist minister and now serves as a minister of the Uniting Church in Australia. His work as a parish minister spanned 17 years in rural, industrial and developing urban areas.

His ministry has been characterised by a healthy balance between education, evangelism, pastoral care and social concern. It is this perspective that John carried with him into the 14 years in which he was involved in full-time Christian education for his church in NSW. During this time he served as State Youth Director, Director of Adult Education and Founding Director of the ELM Centre, the lay training centre of the Uniting Church in NSW. More recently, John has served as part-time Minister for leadership development in an inner-city parish in Sydney.

John's main interests lie in the area of church growth and renewal, especially the role of small groups in bringing new life to the church. He has written 15 books, the majority of which deal with the role of the small group in the Christian community.

His extensive practical experience gives authenticity and credibility to all his training courses. He is in great demand by both secular and church bodies for lecturing, consulting and training.

He has conducted training events in Australia, England, Western and Eastern Europe, USA, India, Pakistan, Papua New Guinea, Indonesia and many South Pacific areas.

John now spends most of his time involved in specialist ministries both in Australia and overseas.

By the same author:

How to Commence Christian Cells in the Local Church
    (1964)
Lay Witness Teams (1972)
Youth Outreach and Evangelism (1975)
How to Communicate Your Faith (1975)
Christian Lifestyle Discovery Through Small Groups (1977)
Guidelines for Small Groups (1976)
Learning and Praying in Small Groups (1976)
Keeping Group Life Vital (1976)
Celling Youth and Adults (1976)
Building Small Groups in the Christian Community (1978)
Creative Ideas for Small Groups (1978)
Survival Kit for Christian Disciples (1979)
Nurturing New Disciples in Small Groups (1980)
Caring for New Christians (co-author with Dr Eddie Gibbs,
    1982)
Caring for People (1980)

"John Mallison's teaching, training of pastors and his writings have given depth and Biblical credibility to the small group movement. An amazing resource, distilling 35 years of ministry."

Lyman Coleman
Serendipity House
Littleton USA

"John Mallison provides both a sufficiently large vision and highly effective tactics to meet the urgent pastoral challenge of developing smaller groupings of believers in the church. I know of no other book which is anything like as useful."

Rev A L Doherty
Director of Adult Education
Catholic Archdiocese of Sydney

"Full of practical advice and wise insights gained from decades of experience. A rich resource . . . it is basic enough to be helpful to beginners yet thorough enough to help stretch those with years of experience."

Professor Roberta Hestenes
Eastern College USA

"John Mallison's writing is always inspirational and practical . . . This book will be of tremendous help to ministers and lay people who are committed to establishing and continuing small groups."

Rev John E Mavor
Moderator Queensland Synod
Uniting Church in Australia

"Timely and full of experience for those who want to learn how to start and keep alive the vital ministry of contact at a personal level with people . . . a resource book for all clergy and lay people."

Archbishop David Penman
Anglican Diocese of Melbourne